READING
CONNECTIONS

READING
CONNECTIONS

MARIANNE C. REYNOLDS

Mercer County Community College

Wadsworth Publishing Company

I(T)P ™ An International Thomson Publishing Company

Belmont • Albany • Bonn • Boston • Cincinnati • Detroit • London • Madrid • Melbourne
Mexico City • New York • Paris • San Francisco • Singapore • Tokyo • Toronto • Washington

English Editor: Angela Gantner Wrahtz
Assistant Editor: Lisa Timbrell
Editorial Assistant: Kate Peltier
Production: Del Mar Associates
Designer: John Odam
Print Buyer: Barbara Britton
Copy Editor: Robin Witkin
Cover Designer: Cassandra Chu
Cover Art: Bonnie Timmons/The Image Bank
Compositor: G&S Typesetters, Inc.
Printer: Courier Companies, Inc.

Chapter Opening Photos
1: Courtesy of The Missouri Historical Society, neg.# Groups 52A; **41:** The Bettmann Archive; **105:** Caufield & Shook Collection, Photographic Archives, University of Louisville, neg.# CS 104424; **157:** Caufield & Shook Collection, Photographic Archives, University of Louisville, neg.# CS 71790.

Printed in the United States of America
  2 3 4 5 6 7 8 9 10—01 00 99 98 97 96 95

For more information, contact Wadsworth Publishing Company:

Wadsworth Publishing Company
10 Davis Drive
Belmont, California 94002, USA

International Thomson Editores
Campos Eliseos 385, Piso 7
Col. Polanco
11560 México D.F. México

International Thomson Publishing Europe
Berkshire House 168-173
High Holborn
London, WC1V 7AA, England

International Thomson Publishing GmbH
Königswinterer Strasse 418
53227 Bonn, Germany

Thomas Nelson Australia
102 Dodds Street
South Melbourne 3205
Victoria, Australia

International Thomson Publishing Asia
221 Henderson Road
#05-10 Henderson Building
Singapore 0315

Nelson Canada
1120 Birchmount Road
Scarborough, Ontario
Canada M1K 5G4

International Thomson Publishing Japan
Hirakawacho Kyowa Building, 3F
2-2-1 Hirakawacho
Chiyoda-ku, Tokyo 102, Japan

Library of Congress Cataloging-in-Publication Data

Reynolds, Marianne Clifford.
    Reading connections / Marianne C. Reynolds.
        p.   cm.
    Includes bibliographical references.
    ISBN: 0-534-24456-4
    1. Reading (Higher education)—United States. 2. College readers.
  I. Title
  LB2395.R49 1994
  428.4′07′11—dc20   94-31933
                                                CIP

FOR TOM AND IAN

Preface

The instruction and practice opportunities found in *Reading Connections* combined with classroom instruction and serious study will prepare students to tackle the demands of college work. This text differs from others in that all of the skills and strageies are taught in the context of a particular academic theme. The four themes are gender, environment, civil rights, and business. Each begins with vocabulary exercises that teach the meanings of words students will meet in their readings. Skill development, such as expressing the main idea, identifying details, or making inferences, is integrated into the content of each theme. Students learn and practice with short passages and then apply these strategies to longer readings on the same topic. As students work through each theme, they increase their background knowledge and the context into which they can incorporate new information. By studying organizational patterns, students learn how authors organize information. Then students also learn to organize information, as they learn to outline, map, summarize, and take notes.

Ideally, instructors will follow an instructional pattern that includes

- instruction—explanation and modeling by the instructor

- example—large-group activity, the instructor helps the class work through a sample

- collaborative learning—students work together in pairs or small groups

- independent application—students work on their own in class or at home

- testing—students demonstrate proficiency

This text is designed to be used to the fullest. Students are encouraged to highlight or underline, make notes, and write answers in the book. Space has been provided for answers, including the writing exercises, which are important culminating activities.

None of the material has been "watered down." Rather, students are provided with the support they need to tackle the college academic work they will meet as they work toward their degrees.

I wish to thank the following reviewers for their helpful suggestions and guidance in the preparation of this book: Joy Bennett, University of Arkansas, Little Rock; Suzanne M. Forster, University of Alaska, Anchorage; Maryann Heidinger, Elmhurst College; Margaret Faye Jones, Nashville State Technical Institute; Wendy Paterson, Buffalo State College; Joyce Ritchey, El Paso Community College; Meritt W. Stark, Jr., Henderson State University; and Joanne W. Vaughan, Southwest Baptist University.

Marianne C. Reynolds

The Successful College Student

Each year, thousands of students enter college. Their experiences range from great success to total disaster. Why do some students succeed while others do not? Surveying students reveals that most believe that "smartness" is a fairly permanent characteristic, like being tall or being Latino.

Teachers, on the other hand, believe that success in college depends more on what you do than what you are. College professors expect their students to be independent and resourceful. They know that the smart student who didn't read the assigned chapter will fail the exam, and the conscientious student who studied will pass.

What does it mean to be a conscientious student? It means taking the time to concentrate, read, study, and review. But even the most willing student will fail, if he or she doesn't know reading and study strategies. The instruction, readings, and exercises in this book will help you learn how to read and study effectively. You will also have an opportunity to practice as you learn.

Each of the four units in this text centers on a theme, and each theme reflects a field of study that can be pursued in college. The first theme, *gender,* concentrates on readings from the social sciences, particularly psychology and sociology. The second theme, *environment,* combines science and social responsibility. The third theme, *civil rights,* presents the civil rights movement from a historical perspective. The fourth and final theme, *business,* explores various aspects of the business world, such as liability, marketing, and consumerism. As you learn about each theme, you will expand your vocabulary and develop strategies for understanding text. The vocabulary words and reading skills that are covered in each unit focus on the theme. As you practice these skills, you will be gaining more information about the topic you are studying. All of the skill development exercises are also based on thematic readings. At the end of each thematic unit, longer reading selections allow the more able readers to apply what they have learned to passages similar to those they will meet in their major courses. Some instructors may choose to work through each theme completely, and others may choose to concentrate on skill development first, saving the longer reading selections for the end of the semester.

The reading strategies you will acquire will help you learn how to use your textbooks effectively. For example, you will learn how to highlight or underline your text. You will also learn how to write margin notes that will serve as signals to the content of each section of the reading. College textbooks are expensive investments. To make the most of them, you need to be actively involved with the material they contain. In high school, you were told not to mark in your books; in college, however, you should use them to the fullest. In most cases, each exercise provides space for you to write your answers. Unless your instructor asks you to write on a separate sheet of paper, do all of your work in the book. You will find space for your writing exercises, too. If you get into the habit of really using your textbook now, you will be ready to tackle the most difficult college textbooks you will meet in your advanced courses.

Rise to the challenge and enjoy your reading.

Contents

Gender

Individuals are identified by sex or gender from the moment they are born, and sometimes before. The news of a birth is often followed by the question "Is it a girl or a boy?" When asked to describe themselves, young children commonly give gender and age the most importance: "I am a six-year-old girl" or "I'm a seven-year-old boy." Children's dress, toys, and behavior usually reflect their gender as well. Psychologists and sociologists have long wondered whether gender differences are biological or sociological. That is, are males and females born with different preferences and characteristics or do they learn gender roles from society?

As you work on this theme, you will be introduced to vocabulary words that often come up when discussing gender. You will also read a variety of selections that will add to your knowledge of this topic. Then, based on your reading, you will have the opportunity to refine your ideas. Finally, you will be asked to write about certain aspects of gender.

THEME FOCUS	
TOPIC:	GENDER
RELATED VOCABULARY	
SKILLS:	IDENTIFYING TOPICS
	MAIN IDEA
	DEFINITION/EXAMPLE ORGANIZATIONAL PATTERN
	FACT VERSUS OPINION

SKILL DEVELOPMENT: EXPANDING YOUR VOCABULARY

EXERCISE 1

Words in Context

This section contains exercises that introduce you to vocabulary that is specific to our topic, gender.

The underlined words in the following sentences appear in the passages you will read in this section of your text. They are presented in context here to help you figure out their meanings. Write the meaning of the underlined word after each sentence.

1. Certain activities, like sports and military training, are designed to develop <u>aggression</u> in the participants.

   _____

   _____

2. Children who are treated kindly and are encouraged to be gentle and generous often become <u>altruistic</u> adults. _____

   _____

3. A parent's <u>aspirations</u> for his or her child may not match the child's plans for the future. _____

   _____

   _____

4. <u>Assessing</u> a student's ability on the basis of a single test score is a dangerous practice. _____

   _____

   _____

5. In some societies, <u>compensation</u> for work performed may be in the form of food, clothing, or services, rather than money. _____

   _____

   _____

6. Diego purchased two stereo <u>components</u> in December and hoped to save $150 by June to add to the system. _____

   _____

   _____

7. The experiment that led to the cure of one of our most serious diseases was the <u>conception</u> of two brilliant Asian scientists. _____

   _____

   _____

8. In many households, the <u>domestic</u> chores are divided unequally, with the woman completing most of them. _____

   _____

9. The principles of economics become clearer when Professor Samuels <u>elaborates</u> on each point and provides examples. _____

   _____

   _____

10. Although his family had expected him to major in engineering, Leroy's high school art teacher influenced him to study <u>esthetics</u>. _____

_____

_____

11. The sight of his seriously injured cat <u>evoked</u> bitter tears from Carlos. _____

_____

_____

12. Her tennis opponent's <u>hostility</u> amazed Marta as she returned one vicious shot after another. _____

_____

_____

13. Arriving late for a formal awards ceremony <u>inhibits</u> even the most confident guest. _____

_____

_____

14. Regardless of how valued her friendships were, Tawanda felt she owed her first loyalty to her <u>kin</u>. _____

_____

_____

15. Four minutes after the veterinarian administered the <u>lethal</u> injection to the vicious dog, she pronounced him dead. _____

_____

_____

16. <u>Mundane</u> tasks, which require little thought and must be repeated often, should be divided fairly among members of the household. _____

_____

_____

17. Under a democratic system of government, the will of the majority <u>prevails</u>. _____

_____

_____

18. After two hours of playing with no repetitions, Kesha's parents' friends were amazed by her <u>repertoire</u> of piano music. _____

_____

19. As the scenes in the horror movie became more gruesome, Juan <u>unconsciously</u> moved closer to his mother. _____

_____

20. Because of the <u>variability</u> of the weather, Bridget's travel agent advised her to pack both shorts and sweaters for her trip. _____

_____

_____

EXERCISE 2

Definitions

Match the words in column A to their definitions in column B.

PART 1

COLUMN A	COLUMN B
____ 1. domestic	a. offensive action, forcefulness
____ 2. component	b. something given in payment
____ 3. prevail	c. element or part of something
____ 4. compensation	d. relating to the home or household
____ 5. lethal	e. to predominate; to be widespread
____ 6. inhibit	f. to call forth; to produce (feelings, memories)
____ 7. evoke	g. to restrain from free expression
____ 8. aggression	h. blood relatives
____ 9. kin	i. deadly
____10. aesthetics (esthetics)	j. the study of beauty in nature and art

PART 2

COLUMN A	COLUMN B
____ 1. elaborate	a. unselfish, concerned for others
____ 2. hostility	b. desire, hope, ambition
____ 3. variability	c. to estimate or to judge the value
____ 4. unconsciously	d. something created; an idea or notion
____ 5. altruistic	e. to work out in detail; to expand
____ 6. mundane	f. antagonism, unfriendliness
____ 7. conception	g. everyday, ordinary
____ 8. repertoire	h. all the works an artist or company performs
____ 9. aspiration	i. without being aware
____10. assess	j. changeability

Word parts (prefixes, suffixes, and roots) appear often in English words. They are so common that learning their meanings should help you figure out many words. In addition, you will meet the words used in the examples in this exercise in the readings that follow.

In this exercise, you are introduced to a word part and provided with its definition and a sample word. You are then given the definition of another word that includes this word part. With a fellow student, try to figure out what the missing word is and write it in the space provided. The first one is done for you.

EXERCISE 3

Word Parts

WORD PART	DEFINITION	EXAMPLE WORD
1. anthrop	human	anthropology: the study of human beings
	one who studies humans and their cultures	*anthropologist*
2. bene	good	beneficiary: a person who receives benefits
	something that is good; an advantage	_____
3. bio	life	biological: related to the study of living matter
	a written account of another person's life	_____
4. cep, cap	take, receive	conception: the act of conceiving; an idea
	party for wedding guests	_____
5. co, com	with, together	communicate: to talk with another
	a group of people who meet to plan something	_____
6. contra	against	controversy: argument; disagreement
	to say the opposite	_____
7. corp	body	incorporate: to include as a part
	dead body	_____
8. dis	not, reverse	discourage: to deprive of hope
	no longer available or produced	_____
9. ego	I, self	egoistic: self-centered, selfish
	conceited, boastful person	_____
10. equi	equal	equally: in an identical manner
	statement or problem to solve in algebra	_____
11. ex, e	out of	external: pertaining to the outside
	a way out	_____

12. gen	produce or create	gender: social classification of masculine or feminine
	a machine that converts energy	_____
13. im, in	not	insignificant: not serious, without consequence
	not able to move	_____
14. inter	between	interact: to act upon one another
	to meddle or take part in others' affairs	_____
15. intra	within	intraspecific: occurring within a species
	sports event involving students from the same school	_____
16. nat	birth	innate: inborn; existing in one since birth
	born in a particular place	_____
17. non	not	nonexistent: having no life or being
	not creating or producing	_____
18. ology	study of	ecology: study of organisms and environment
	study of people in groups	_____
19. op	against	opposite: contrary or radically different
	to govern or rule harshly	_____
20. poten	power	potential: possible, capable of becoming
	powerful, mighty	_____
21. pre	before	predisposition: a prior tendency or bias
	word part at the beginning of a word	_____
22. pro	forward, ahead	project: something planned or devised
	to advance in rank; to move to a higher position; to advocate purchasing something	_____
23. psych	mind	psyche: the human soul, spirit, mind
	study of mental processes	_____
24. re	back, again	retreat: to withdraw or go back
	to go and to come back again	

25. super	over, above	superior: above average, excellent
	a person in charge of other workers	_____
26. un	not	unconsciously: without awareness
	not meaning to, not on purpose	_____
27. uni	one	universal: used or understood by all
	an identifying outfit worn by members of a profession	_____
28. vers, vert	turn	reversible: able to be turned or changed back
	to change to a different religion	_____
29. vis, vid	see	visible: able to be seen or observed
	a set for receiving broadcasts	_____
30. voc, vok	call	evoke: to call up or produce (memories, feelings)
	a career or profession	_____

SKILL DEVELOPMENT: IDENTIFYING MAIN IDEAS

Determining the main idea of a sentence, paragraph, textbook chapter, story, or movie sounds easy. Teachers begin talking to children about main ideas at the beginning of elementary school. College professors also expect students to find main ideas, although they may phrase their questions in a different way.

What is easy for most students to identify is the topic, or subject, of their reading. For example, "I read about food, dancing, or pollution." But identifying the topic is only the first step toward arriving at the main idea. There are several reasons it is important for good readers to identify and express the main idea: (1) it forces the reader to get involved in the reading material; (2) it provides the reader with an excellent way to relate information to someone else; and (3) it serves as a measure of the reader's understanding of the text.

Let's take one of the topic examples mentioned before—food— and look at three main idea statements.

1. Americans are switching to low-fat, high-fiber diets.

2. Civil wars and drought have had such devastating effects on the food supply in Africa that famine is widespread.

3. Asian spices are finding their way into classic French cooking.

You can imagine how different each of these passages would be.

The first one would talk about how health conscious Americans are becoming. It might include some examples of low-fat, high-fiber foods or a sample menu.

The second passage would discuss the absence of food. From the main idea statement, you could expect to read about the causes and effects of the food shortage.

The third passage would talk about cooking. It might include some recipes or some descriptions of Asian spices.

From these examples, you can see that the topic (food, in this case) is more general and briefer than the main idea. The main idea statement tells what is said about the topic. It is specific and informative, and it is written as a complete sentence.

EXERCISE 4

Identifying Topics and Main Ideas

In the following pairs, pick out the topic (*T*) and the main idea (*MI*). The first is done for you as an example.

MI   The incumbent (officeholder) always enjoys an advantage over the challenger.

T   Political campaigns

1. _____ Crime reports

   _____ In 1991, New York City reported a decrease in crime reports in every category.

2. _____ Neighborhood clinics are filling a need for women who prefer not to use a hospital to give birth.

   _____ Alternative child-delivery sites

3. _____ Nuclear power plant accidents cause panic in the surrounding areas.

   _____ Nuclear power plants

4. _____ Airline fares

   _____ Fares for air travel are usually higher around holiday time.

5. _____ Conservation may harm fishermen in the short term.

   _____ Limits on catch size, net mesh size, and days at sea may conserve fish but will cut down on fishermen's profits.

6. _____ Except for professional chefs, most men are not considered good cooks.

   _____ Gender-role expectations

7. _____ The disadvantages of stereotyping

   _____ People may characterize a whole group of people as unreliable because one of its members was not dependable.

8. _____ The nursing profession

_____ After years of receiving inadequate pay, nurses finally earn professional salaries.

9. _____ In the 1960s, for the first time, men felt free to wear jewelry and grow long hair.

_____ Male and female roles in the 1960s

10. _____ Aggression in sports

_____ For years, girls were prohibited from playing hockey because the sport is so aggressive.

Consider the second sample topic, dancing. Try to narrow the topic by listing four specific kinds of dancing:

EXERCISE 5

Writing Main Idea Statements

1. _____

2. _____

3. _____

4. _____

Assume that you have read an article about each type of dance. Now take each specific dance and try to write a main idea sentence about it. For example, if aerobic dancing is one of my four types, my main idea sentence might read as follows:

Aerobic dancing is a popular way to exercise.

Here are some suggestions for your main idea sentences:

5. Write a sentence about the popularity of dance type 1. _____

_____

_____

6. Write a sentence about a performance of dance type 2. _____

_____

_____

7. Write a sentence about the ease or difficulty of learning dance type 3. _____

_____

_____

8. Write a sentence about who enjoys dance type 4 or where it might be seen. _____

_____

_____

EXERCISE 6

Sentence Restatements

To see if you've understood what you've heard or read, it is useful to paraphrase—that is, to state the ideas in your own words. This practice helps you figure out what the words mean and learn the information. It also helps your listener or teacher appreciate your understanding of the text.

In this exercise, you will read five sentences that are a bit long and complicated. They all relate to the theme of this unit. With a fellow student, try to restate the main idea in your own words. Write your restatement in the space following each sentence. The first is done for you as an example.

> *Example:* In the absence of artificial birth control, for example, beliefs and practices that limit heterosexual intercourse may be adaptive in contributing to population control. (*Cultural Anthropology,* 4th ed., by Serena Nanda [Belmont, Calif.: Wadsworth, 1991], p. 100.)

> *Restatement:* In places where birth control is not available, too many babies might be born if sexual activity is not limited.

1. The fact that some societies have taken an egalitarian approach to gender relations makes it clear that most of the differences we can see between the sexes in most societies are cultural, not biological (O'Kelly and Carney, 1986). (*Sociology,* 4th ed., by Rodney Stark [Belmont, Calif.: Wadsworth, 1992], p. 165.)

   _____

   _____

2. Economist Ann Markusen observed that ideally, in a democracy, everyone affected by the economy should be represented on decision-making boards: single moms, nurses, senior citizens and so on. Appointing only bankers to the Federal Reserve Board is rather like picking National Rifle Association members to draft gun control laws. ("Quieting New Networks," by Mary Kay Blakely [New York: Lang Communications, March/April 1992], *Ms.* II, 5 [21].) _____

   _____

   _____

3. The researchers suggest, for example, that the increasing rate of female employment and the effects of the feminist movement may have allowed women to increasingly base their social class identifications on their own accomplishments, rather than on their male relatives'. (*Sociological Ideas,* 3rd ed., by William C. Levin [Belmont, Calif.: Wadsworth, 1991], p. 301.) _____

   _____

   _____

4. Researchers cited in the report also found that girls had less confidence in their math abilities than boys did, and that as their confidence diminished, so did their performance. ("Bias Against Girls Is Found Rife in Schools, With Lasting Damage," by Susan Chira [New York: New York Times Company, Feb. 12, 1992], p. A23.) _____

   _____

   _____

5. Often, the achievements of successful women are widely publicized, perhaps unintentionally giving the impression of great gains. (*Sociology: Concepts and Characteristics,* 7th ed., by Judson R. Landis [Belmont, Calif.: Wadsworth, 1989], p. 194.) _____

_____

_____

As you identify and express the main ideas of paragraphs, you must do a bit more than paraphrase. A paragraph has a topic and consists of several sentences. To figure out the topic, ask yourself what the paragraph is about. Once you determine the topic, ask what is said about it. You may find that one sentence states the main idea, or you may have to use information from several sentences. In the next exercise, you will read each paragraph, identify the topic, and state the main idea in your own words. The first one is done for you as an example.

EXERCISE 7

Main Ideas of Paragraphs

Example:

Children take behavioral cues from other adults and from television characters. They tend to imitate adults of their own sex more than adults of the opposite sex, even when the behaviors are fairly trivial. In one experiment, children watched adults choose between an apple and a banana. If all the men chose one and all the women chose the other, the boys who were watching wanted what the men had chosen and the girls wanted what the women had chosen (Perry T. Bussey, 1979). In other words, children learn about gender roles and sex stereotypes by observation. (*Introduction to Psychology,* 3rd ed., by James W. Kalat [Belmont, Calif.: Wadsworth, 1993], p. 312.)

Your first step is to identify the topic. In this paragraph, and in most others, the first and last sentences give you clues about the topic. You could use one of several phrases from either of these sentences as your topic, and you would be right. For example:

1. Gender roles

2. Sex stereotypes

3. Behavioral cues

If these terms are unfamiliar or confusing to you, you might state the topic in your own words such as:

4. Children watching adults

5. Children imitating adults

6. Learning by observation

Any of these choices would be correct. Notice that six different topics are identifiable for one paragraph. All of the choices are related, and you might use more than one as you express the main idea in a sentence. Stating the main idea specifically is important if you need to tell someone what the paragraph is actually about.

The second step is to ask, What does the paragraph say about the topic? Let's start with topic 4, which seems to be stated most simply. What does the paragraph say about children watching adults? As you read the paragraph, you probably appreciated the author's example about picking fruit. Even though that illustration may have clarified the point for you, the paragraph is not about picking fruit. The experimenters could have chosen many other examples to illustrate the same point. They could have asked the adults to choose a favorite color or to demonstrate a sport. The point is that the boys wanted to have what the men chose. We could state the main idea this way:

1. Boys and girls tend to watch and imitate members of their own sex.

This main idea statement is acceptable and explains topics 4, 5, and 6.

The first three topics have emphasized the terminology found in the paragraph. Your psychology professor may agree with the main idea stated above, but he or she may also want you to demonstrate your understanding of the terms used. For example:

What are *gender roles* and *sex stereotypes*?

You will learn through your reading in this unit that both terms refer to the expectations our society has for males and females to behave in a particular way. Or:

What are *behavioral cues*?

Cues are prompts, hints, or suggestions about what we are supposed to do. Actresses use cues to tell them when to appear on stage. Your date may give you a cue when he or she wants to leave a party. *Behavioral cues* are signals that tell us how to behave. Let's try some main idea statements using these terms.

2. Children live up to their gender roles by behaving like adults of their own sex.

3. Sex stereotypes encourage boys to imitate men and girls to imitate women.

4. Children take their behavioral cues from adults of their own sex.

All of these main idea statements are acceptable. Each tells what the paragraph is about. The advantages in expressing the main idea in your own words (rather than selecting from multiple choices) are that you show a real understanding of the paragraph and have some flexibility in how you express it.

For each of the following five paragraphs, identify the topic. Then, work with a fellow student to identify and to express the main idea of each paragraph. Write it in your own words below the paragraph.

1. On the average, males behave differently from females in many ways. Men are more likely than women to hit one another (Eagly & Steffen, 1986) and to swear. Women tend to know more than men do about flowers. Men and women generally carry books and packages in different ways. (*Introduction to Psychology,* 3rd ed., by James W. Kalat [Belmont, Calif.: Wadsworth, 1993], p. 266.)

    a. Topic: _____

    b. Main idea: _____

    _____

    _____

2. What made me want to puke in my history teacher's lap was one particular habit—he called all the girls in my class "Beautiful ," "Adorable," "Gorgeous." I finally confronted him after class one day and asked if it was really too much to drop all the honey-cookie-pieface-lambchop stuff, adding that I considered it sexist and demeaning. Mr. Lecherman's eyes nearly popped out of his head. When I pointed out that none of the guys in my class were "Hot Harold" or "Studmuffin Stan," he whined, "But I'm not interested in guys!" (And I'm not interested in 50-year-old history teachers.) ("High School Letdown" by Miranda J. Van Gelder, *Ms.* II, 5 [p. 94].)

    a. Topic: _____

    b. Main idea: _____

    _____

    _____

3. The results of gender-role typing are many and varied, and not all the benefits are for males. The male is restricted in how he may show emotion: He is strong and silent, he does not show weakness, and he keeps his feelings under careful rein, at least outwardly. The female has far greater freedom to express emotion. (*Sociology: Concepts and Characteristics,* 7th ed., by Judson R. Landis [Belmont, Calif.: Wadsworth, 1989], p. 191.)

    a. Topic: _____

    b. Main idea: _____

    _____

    _____

4. Rapid change had affected women's lives after World War II. Most significant was the increased participation of women in the work force. In 1947, only about 27 percent of workers in the labor force were women. In 1981, women constituted about 43 percent of the labor force. Put another way, in 1947 about 30 percent of women worked. In 1981 almost 50 percent worked. Many of them joined the labor force to maintain their family's standard of living. (*The Pursuit of Liberty: A History of the American People,* 2nd ed., by R. Jackson Wilson et al. [Belmont, Calif.: Wadsworth, 1990], p. 1093.)

   a. Topic: _____

   b. Main idea: _____

   _____

   _____

5. School is still a place of unequal opportunity, where girls face discrimination from teachers, textbooks, tests and their male classmates, according to a report being released today that examined virtually all major studies on girls and education. ("Bias Against Girls is Found Rife in Schools, With Lasting Damage," by Susan Chira, *New York Times,* Feb. 12, 1992, p. 1.)

   a. Topic: _____

   b. Main idea: _____

   _____

   _____

SKILL DEVELOPMENT: IDENTIFYING ORGANIZATIONAL PATTERNS

Nonfiction writers, particularly textbook authors, often organize the information they present in particular ways or patterns. In many cases, such patterns help the reader understand the logic of the material as it is presented. For example, a history text may present information in chronological or sequential order. Since historians are interested in the time order of events, a chronological pattern is an appropriate choice. You will see examples of the chronological, listing, process/description, comparison/contrast, and cause/effect patterns later in this book.

Right now, we will look at the *definition/example* pattern. Authors often use this pattern to introduce a term or a topic. You will find it used in almost any subject area. Typically, an author defines a term or a topic and then provides an explanation and examples. You have probably used the definition/example pattern yourself. Perhaps you defined a work term to a new employee and then gave an example of how it is used. For example, "palletizing" may mean stacking pallets in a store room, or "cashing out" may mean counting the money in your cash register at the end of the day.

The following paragraph from a sociology textbook is an example of the definition/example pattern. As you read, look for the topic, the definition, and examples.

GENDER-ROLE SOCIALIZATION

One important process associated with sex-role learning (that is, learning to behave as a male or female) is *imitation of a same-sex role model*. In play, for example, girls most frequently imitate the domestic activities of their mothers or elder females who stand in this relation to them; boys imitate their fathers or other males. This imitation is subtly encouraged along the lines of sex even when it is not a consequence of direct teaching. Girls and boys are both discouraged from imitating activities culturally considered appropriate for the opposite sex and rewarded for imitating activities considered culturally appropriate for their own sex.

Notice that the key term is indicated in *italics*. Some authors will provide this type of visual clue (*italics*, underlining, or **boldface**); others will not.

The author also tells us that *imitation of a same-sex role model* is "an important process." We can find the definition of the key term in the first sentence: *imitation of a same-sex role model* is one important process associated with sex-role learning. You are probably already familiar with the term *role model* as someone who is admired and sometimes imitated. Professional athletes, teachers, and community volunteers are sometimes described as *role models* and positive influences on young people.

Next, consider the author's examples that help make the term and its definition clearer. She says that girls imitate mothers and that boys imitate fathers. She also says that boys are discouraged from imitating women, and that girls are discouraged from imitating men. Think of some examples of your own, and recall what you already know about some of these terms. You have probably heard the term *imitate* before. Write down what it means to you: _____

_____

_____

Now write down an example of boys imitating men or girls imitating women: _____

_____

_____

Excerpt from *Cultural Anthropology,* 4th ed., by Serena Nanda (Belmont, Calif.: Wadsworth, 1991), p. 136.

After you find a definition in a text, it is always wise to state it in your own words. For example:

> *Imitation of a same-sex role model* is one way girls and boys learn to act female or male as they behave the same way as adults of the same sex.

Look at another related example of the definition/example pattern before you try some on your own. Remember this pattern includes a term or phrase, its meaning, and a sample or example. Although sometimes authors omit examples, readers often find them very helpful. The example usually follows the definition, but at times the example may come first. As you read the following example, try to identify the key term or phrase, its definition, and the example.

> When you join a religious organization, a fraternity, or a sorority, or when you start a new job, you discover that the people already there observe certain customs. They will explain some of those customs to you, but the only way you will learn about others is by watching. Those who already know the customs serve as models (or examples) for you; when you copy their example, we say that you are **modeling** your behavior after theirs, or that you are **imitating.** (*Introduction to Psychology,* 3rd ed., by James W. Kalat [Belmont, Calif.: Wadsworth, 1993], p. 311.)

Notice that the two key terms come at the end of the paragraph and that they seem to be interchangeable. In the psychology text from which this paragraph was taken, the terms *modeling* and *imitating* were printed in boldface to emphasize their importance.

You should also be able to pick out the definition. You might write it this way:

> *Modeling* is copying the examples set by people who already know the customs.

We can use the same definition for the term *imitating*. The author provided examples at the beginning of the paragraph. Those examples include copying the people you meet when you join a religious organization, a fraternity or sorority, or start a new job. We also learned about the term *imitation* in the first sample paragraph we looked at. In that case, we learned about a particular kind of imitation. In this paragraph, the term is used and defined in a more general way.

Think of your own example of *modeling* or *imitating* and write it here: _____

_____

Now try working with the definition/example pattern on your own.

The following paragraphs further illustrate the *definition/example* pattern. After you read each one, write down the key term or phrase, the definition, the example (if the author includes one), and your own example.

1. For many years, psychologists assumed that most children grew up in a so-called traditional family, which consisted of a working father, a housekeeping mother, and one or more children. Today, only a small percentage of children in the United States and Canada grow up in such a family. An estimated 50 percent of all children eventually experience the divorce of their parents. A clear majority of mothers have at least a part-time job, and children grow up in a great variety of home environments. (*Introduction to Psychology,* 3rd ed., by James W. Kalat [Belmont, Calif.: Wadsworth, 1993], p. 263.)

   a. Key term or phrase: _____

   b. Definition: _____

   _____

   c. Is there an example given in the paragraph? _____

   _____

   d. Give your example of a so-called nontraditional family: _____

   _____

2. Increasingly during the 1970s, disputes over women's roles focused on the proposed Equal Rights Amendment to the Constitution. Little more, in fact, than a ratification of the rights to equal treatment that many women already enjoyed and that most Americans supported, the ERA came to symbolize those changes in modern society that more conservative Americans opposed. Although the amendment failed in 1982, public opinion supporting it did not diminish. (*The Pursuit of Liberty: A History of the American People,* vol. 1, 2nd ed., by R. Jackson Wilson et al. [Belmont, Calif.: Wadsworth, 1990], p. 1094.)

   a. Key term or phrase: _____

   b. Definition: _____

   _____

   c. Is there an example given in the paragraph? _____

   _____

   d. Give an example of a change in the role of women that more conservative people might find objectionable. _____

   _____

3. <u>Sex</u> refers to the *biological* differences between male and female, particularly the visible differences in external genitalia and the related differences in the role each sex plays in the reproductive process. <u>Gender</u> refers to the *social* classification of masculine and feminine. Every society gives cultural recognition to the sexual division of the species into male and female. Cultures differ, though, in what they consider masculine and feminine. Some male/female differences in behavior appear to be very widespread, however. Males, for example, have been observed to be more likely to initiate activity than females in various cultures. Females also have been observed to be more altruistic than males. (*Cultural Anthropology,* 4th ed., by Serena Nanda [Belmont, Calif.: Wadsworth, 1991], p. 100.)

a. Key terms or phrases: _____

b. Definitions: _____

_____

c. Are there examples given in the paragraph? _____

_____

d. Give an example of a behavior you think of as either masculine or feminine. _____

_____

4. Betty Friedan first confronted the "problem that had no name" in 1956–57 when she compiled and ana-
   lyzed questionnaires for her fifteenth reunion at Smith College. Six years later, she expanded on the themes
   she had seen in her classmates' lives in her book, *The Feminine Mystique.* "As she made the beds, shopped
   for groceries, matched slipcover material, ate peanut butter sandwiches with her children, chauffeured cub
   scouts and brownies, lay beside her husband at night—she was afraid to ask even of herself the silent question— 'Is this all?'" The root of the dissatisfaction, Friedan argued, lay in the postwar ideal of the feminine
   mystique: the ideology that "the highest value and only commitment for women is the fulfillment of their
   own femininity." (*Modern American Women: A Documentary History,* by Susan Ware [Belmont, Calif.: Wadsworth, 1989], p. 286.)

   a. Key term or phrase: _____

   b. Definition: _____

   _____

   c. Are there examples given in the paragraph? _____

   _____

   d. How do you think the feminine mystique might have affected young, unmarried women in the 1950s
      and 1960s? _____

   _____

5. Judy B. Rosener's study of 456 successful female executives revealed that men and women use very different leadership styles. Men prefer a "command and control" style in dealing with subordinates. They rely
   on orders, appeals to self-interest, rational decision-making and rewards. Women prefer to work "interac-
   tively," sharing power and information, motivating by appeals to organizational goals and promoting em-
   powerment. ("The Debate over La Difference," by Barbara Presley Noble, *The New York Times,* Aug. 15,
   1993, Business, p. 6.)

   a. Key terms: _____

   b. Definitions: _____

   _____

   c. Are there examples given in the paragraph? _____

   _____

   d. Give an example of differences you have observed between men and women in leadership roles. _____

   _____

6. Adolescents, realizing that they must make decisions within a few years, face an <u>identity crisis</u>. The search for identity or self-understanding may lead an adolescent in several directions (Marcia, 1980). <u>Identity foreclosure</u>, for example, is the passive acceptance of a role defined by one's parents. Until fairly recently, identity foreclosure was the norm for most young women. Parents and society both decreed, "You will be a full-time wife and mother." Today, young women have greater freedom to choose what to do with their lives. That greater freedom has made it more likely that they will experience an identity crisis during adolescence. (*Introduction to Psychology,* 3rd ed., by James W. Kalat [Belmont, Calif.: Wadsworth, 1993], p. 252.)

   a. Key terms or phrases: _____

   b. Definitions: _____

   _____

   c. Are there examples given in the paragraph? _____

   _____

   d. How does an identity crisis differ from identity foreclosure? _____

   _____

After you finish this exercise, you will read Selection 1, "Stereotyping." Many times, you are familiar with terms or phrases because you have heard them before. You may not be able to provide a clear definition, but you have a sense of the word's meaning and may be able to give some examples. This is probably the case for the word *stereotyping.* As a prereading activity, this exercise will help you distinguish facts from stereotypes. Your instructor may ask you to work with fellow students as you categorize each statement. If you work alone, make sure you compare your answers with a classmate to see if you agree. After completing the exercise, see if you can come up with a working definition of the word *stereotype.* Then you can check your definition with the one offered in Selection 1.

After you read each of the following statements, decide if it is factual or if it includes a stereotype. If it is factual, put an *F* in the first blank. If it is a stereotype, put an *S* in the first blank. Next, for the stereotypes (*S*), tell whether you agree (*A*) or disagree (*D*) with the statement by marking your answer in the second blank. A sample is provided for you.

EXERCISE 9

Prereading Activity: Distinguishing Facts from Stereotypes

   _S_ Women's sports events are not as much fun to watch as men's events.
   _A_

_____ 1. Boys like math classes better than girls do.

_____

_____ 2. There are more boys than girls enrolled in high school math classes.

_____

_____ 3. Most day-care workers and nursery-school teachers are women.

_____

_____ 4. Children should be cared for by women until they are at least two years old.

_____

_____ 5. Females are more emotional than males.

_____

_____ 6. Male police officers with female partners are at a disadvantage.

_____

_____ 7. There are more female nurses than male nurses.

_____

_____ 8. By the time players are nine or ten years old, most sports teams are restricted to boys or girls.

_____

_____ 9. Boys are more competitive and aggressive than girls are.

_____

_____ 10. Women prefer to stay at home rather than work while their children are young.

_____

Compare your answers with a fellow classmate. Discuss why you decided certain statements were stereotypes.

1. What do the stereotypes have in common? Write your answer below.

_____

_____

2. What does the term _stereotype_ mean to you? Write your answer below.

_____

_____

_____

SKILL DEVELOPMENT: GUIDED READING

As you read, finding the main idea becomes one step in the process of understanding the text. You will need a general overview of the material—the main idea—plus an understanding of the major and minor points. Think of the major points as the main ideas of each paragraph and of the minor points as details to support each point.

Before taking on a passage, you should have a strategy to guide your reading. Try to structure your activity with the following steps:

1. Recall as much background information about the topic as you can.

2. Preview the article to see what it's about.

3. Engage your interest with an eagerness to learn.

4. Relate the new information to what you already know.

5. Look for new vocabulary terms and their definitions.

6. Make up your own questions.

7. Read to find the answers.

8. Underline or highlight the answers, or write them down.

9. Quiz yourself when you are finished.

These nine steps probably represent more than you are used to doing during your reading. They do take time, but I guarantee you will understand more and remember the information for a longer time if you follow them. Consider some of the reasons I recommend these steps.

Step 1 helps you establish a framework for your reading. If you already know something about the topic, recalling that information will help you deal with the new reading material. For example, if you are knowledgeable about fishing, you would be better able to appreciate an article about lures if you could compare those described to ones you have used. Also, you can predetermine if a passage will be easy or difficult for you.

Step 2 encourages you to preview—take a look before you jump in. A preview lets you see how long the passage is, whether it is divided into sections, or if the author provides subheadings, italicized or boldfaced words, or other aids. You may be able to tell if the text is straightforward or indirect so that you can adjust your reading attitude. For example, you shouldn't read a poem the same way you study a chapter in your chemistry textbook. When you preview, look at the title, the headings, and the subheadings. Read the first and the last paragraphs. Read the first line of every paragraph. This should take no more than a few minutes, but it should give you a sense of what the reading will be like.

Step 3 is a tough one, and no one else can do it for you. It is very important to "get yourself up" for your reading. Students frequently make two comments about their reading: (1) "I do better with material that interests me," and (2) "Much of what I read, I find boring." The logical conclusion is to be more interested in what you read. If you can't control the choice of reading material, try to adjust your attitude. Approach passages positively, expecting to learn something interesting.

Step 4 suggests that you add the new information to the old. Fit the new pieces into the jigsaw puzzle you are assembling in your mind. You should have no trouble with this step in this textbook since the readings in each unit are centered around a single theme.

Step 5 asks you to expand your word knowledge. In some cases, words and definitions are provided before the reading. In other cases, you will need to learn the terminology introduced and defined in the passage.

Step 6 advises you to ask questions before you read. The easiest way to create a question is to use the heading. For example, if the heading is "Stereotypes Affect Behavior," you can use the question words *What* or *How* or *Why* to make up your own questions.

What are stereotypes?

How do stereotypes affect behavior?

Why do stereotypes affect behavior?

Step 7 capitalizes on the questions you raised in step 6. If you start reading with questions in mind, your reading is directed and purposeful. In some cases, authors provide questions at the end of a reading. You may want to read those questions *before* you start reading, so your attention will be focused on the important points.

Logically, in step 8, you do something with the information you found—underline it, highlight it, or write it down. This will help you become more involved in the reading process and should help you remember the information.

The purpose behind step 9 is to see if you learned the information, and it can be handled in several ways. You may choose to answer questions, to write an outline or summary, or to make notes from memory.

SELECTION 1

The selection that follows deals with stereotyping, an issue closely related to gender. When a person judges others on the basis of their membership in a group, he or she is stereotyping. People often make stereotypical judgments on the basis of gender. For example, if a small child is crying, many people would expect a woman, regardless of her relationship to the child, to be more likely to offer comfort than a man. As you work through this selection, your task is to understand what stereotyping means, to relate to the examples provided, and to think of some examples of your own. Finally, you will consider how stereotyping relates to gender.

STEREOTYPING

Perhaps the most commonly known barrier to accurate judgment of others is our tendency to stereotype. *Stereotyping* is an oversimplified opinion or uncritical judgment of others. It often involves assigning characteristics to individuals solely on the basis of their membership in a certain class or category. Stereotyping is a perceptual shortcut. We are likely to develop generalized opinions about any group we come in contact with. Subsequently, any number of perceptual cues—skin color, style of dress, a religious medal, gray hair, gender, and so on—can lead us to automatically project our generalized opinions onto a specific individual.

Stereotyping contributes to perceptual inaccuracies by ignoring individual differences. Stereotyping causes us to assume characteristics just because a person happens to be a member of the stereotyped group. For instance, if Dave held a stereotype that stockbrokers are <u>unethical</u>, that would not mean that Denise, a highly principled woman, is unethical even if we discover that a majority of stockbrokers are unethical. You may be able to think of instances when you have been the victim of a stereotype based on your gender, age, ethnic heritage, social class, physical characteristics, or other qualities. If so, you know how damaging and unfair stereotypes can be.

Read the first paragraph and <u>underline the definition of stereotyping and some of its consequences</u>. Do not underline the example.

Answer the following questions based on your reading and experience.

1. Define stereotyping according to the text. _____

   _____

2. Write a definition in your own words. _____

   _____

3. What example does the author provide to illustrate stereotyping?_____

   _____

   _____

4. Write your own example: All _____ are _____ .

5. What is the meaning of the word *unethical*?_____

   _____

If stereotypes are often inaccurate, why do they persist? There are at least two good reasons. First, we tend to believe that stereotypes are helpful. Although people may learn to go beyond a stereotype in forming opinions of individuals, stereotypes provide a working hypothesis. That is, when encountering a person from a different race or culture, we are likely to attribute characteristics of our stereotype to the person. We then act as

Read the next section to learn about why stereotypes persist.

Excerpts from *Communicate,* 7th ed., by Rudolph F. Verderber (Belmont, Calif.: Wadsworth, 1993), pp. 48–49.

if our stereotype is accurate until we get sufficient information to judge that person as an individual. In short, it is easier to base our perceptions of a person or group of people on a stereotype than to take the time to really learn about each individual we encounter.

In addition, it provides some people with a certain comfort to believe that blacks are lazy, whites racist, old people stubborn, Italians naturally hot-headed, or women too emotional to be capable of reasoning under stress. Such generalizations enable the person to "know" how to treat new acquaintances.

Answer the following question based on your reading.

6. What are the reasons stereotypes exist?

a. _____

_____

b. _____

_____

Read the next section to understand the relationship between stereotyping and prejudice.

Stereotyping and prejudice go hand in hand. <u>Prejudice</u> is an unjustified attitude toward a person or group. For instance, Laura discovers that Wasif, a man she has just met, is a Muslim. She would be stereotyping him if she viewed him solely in terms of her perception of Muslims' beliefs about women rather than in terms of his individual behavior. Moreover, to the extent that Laura permits her stereotype to govern her responses to Wasif, she will be guilty of prejudice. In this case, Wasif may never get the chance to be known for who he really is.

Answer the following questions based on your reading.

7. What is prejudice? _____

_____

8. What is the relationship between prejudice and stereotyping? _____

_____

Read the following section to learn about sexism.

One form of prejudice that causes major problems in relationships is sexism. <u>Sexism</u> is any behavior, however insignificant, that limits either men or women to rigid, stereotypic roles based solely on their sex. In our society, sexism comes under heaviest attack when it limits the economic and social opportunities of women. Nevertheless, sexist attitudes and behaviors are not confined to men's behavior toward women. The attitudes men have about how other men should behave, the attitudes women have about men, the attitudes women have about other women, as well as the accompanying behavior, all can be sexist. For example, many women never think of paying their own way on a date. That is sexist.

Similarly, many women believe that all women should stay home with small children. That is sexist. And many men believe women have no place in an executive office unless they have memo pads or vacuum cleaner in their hands. That is sexist. Some men think a man (but not a woman) who cries is weak. That, too, is sexist. In all these cases, we invite tension and misunderstandings in relationships because we treat others not as individuals but as members of one or the other sex.

Answer the following questions based on your reading.

9. What is sexism? _____

_____

10. Who can be guilty of sexism? _____

_____

11. What problems can sexism cause? _____

_____

12. Give your own example of sexist behavior. _____

_____

Because gender stereotypes are deeply <u>ingrained</u> in our culture, very few people manage to completely avoid behaving or thinking in a sexist manner. By becoming aware of our own sexist attitudes and behaviors, we can guard against inhibiting communication. We can avoid automatically assuming that other people feel and act the same way we do. We can also guard against saying or doing things that offend people and <u>perpetuate</u> outdated sex-role stereotypes. If people are confronted with enough information over a long enough period of time, their attitudes may change.

Read the last paragraph for some advice about avoiding sexism.

Answer the following questions based on your reading.

13. What does the word *ingrained* mean? _____

_____

14. What does the word *perpetuate* mean? _____

_____

15. How will gender stereotypes change? _____

_____

WRITING EXERCISE

Discuss stereotyping in a paragraph that includes a definition, some examples, and the problems associated with it. (Use your answers to the comprehension questions as the basis for your writing.)

_____

_____

_____

_____

_____

_____

EXERCISE 10

Applying Stereotyping to Gender

This exercise may help you decide whether you or others stereotype people according to gender. Do you assume that individuals will behave or think a certain way because they are male or female?

In column A, list five characteristics that you (or others) consider predominantly female. In column B, list five characteristics that you (or others) consider predominantly male.

A. FEMALE CHARACTERISTICS	B. MALE CHARACTERISTICS
1. _____	1. _____
2. _____	2. _____
3. _____	3. _____
4. _____	4. _____
5. _____	5. _____

Compare your list with a classmate's list. Do you see similarities or a pattern?

WRITING EXERCISE

Write a descriptive paragraph about someone you admire and know well. Include five characteristics and an example of each. For example:

> My sister Rochelle is very generous. She brings my children gifts whenever she visits.

_____

_____

_____

_____

_____

_____

Exchange your paragraph with a classmate. After you read each other's paragraphs, list the characteristics your partner included and indicate whether you consider them male (*M*), female (*F*), or neutral (*N*).

1. _____

2. _____

3. _____

4. _____

5. _____

Do you think there is a male or female personality? Do you think we stereotype males and females? _____

_____

_____

SKILL DEVELOPMENT: DISTINGUISHING FACTS FROM OPINIONS

Careful readers distinguish facts from opinions as they read. They know some writers are interested in persuading readers to accept a particular point of view. Astute readers will test statements as they read. For example, to determine if the statement is a fact, they may ask the following questions:

1. Can the statement be proven?   Yes

2. Can the statement be supported?   Yes

3. Can anyone disagree with it?   No

These answers show that the statement is a fact.

Let's use these sentences about spinach as an example.

A. Spinach is a nutritious vegetable.

B. Spinach is a delicious vegetable.

Can sentence A be proven? Yes. We could find out about the vitamins and nutritional benefits spinach provides. Can the statement be supported? Yes. A dietitian may have some statistics about the positive long-term effects of spinach in a person's diet. Can anyone disagree with sentence A? No.

Sentence B, on the other hand, is a matter of personal taste or opinion. Can the statement be proven? No. Spinach-haters cannot be convinced that the vegetable is delicious. Nor can they be considered wrong. Can the statement be supported? No. In fact, you may find more support for the unpleasant taste of spinach. Finally, can anyone disagree with the statement? Yes. Of course, differences of opinion about food are acceptable.

EXERCISE 11

Fact Versus Opinion Statements

Next to each of the following statements, write an *F* for fact or an *O* for opinion.

_____ 1. Spring is the most pleasant season of the year.

_____ 2. The average rainfall is 3.8 inches per month.

_____ 3. More people watch the news at 6:00 P.M. than at 11:00 P.M.

_____ 4. Tom Brokaw is the most intelligent newscaster.

_____ 5. Physics is more difficult than chemistry.

_____ 6. Men in the 1950s were happier than men in the 1970s.

_____ 7. Strong women may be attracted to weak men.

_____ 8. The preadolescent growth spurt usually occurs earlier in females than in males.

_____ 9. Shorter men tend to be more aggressive.

_____ 10. More male students than female students enroll in higher-level math courses.

EXERCISE 12

Writing Fact and Opinion Statements

In this exercise you will be writing sentences that are either facts or opinions. If you are asked to write a factual statement, you should be able to prove it. If anyone can disagree with the statement, it is an opinion.

1. Write a factual statement about men as caregivers for children. _____

_____

2. Write an opinion statement about women as caregivers for the elderly. _____

_____

3. Write a factual statement about the salaries of men and women. _____

_____

4. Write an opinion statement about the salaries of men and women. _____

_____

5. Write a factual statement about men and sports. _____

_____

6. Write an opinion statement about women and sports. _____

_____

7. Write a factual statement about men and clothing styles or costs. _____

_____

8. Write an opinion statement about women and clothing styles or costs. _____

_____

9. Write a factual statement about women and politics. _____

_____

10. Write an opinion statement about men and politics. _____

_____

At times, writers will include a fact and an opinion in the same sentence. Often, this is an attempt to influence the reader. The careful reader can distinguish which part of the sentence is factual and which part is not. Consider the following example.

> Men hold most of the highest positions in large corporations because they are more logical and efficient than women.

There are two parts to this sentence. Circle the word *because*. It divides the sentence in two. Now apply the three-question test to both parts of the sentence.

1. Can the statement be proven?

2. Can the statement be supported?

3. Can anyone disagree with it?

You will see that the first part, "Men hold most of the highest positions in large corporations," is a fact. It can be proven, supported, and no one can disagree with it. The second part, "they [men] are more logical and efficient than women," is an opinion. It can neither be proven nor supported, and many would disagree with it.

There may be many reasons that men occupy most executive positions. Perhaps men hire men, or women are not provided opportunities to advance in some companies. If you believed the second part of the sentence because the first part is factual, you would have been misled.

The following statements contain facts and opinions. Underline the opinion section of each one.

EXERCISE 13

Mixed Fact and Opinion Statements

1. Women have fewer heart attacks than men because they take better care of their bodies.

2. As indicated by their higher scores on the spelling test, fourth-grade girls are smarter than fourth-grade boys.

3. Since they can't handle heavy stockpots and feel the effects of excessive heat in the kitchen, women rarely hold the position of head chef in first-class restaurants.

4. Men are offered more transfer promotions because they are more willing to move than women are.

5. We need more women in government to represent women who make up the majority of voters.

6. Geraldine Ferraro, one of the brightest representatives from the state of New York, was the first woman to run for the vice-presidency of the United States.

7. *Murphy Brown,* a popular situation comedy, should not have tackled the issue of unwed mothers.

8. The number of fathers who are delinquent with child-support payments is due to the irresponsibility of men in general.

9. Reluctant to appear defensive, the politician continued to smile and shake hands as demonstrators heckled him.

10. Football, a high-contact sport, is too dangerous for women.

SELECTION 2

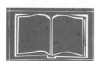

This selection provides some very important information about our theme. You can tell from the title that the passage will discuss how gender roles develop. You can assume from the word *development* that gender roles grow and may change. To help you focus on the important points, you should turn the title into a question or two and read to find the answers.

What are gender roles?

How do they develop?

You will be asked questions after each section of the reading passage. You may discuss your answers with a fellow student before you write them in the space provided.

The first paragraph introduces the topic, and the second provides a definition and the answer to your first question.

THE DEVELOPMENT OF GENDER ROLES

Men and women differ on the average in many social behaviors. The question is: Why? Chances are there are several reasons. Biology is probably one factor. Competition among males for status is widespread in the animal kingdom; it is probably part of our basic nature. But people are also molded by culture. Even if males are biologically predisposed to be more <u>aggressive</u> or females to be more cooperative, their culture channels the ways they express those tendencies.

In one way or another, each society teaches its children how they are expected to behave. In particular, it prepares boys for the tasks that will

Excerpts from *Introduction to Psychology,* 3rd ed., by James W. Kalat (Belmont, Calif.: Wadsworth, 1993), pp. 268–269.

be expected of men, and it prepares girls for the tasks expected of women. That is, it teaches them their gender role. A gender role is the psychological aspect of being male or female, as opposed to sex, which is the biological aspect. <u>Gender role</u> is the role each person is expected to play because of being male or female.

Answer the following questions based on your reading.

1. What are gender roles? _____

_____

You probably copied the definition from the passage. Now see if you can explain it in your own words to a fellow student. You will need to consider the terms *psychological* and *biological*. You may also wish to provide an example.

2. What does the word *aggressive* mean? _____

_____

When we say that "society" teaches children their gender role, that does not necessarily mean that *adults* teach children their gender role, or that *anyone* teaches gender roles deliberately or intentionally. Adults, especially parents, do teach children gender roles to some extent. Parents dress boys differently from girls, give them different toys, and offer them different kinds of experiences. The choice of toys, in turn, <u>determines</u> how much the parents talk with the children while they are playing. When parents and their children play with dolls, they talk a great deal. When they play with cars and trucks, they talk less (O'Brien & Nagle, 1987).

Adults also teach gender roles by example. Boys tend to imitate their fathers, and girls tend to imitate their mothers. Television presents certain images of what men and women do. Children also pay attention to role models outside the home. For example, a girl who goes to a female pediatrician may think of becoming a doctor herself.

Read the next two paragraphs to learn about how children learn their gender roles. As you read, look for several different ways children learn gender roles. Underline and number each one.

Answer the following questions based on your reading and on your own experience.

3. Name three ways parents teach their children gender roles:

   a. _____

   b. _____

   c. _____

4. In the preceding paragraph, what does the word *determines* mean? _____

   _____

5. According to the author, what effect does the choice of toys have on developing gender roles? Can you give your own example as well? _____

   _____

   _____

6. According to the author, what two other ways do children learn their gender roles?

   a. _____

   b. _____

Read the next two paragraphs to learn about yet another way children learn their gender roles.

However, in our society, most adults do *not* teach boys that they are supposed to fight with one another. In fact, they usually try to curb the fighting. Little boys tend to be bossy and aggressive toward little girls if they think no adults are watching. With an adult present, they become more cooperative (Powlishta & Maccoby, 1990).

And yet, clearly, little boys do learn to compete and fight with one another, even if adults are trying to tell them to stop. Where does this part of their gender role come from? From whom are they learning it? Quite simply, they learn it from other children. Children have a "playground culture" of their own. Each cohort of children teaches the slightly younger set what is expected of them. Even parents who try to raise their sons and daughters exactly the same find that their children come back from the playground with strong prejudices of what boys do and what girls do.

Answer the following questions based on your reading and on your experience.

7. From what other source do children learn their gender roles? _____

_____

8. What does the word *curb* mean as used by the author? _____

_____

9. Give an example you have observed illustrating how children learn their gender roles from other children.

_____

10. What word could you substitute for *cohort* in the passage? _____

_____

Gender roles are not necessarily harmful, but they sometimes limit the choices children feel will be open to them later in life. Imagine an artistically <u>inclined</u> boy who is told "real men like sports, not art." Or imagine a girl who wants to become an electrical engineer until someone tells her that "engineering is not a good career for a woman." Ideally, children (and adults) should feel free to develop their own interests and talents, whatever they may be.

Read the last paragraph to learn about one disadvantage of gender roles.

Answer the following questions based on your reading and on your experience.

11. What problem do gender roles cause? _____

_____

12. What does the word *inclined* mean as the author uses it? _____

_____

13. Can you think of certain professions or jobs that are usually held by men? Can you think of any careers that are often recommended to women? _____

_____

14. Give an example you have observed where a man was expected to do something but a woman was not. It may be a social, family, or work-related expectation. _____

_____

15. Describe a situation in which a woman is expected to behave in a particular way just because of her gender role. _____

_____

WRITING EXERCISE

Explain what gender roles are and how they are learned.

_____

_____

_____

_____

_____

_____

SELECTION 3

In the United States today, there are laws against discrimination in the workplace. Employers are not permitted to deny job opportunities to anyone because of sex, race, religion, or other factors unrelated to the job qualifications. This was not always the case. The excerpt that follows is taken from a book that describes the employment history at *The New York Times*. As you read, try to understand what the situation was like in the newspaper business in the 1930s and compare it to today's situation.

Read the first paragraph to find out about Adolph Ochs, publisher of *The New York Times* from 1896 to 1935.

WOMEN

To the end of his life in 1935, Ochs agreed with the outdated views of James Gordon Bennett, the cross-eyed, cross-grained owner of the *New York Herald* from 1835 to 1872. Bennett was probably the worst <u>misogynist</u> among publishers in the nineteenth century: he strode into his office one day and bellowed, "Who are these females? Fire them all!" Ochs, who was a Southern gentleman as well as a dictator, would never have expressed such an attitude so rudely. But he carried Bennett's Victorian notions straight into the twentieth century. He believed women belonged at home and certainly not on a newspaper; he fought personally and in his paper's editorials against women's right to vote.

Answer the following questions based on your reading.

1. What opinions about women did Adolph Ochs have? _____

_____

2. What do you think the word *misogynist* means? _____

_____

3. What would happen today if an employer expressed such an attitude? _____

_____

Excerpts from *The Girls in the Balcony: Women, Men and The New York Times,* by Nan Robertson (New York: Random House, 1992), pp. 46, 20.

Her talent shone forth in her very first stories for the *Times*. "She put a glow on everything she wrote," said James B. Reston, one of the most idolized reporters of his time, and of the *Times*. Adolph Ochs found her charming, and a writer of unusual power and grace. But he would not welcome Anne O'Hare McCormick on his staff.

His son-in-law and successor as publisher, Arthur Hays Sulzberger, could hardly wait to do the deed. Sulzberger had been secretly promising Mrs. McCormick a permanent arrangement since 1934, while Ochs was isolated in his second nervous breakdown and Sulzberger was acting in his place. Finally, on June 1, 1936, a year after Ochs's death, the new publisher put her on his payroll. She was fifty-six years old. He immediately named her the first woman member of the editorial board and soon gave Anne McCormick her own column on foreign affairs. Sulzberger called it "my first important official decision." Her peak earnings as a space-rate writer had been $200 for a *Times* magazine article and $62.50 for a daily newspaper piece measuring a column long. Her starting salary was $7,000 a year.

Her Pulitzer came less than a year later. It was not for one superlative piece. It was for distinguished foreign correspondence: her dispatches and features from Europe. Implicitly, the prize was for hundreds of articles written during the fifteen years she had knocked at the door of *The New York Times*.

The next section describes how Adolph Ochs influenced the career of a very talented woman reporter. As you read, contrast the talent described with the treatment Anne McCormick received.

Answer the following questions based on your reading and on your experience.

4. Who admired Anne McCormick's writing? _____

_____

5. Why do you think Adolph Ochs allowed Anne McCormick to contribute articles to the paper but would not put her on staff, even though he liked her and appreciated her writing? _____

_____

_____

6. Can you think of any contemporary examples of people who believe certain careers and opportunities are inappropriate for women? Describe them. _____

_____

7. How old was Anne McCormick when she was formally employed by *The New York Times*? Why is this significant? _____

_____

8. Is there a difference today between being a full-time staff person and working part-time or "by the piece" for a company? ("By the piece" is an expression that is often used in factory or garment-center work. The employee who makes shoes or sews zippers on jackets is paid according to how many "pieces" he or she completes.) _____

_____

9. The Pulitzer prize is perhaps the most respected award for journalism. Comment on the timing and the work for which Anne McCormick received it. _____

_____

10. What obstacles did Anne McCormick have to face as she tried to make her career in journalism? _____

_____

WRITING EXERCISE

Write a three-paragraph piece on women in the workplace. In the first paragraph, describe the situation Anne McCormick faced in the newspaper business. In the second paragraph, describe a difficult work situation you or someone you know faced. In the third paragraph, compare and contrast the two situations.

_____

_____

_____

_____

_____

_____

_____

_____

_____

_____

_____

_____

_____

_____

_____

_____

_____

_____

_____

In the last twenty years, the women's movement has directed our attention to problems women have faced in living up to their potential. More recently, the idea that men, too, have experienced discrimination and limitations has come forward. One of the spokesmen for the "men's movement" is Robert Bly. In his book *Iron John,* Bly uses a version of a story found in the folklore and mythology of many cultures to describe some of the difficulties men face today. You will read several excerpts from his work. The first describes the way an American man's situation has changed in recent history. As you read the first excerpt, try to identify the changes that men have experienced as they've moved from one decade to another.

SELECTION 4

MEN

The Fifties man was supposed to like football, be aggressive, stick up for the United States, never cry, and always provide. But receptive space or intimate space was missing in this image of a man. The personality lacked some sense of flow. The <u>psyche</u> lacked compassion in a way that encouraged the unbalanced pursuit of the Vietnam war, just as, later, the lack of what we might call "garden" space inside Reagan's head led to his <u>callousness</u> and brutality toward the powerless in El Salvador, toward old people here, the unemployed, schoolchildren, and poor people in general.

The Fifties male had a clear vision of what a man was, and what male responsibilities were, but the isolation and one-sidedness of his vision were dangerous.

Read the first two paragraphs to learn about the "fifties man."

Answer the following questions based on your reading and on your experience.

1. What was the fifties man like? _____

_____

2. Do you know anyone like that? If so, tell about him, including his age, appearance, and interests. _____

_____

3. According to Bly, what does the word *psyche* mean? _____

_____

4. What does the word *callousness* mean? _____

_____

During the sixties, another sort of man appeared. The waste and violence of the Vietnam war made men question whether they knew what an adult male really was. If manhood meant Vietnam, did they want any part of it? Meanwhile, the feminist movement encouraged men to

Read the next two paragraphs to find out about men in the sixties.

Excerpts from *Iron John: A Book About Men,* by Robert Bly (Reading, Mass.: Addison Wesley, 1990), pp. 2–3.

actually look at women, forcing them to become conscious of concerns and sufferings that the Fifties male <u>labored</u> to avoid. As men began to examine women's history and women's sensibility, some men began to notice what was called their feminine side and pay attention to it. This process continues to this day, and I would say that most contemporary men are involved in it in some way.

There's something wonderful about this development—I mean the practice of men welcoming their own "feminine" consciousness and <u>nurturing</u> it—this is important—and yet I have the sense that there is something wrong. The male in the past twenty years has become more thoughtful, more gentle. But by this process he has not become more free. He's a nice boy who pleases not only his mother but also the young woman he is living with.

Answer the following questions based on your reading and on your experience.

5. What were men like in the sixties? _____

_____

6. Do you know anyone like that? If so, tell about him, including his age, appearance, and interests. _____

_____

7. What does the word *labored* mean in this excerpt? _____

_____

8. How does Bly use the word *nurturing*? _____

_____

Read the next section to learn how men have changed in the seventies.

In the seventies I began to see all over the country a phenomenon that we might call the "soft male." Sometimes even today when I look out at an audience, perhaps half the young males are what I'd call soft. They're lovely, valuable people—I like them—they're not interested in harming the earth or starting wars. There's a gentle attitude toward life in the whole being and style of living.

But many of these men are not happy. You quickly notice the lack of energy in them. They are life-preserving but not exactly life-giving. Ironically, you often see these men with strong women who positively <u>radiate</u> energy.

Here we have a finely tuned young man, ecologically superior to his father, sympathetic to the whole harmony of the universe, yet he himself has little vitality to offer.

The strong or life-giving women who graduated from the sixties, so to speak, or who have inherited an older spirit, played an important part in producing this life-preserving, but not life-giving, man.

Answer the following questions based on your reading and on your experience.

9. Describe the seventies male. _____

   _____

10. Do you know anyone like that? If so, tell about him, including his age, appearance, and interests. _____

   _____

11. What is the meaning of the word *radiate?* _____

   _____

As you answered questions 1, 3, and 5, you were writing down the main ideas of each paragraph or section of the reading. As you answered questions 2, 4, and 6, you applied what you had read to another situation. In other words, you understood the information presented, created your own example, and consequently deepened your comprehension.

Another way to extend your comprehension and appreciation is through making inferences. An *inference* is a conclusion or a judgment based on the information provided plus your own thinking. The writer gives you hints or suggestions, but you do the thinking.

Consider the following sentences from the selection you have just finished reading.

A. "The personality lacked some sense of flow."

B. ". . . but the isolation and one-sidedness of his vision were dangerous."

C. ". . . and yet I have the sense that there is something wrong."

D. "But by this process he has not become more free."

E. "But many of these men are not happy."

12. What is similar about these statements? _____

_____

_____

13. Compare these five statements with your descriptions of fifties, sixties, and seventies men. Are your statements more positive or negative? _____

_____

_____

14. Find these statements in the reading selection and underline them.

15. In the context of the passage, these five statements indicate the writer's opinion about how men have changed. Complete the following inferential statement: Robert Bly seems to believe that men have changed a lot since the 1950s. Although most of these changes are good ones, _____

_____

_____

WRITING EXERCISE

Write a paragraph describing how men have changed from the 1950s to the 1970s.

_____

_____

_____

_____

_____

THEME 2
Environment

For decades we have been taking our natural environment and its resources for granted. Many Americans have grown up with a "throwaway mentality." We have become accustomed to replacing things rather than repairing them, to eating fast food and to producing a lot of garbage. We have overheated our homes and left our lights burning all day, expecting that cheap energy would always be available. In our desire to lead comfortable and convenient lives, we have put the natural environment and its creatures at risk. In our experimentation with chemicals and nuclear energy, we have put ourselves at risk.

As the world's population has grown and as demands for energy have increased, it has become apparent that a change in attitude is needed. Nonrenewable energy sources, such as oil, coal, and natural gas, must be conserved. Disposal methods such as recycling must be developed to cope with the mounds of trash produced by populated areas.

As you work on this theme, you will learn some terminology associated with environmental studies. By reading about selected environmental topics, you will gather information that will help you make thoughtful decisions and recommendations about how we can protect our environment and ourselves. Finally, you will have the opportunity to present your own ideas.

THEME FOCUS

TOPIC: ENVIRONMENT

RELATED VOCABULARY

SKILLS: GLOSSARY USE

IDENTIFYING DETAILS

UNDERLINING OR HIGH-LIGHTING

OUTLINING

MAPPING

IDENTIFYING ORGANIZATIONAL PATTERNS—LIST AND PROCESS DESCRIPTION

SKILL DEVELOPMENT: EXPANDING YOUR VOCABULARY

In this section the exercises will focus on words in context, definitions, and glossary use.

EXERCISE 1
Words in Context

The underlined words in the following sentences appear in the passages you will read in this section of your text. They are presented in context here so that you will be able to figure out their meanings. Write the meaning of the underlined word below each sentence.

---

1. The Endangered Species Act prohibits destroying or changing the <u>habitats</u> of creatures whose existence is threatened by activities that would ruin their homes or surroundings. _____

   _____

2. Critics of the Endangered Species Act say that it creates conflict between <u>ecology</u> and economy. Members of the first group put the environment first, and those who belong to the second favor business interests. _____

   _____

3. The conservation committee hopes to repair <u>watersheds</u> and streams that nurture salmon, one of the forests' most valuable species. _____

   _____

4. What started nearly a decade ago as an attempt to save the spotted owl from <u>extinction</u> has grown into a movement to save the forests for their own sakes. _____

   _____

5. One conservation plan recommends hiring people in rural areas to plant new trees, fix trails, and repair or remove roads that are depositing <u>sediment</u> in nearby streams. _____

   _____

6. "Green Lights," a program to promote energy-efficient lighting, hopes to reduce carbon dioxide by more than 132 million pounds—equal to the <u>emissions</u> from the exhausts of 44 million automobiles.

   _____

7. In the past two years, the Federal Trade Commission has brought charges against eight firms for allegedly making <u>unsubstantiated</u> claims of environmental benefits from consumer products. _____

   _____

8. Small oil companies must find ways to finance new <u>exploration</u>, research, and production. _____

   _____

9. Chain saws have ripped through the equatorial rain forests, and <u>overgrazing</u> by wild and domestic animals threatens to turn African plains to dust. _____

   _____

10. Gardeners seek to improve on nature and tame it, but <u>restorationists</u> try to return to the landscape the very things people find hostile—fire, floods, and "annoying critters" that help keep each ecosystem healthy. _____

_____

11. With hacksaws and <u>herbicides</u>, restorationists are attacking exotic foreign plants that have displaced native vegetation. _____

_____

12. The U.S. Army Corps of Engineers has drawn up plans to <u>regenerate</u> wetlands killed off by flood control projects. _____

_____

13. The diaries of a nineteenth-century doctor have provided Illinois ecologists with a list of plants that once <u>flourished</u> in the state under the shade of oak trees. _____

_____

14. <u>Conservationists</u> often find themselves at odds with local groups who fear that too much attention to protecting the environment may result in a loss of jobs. _____

_____

15. The main reasons for the extinction of the passenger pigeon include hunting and the loss of habitat and food supplies. Many birds also died from infectious disease and severe storms during their annual fall <u>migration</u> to Central and South America. _____

_____

16. About 75 percent of the world's population relies on plants or plant <u>extracts</u> as sources of medicine.

_____

17. <u>Toxic</u> chemicals discharged into the environment by industry can be fatal to humans as they attack the nerve cells. _____

_____

18. Too many visitors to favorite wildlife reserves can damage <u>ecosystems</u> and disrupt the lives of some species. _____

_____

19. About half of all tropical <u>deforestation</u> is taking place in the vast Amazon basin, mostly in Brazil, as trees are cut and areas are burned to clear land to grow crops. _____

_____

20. Even creatures whose homes are not totally destroyed have a hard time coping with the <u>degradation</u> of their habitats as humans and their activities move into their areas. _____

_____

EXERCISE 2

Definitions

Match the words in column A with their definitions in column B.

PART 1	
COLUMN A	COLUMN B
___ 1. habitat	a. area of water supply that feeds a stream or river
___ 2. ecology	b. without proof or confirmation
___ 3. watershed	c. the complete disappearance of a species
___ 4. extinction	d. the process of investigation; trying to discover or to uncover
___ 5. sediment	e. place or area where an organism or population lives
___ 6. emissions	f. deposits or other material that settles to the bottom in water
___ 7. unsubstantiated	g. chemical substance that kills plants
___ 8. exploration	h. substances that are released or given off
___ 9. overgrazing	i. destruction of vegetation in a particular area as animals feed too long
___ 10. herbicide	j. the study of the relationships among organisms and their environment

PART 2

COLUMN A	COLUMN B
_____ 1. restoration	a. poisonous; harmful; deadly
_____ 2. regenerate	b. to bring back to life; to restore; to refresh
_____ 3. flourish	c. to return or to bring back to use or original condition
_____ 4. conservationists	d. seasonal pattern of movement from one area to another
_____ 5. migration	e. removal of many trees without replacement
_____ 6. extracts	f. to grow well or to thrive
_____ 7. toxic	g. people who believe resources should be protected and managed
_____ 8. ecosystems	h. serious damage or corruption
_____ 9. deforestation	i. substances that are removed or drawn forth
_____ 10. degradation	j. a community of different species interacting with one another and the environment

EXERCISE 3

Glossary Use

When you study theme 4, you will learn about the features of a dictionary and will practice using one. In this section of the book, however, you will learn about glossaries and how they can help you extend your vocabulary. Dictionaries and glossaries are similar. Both contain alphabetized lists of words with definitions. The words that are listed are called *entries* whether they are found in a dictionary or a glossary.

There are several important differences between a dictionary and a glossary, however.

- A glossary is found in the back of a book; it is not a book in itself.

- A glossary does not provide as much information as a dictionary. For example, a glossary may not include pronunciation, multiple meanings, or information about the word's origins. What it does provide is a definition that is related to the subject of the book. For example, a glossary in a book about the environment will probably include the word *mantle*. The definition will tell you that it means the "zone of the earth's interior between the core and its crust." If you looked up the word *mantle* in a standard dictionary, the first meaning would probably be "a loose, sleeveless coat." The second definition might be "a facing around a fireplace." Such definitions would not be particularly helpful in environmental studies.

- A glossary also has more technical definitions. If you looked up the word *forest* in a standard dictionary, for example, you might learn that it means "a dense growth of trees covering a large area." The glossary may give you more technical information, such as "a biome with enough average precipitation (at least 76 centimeters, or 30 inches) to support the growth of various species of trees and smaller forms of vegetation." Both definitions are essentially the same, but you might need the glossary definition to determine if a particular area is actually classified as a forest.

- Finally, a glossary may contain words or phrases that have been coined by the subject discipline. These words would not be found in a dictionary. For example, environmentalists came up with *agroforestry*, a word that combines agriculture and forestry to mean "planting trees and crops together." The term *conservation-tillage farming* would not be found in a standard dictionary either, but it is listed in an environmental glossary. It means "crop cultivation in which the soil is disturbed little to reduce soil erosion."

You will find glossaries helpful when you are reading textbooks. As soon as you begin to use a book, check to see if it includes a glossary. Fields such as biology, psychology, sociology, and computer science have developed their own terminologies and vocabularies. Some authors define these terms the first time they are used. Others presume that the readers have some background in the field and expect them to be familiar with technical terms. The glossary can help clarify the meaning of a word. A clear definition may help you understand a paragraph or a chapter. You may also want to use the glossary to review the meanings of words you learned in earlier chapters. Many professors consider a student's familiarity with subject terminology a good indicator of his or her general knowledge of the field. As with general reading, if you are comfortable with vocabulary words in a technical passage, your comprehension will improve. The glossary provides you with another tool to increase your vocabulary knowledge.

Read carefully the following sample glossary page from an environmental textbook, and then answer the list of questions. This exercise is designed to give you some practice in using a glossary.

contour strip mining Cutting a series of shelves or terraces along the side of a hill or mountain to remove a mineral such as coal from a deposit found near the earth's surface. Compare *area strip mining, open-pit surface mining*.

contraceptive Physical, chemical, or biological method used to prevent pregnancy.

conventional-tillage farming Making a planting surface by plowing land, disking it several times to break up the soil, and then smoothing the surface. Compare *conservation-tillage farming*.

convergent plate boundary Area where Earth's lithospheric plates are pushed together. See *subduction zone*. Compare *divergent plate boundary, transform fault*.

core Inner zone of the earth. It consists of a solid *inner core* and a liquid *outer core*. Compare *crust, mantle*.

cost-benefit analysis Estimates and comparison of short-term and long-term costs (losses) and benefits (gains) from an economic decision. If the estimated benefits exceed the estimated costs, the decision to buy an economic good or provide a public good is considered worthwhile.

critical mass Amount of fissionable nuclei needed to sustain a branching nuclear fission chain reaction.

critical mineral A mineral necessary to the economy of a country. Compare *strategic mineral*.

crop rotation Planting a field, or an area of a field, with different crops from year to year to reduce depletion of soil nutrients. A plant such as corn, tobacco, or cotton, which removes large amounts of nitrogen from the soil, is planted one year. The next year a legume such as soybeans, which add nitrogen to the soil, is planted.

crown fire Extremely hot forest fire that burns ground vegetation and tree tops. Compare *ground fire, surface fire*.

crude birth rate Annual number of live births per 1,000 persons in the population of a geographical area at the midpoint of a given year. Compare *crude death rate*.

crude death rate Annual number of deaths per 1,000 persons in the population of a geographical area at the midpoint of a given year. Compare *crude birth rate*.

crude oil Gooey liquid consisting mostly of hydrocarbon compounds and small amounts of compounds containing oxygen, sulfur, and nitrogen. Extracted from underground accumulations, it is sent to oil refineries, where it is converted into heating oil, diesel fuel, gasoline, tar, and other materials.

crust Solid outer zone of the earth. It consists of *oceanic crust* and *continental crust*. Compare *core, mantle*.

cultural eutrophication Overnourishment of aquatic ecosystems with plant nutrients (mostly nitrates and phosphates) because of human activities such as agriculture, urbanization, and discharges from industrial plants and sewage treatment plants. See *eutrophication*.

DDT Dichlorodiphenyltrichloroethane, a chlorinated hydrocarbon that has been widely used as a pesticide.

death rate See *crude death rate*.

debt-for-nature swap Agreement in which a certain amount of foreign debt is cancelled in exchange for local currency investments that will improve natural resource management or protect certain areas from harmful development in the debtor country.

deciduous plants Trees, such as oaks and maples, and other plants that survive during dry seasons or cold seasons by shedding their leaves. Compare *coniferous trees, succulent plants*.

decomposer Organism that digests parts of dead organisms and cast-off fragments and wastes of living organisms by breaking down the complex organic molecules in those materials into simpler inorganic compounds and absorbing the soluble nutrients. Most of these chemicals are returned to the soil and water for reuse by producers. Decomposers consist of various bacteria and fungi. Compare *consumer, detritivore, producer*.

deep ecology See *sustainable-Earth worldview*.

defendant The individual, group of individuals, corporation, or government agency being charged in a lawsuit. Compare *plaintiff*.

deforestation Removal of trees from a forested area without adequate replanting.

degradable pollutant Potentially polluting chemical that is broken down completely or reduced to acceptable levels by natural physical, chemical, and biological processes. Compare *biodegradable pollutant, nondegradable pollutant, slowly degradable pollutant*.

degree of urbanization Percentage of the population in the world, or a country, living in areas with a population of more than 2,500 people (significantly more in some countries). Compare *urban growth*.

delta Buildup deposit of river-borne sediments at the mouth of a river.

demographic transition Hypothesis that countries, as they become industrialized, have declines in death rates followed by declines in birth rates.

demography Study of characteristics and changes in the size and structure of the human population in the world or other geographical area.

depletion time How long it takes to use a certain fraction—usually 80%—of the known or estimated supply of a nonrenewable resource at an assumed rate of use. Finding and extracting the remaining 20% usually costs more than it is worth.

desalination Purification of salt water or brackish (slightly salty) water by removing dissolved salts.

desert Biome where evaporation exceeds precipitation and the average amount of precipitation is less than 25 centimeters (10 inches) a year. Such areas have little vegetation or have widely spaced, mostly low vegetation. Compare *forest, grassland*.

desertification Conversion of rangeland, rain-fed cropland, or irrigated cropland to desertlike land, with a drop in agricultural productivity of 10% or more. It is usually caused by a combination of overgrazing, soil erosion, prolonged drought, and climate change.

desirability quotient A number expressing the results of risk-benefit analysis by dividing the estimate of the benefits to society of using a particular product or technology by its estimated risks. See *risk-benefit analysis*. Compare *cost-benefit analysis*.

detritivore Consumer organism that feeds on detritus, parts of dead organisms and cast-off fragments and wastes of living organisms. The two principal types are *detritus feeders* and *decomposers*.

detritus Parts of dead organisms and cast-off fragments and wastes of living organisms.

detritus feeder Organism that extracts nutrients from fragments of dead organisms and cast-off parts and organic wastes of living organisms. Examples are earthworms, termites, and crabs. Compare *decomposer*.

deuterium (D: hydrogen-2) Isotope of the element hydrogen, with a nucleus containing one proton and one neutron, and a mass number of 2. Compare *tritium*.

developed country See *more developed country*.

dieback Sharp reduction in the population of a species when its numbers exceed the carrying capacity of its habitat. See *carrying capacity, consumption overpopulation, overshoot, people overpopulation*.

differential reproduction Ability of individuals with adaptive genetic traits to produce more living offspring than individuals without such traits. See also *natural selection*.

discount rate How much economic value a resource will have in the future compared with its present value.

dissolved oxygen (DO) content (level) Amount of oxygen gas (O_2) dissolved in a given volume of water at a particular temperature and pressure, often expressed as a concentration in parts of oxygen per million parts of water.

divergent plate boundary Area where Earth's lithospheric plates move apart in opposite directions. Compare *convergent plate boundary, transform fault*.

diversity Variety. See *biological diversity*.

DNA (deoxyribonucleic acid) Large molecules that carry genetic information in living organisms. They are found in the cells of organisms.

doubling time The time it takes (usually in years) for the quantity of something growing exponentially to double. It can be calculated by dividing the annual percentage growth rate into 70. See *rule of 70*.

drainage basin See *watershed*.

dredge spoils Materials scraped from the bottoms of harbors and streams to maintain shipping channels. They are often contaminated with high levels of toxic substances that have settled out of the water. See *dredging*.

dredging Type of surface mining, in which chain buckets and draglines scrape up sand, gravel, and other surface deposits covered with water. It is also used to remove sediment from streams and harbors to maintain shipping channels. See *dredge spoils*.

drift-net fishing Catching fish in huge nets that drift in the water.

drip irrigation Using small tubes or pipes to deliver small amounts of irrigation water to the roots of plants.

drought Condition in which an area does not get enough water because of lower than normal precipitation, higher than normal temperatures that increase evaporation, or both.

dust dome Dome of heated air that surrounds an urban area and traps and keeps pollutants, especially particulate matter in suspension. See also *urban heat island*.

Earth capital Earth's natural resources and processes that sustain us and other species.

earthquake Shaking of the ground resulting from the fracturing and displacement of rock, producing a fault, or from subsequent movement along the fault.

ecological diversity The variety of forests, deserts, grasslands, oceans, streams, lakes, and other biological communities interacting with one another and with their nonliving environment. See *biological diversity*. Compare *genetic diversity, species diversity*.

ecological niche Total way of life or role of a species in an ecosystem. It includes all physical, chemical, and biological conditions a species needs to live and reproduce in an ecosystem. See *fundamental niche, realized niche*.

ecological succession Process in which communities of plant and animal species in a particular area are replaced over time by a series of different and usually more complex communities. See *primary ecological succession, secondary ecological succession*.

ecology Study of the interactions of living organisms with one another and with their nonliving environment of matter and energy; study of the structure and functions of nature.

From *Living in the Environment*, 7th ed., by G. Tyler Miller, Jr. (Belmont, Calif.: Wadsworth, 1992), glossary p. 3.

Answer the following questions based on the glossary entries and your own knowledge.

1. Write a definition of the word *crust* as you would use it in ordinary conversation. _____
   _____

2. What is the glossary definition of crust, and how does it differ from your definition? _____
   _____

3. What is the difference between *conservation-tillage farming* (as defined in the introduction to this exercise) and *conventional-tillage farming* (as defined in the glossary)? _____
   _____

4. Where would a *crown fire* occur? _____
   _____

5. Where would you look for information about the word *diversity*? _____
   _____

6. Would you be more likely to find a *dust dome* in the metropolitan Denver area or on a farm in Kansas?
   _____

7. In what two ways is *dredging* used? _____
   a. _____
   b. _____

8. What concern would you have for a particular type of bird that experienced *dieback*? _____
   _____

9. Tell how *decomposers* and *detritus feeders* are alike and how they are different.
   a. _____
   b. _____

10. How would you define the word *desert* as you would use it in ordinary conversation? _____
    _____

11. What additional information about the word *desert* does the glossary provide? _____
    _____

12. For what purpose might you use *desalination*? _____
    _____

13. Why is *crop rotation* a good idea? _____
    _____

14. Write a definition for the word *core* as you would use it in ordinary conversation. _____
    _____

15. What additional information about the word *core* does the glossary provide? _____
    _____

SKILL DEVELOPMENT: IDENTIFYING DETAILS

When you read, try to grasp the main point or idea of a passage as you strive to understand the author's message. Then focus on the details of the reading. Details provide explanation, support, or examples. Some details are crucial to understanding the passage. In fact, a missed detail can lead to a serious misunderstanding of the author's intent. Other details may be less significant and may even be repetitious. It is the reader's job to identify the important details and use them to understand the passage.

The following passage contains details that explain the author's main point. Since the passage is an excerpt from a newspaper article, the headline provides clues about the topic and the main idea. Reporters often find themselves short of space, so they try to make their headlines as short and specific as possible. In translating the headline to a main idea sentence, try to add words that will clarify the main point.

As you read the passage, focus on the author's main point. After you finish reading, you will answer a series of questions that will help you locate the important details.

EXERCISE 4
Locating Details

SEA-DUMPING BAN: GOOD POLITICS, BUT NOT NECESSARILY GOOD POLICY

For millions of people from Montauk to Maryland, the broiling summer of 1988 will be hard to forget. It was the hottest year ever recorded. Repulsive trash slicks covered the Eastern shoreline. And borne upon a tide of public outrage, garbage emerged as a potent political issue.

In New York and New Jersey, where most of the waste appeared, health officials closed beaches by the score, depriving sweltering people of relief. Pictures of used syringes, dead dolphins and human excrement scattered across the sand became a staple of the news.

Anger required action. So that fall, without registering a single vote of opposition, Congress banned the dumping of sewage into the ocean. The law prohibited New York City from dropping its processed waste into the sea and forced officials to find costly new ways to get rid of it.

THE RUSH TO BAN

"This is a turning point in human history," said a euphoric Representative William J. Hughes, Democrat of New Jersey, after the vote. Other officials agreed, rushing to embrace the law as one of the most important environmental measures ever enacted.

There was just one problem.

Ocean dumping had absolutely nothing to do with the garbage that washed up on the sand that year. In fact, the problems that caused the

---

By Michael Specter, *The New York Times*, March 23, 1993, p. 1.

mess on the beaches in 1988—overtaxed sewage systems—were largely ignored, and the health risks they present are as serious as they have ever been.

Most scientists agree that using the sea as a garbage can was unpleasant and are pleased that it is no longer legal. Still, some argue that dumping sewage in the Atlantic Ocean 106 miles from the shore—which saved New York and other cities billions of dollars over the years—is less hazardous than most of the disposal methods that have replaced it.

1. State the topic of the passage. What is it about? _____

_____

2. Write the main idea of the passage in a complete sentence in your own words. _____

_____

Compare your first two answers with a fellow student to see if they are similar. The next four questions will help you look for the details that are specifically stated in the passage.

3. What time period does the article discuss? _____

_____

4. What problem occurred at that time? _____

_____

5. How did people react to the problem? _____

_____

6. What did lawmakers do to try to solve the problem? _____

_____

The last four questions will lead you to details that support the article's main idea; that is, that forbidding sewage dumping in the ocean may *not* solve the problem of polluted beaches.

7. Write the sentence that tells you the author is not as enthusiastic about the new law as the officials are. (*Hint:* The author makes it a paragraph by itself so that it stands out.) _____

_____

8. Why isn't the ocean dumping ban a solution to the problem? _____

_____

9. How far from shore had New York City wastes been dumped? _____

_____

10. The author mentions two problems with the disposal methods that have replaced ocean dumping. What are they?

a. _____

b. _____

Some of the details mentioned in the article did not show up in the questions because they are minor details. They may make the passage easier or more enjoyable to read, but they are not critical to understanding it. Some examples of minor details include pictures used on the news to show the problem and Representative Hughes's comment.

WRITING EXERCISE

Write a paragraph that explains the author's position on prohibiting dumping waste into the ocean. Your first sentence should state the main idea. Then use some of the details you identified to support this point. (*Hint:* Your answers to questions 3, 4, 6, and 8 should be particularly helpful.)

_____

_____

_____

_____

_____

EXERCISE 5

Underlining or Highlighting Important Points

Many students have successfully used underlining or highlighting as a reading and study strategy. It helps maintain concentration by forcing readers to interact with the material as they decide which points are important. Their comprehension often improves as they make a greater effort to understand what they are reading. When it comes time to review for a quiz or a test, half of the work has been done because the important points have already been identified.

High school students are usually discouraged from marking in their textbooks, because the books belong to the school district and are used to educate future classes. First-year college students may find it difficult to write in their books. Once they get in the habit of underlining or highlighting, however, they soon realize its benefits and recommend it to others. As you try to develop the "underlining or highlighting habit," keep these benefits in mind:

1. Helps your concentration.

2. Encourages you to interact with the material.

3. Improves your comprehension.

4. Eases the review process.

The following passage is about forests. As you read, you will notice that the author includes much detailed information. You should also notice that the passage is divided into sections. Your first task is to identify the main idea of each section. After you finish reading, you will be guided through the underlining or highlighting process. Most passages contain *major* and *minor details*. The *major details* are important; they develop and explain the main idea. The *minor details* add interest and information, but they are not essential.

1. ARE OUR FORESTS AN ENDANGERED SPECIES?

For centuries, humans have taken forests for granted. We assumed these vast areas of trees would always provide wood, food, shade, and recreation. Because forests seem large and plentiful, the threat to their existence can seem remote. In the lower forty-eight states, forests make up one-third of the land area. Forests and jungles combined cover 37 percent of the earth's surface. We are beginning to realize, though, that without conservation measures, the survival of our forests may be in jeopardy. The fact that trees take from 20 to 1,000 years to mature should help us realize that the forest is a valuable resource to be preserved.

2. A VALUABLE RESOURCE

In the natural scheme of things, forests perform many valuable functions. The trees and other vegetation absorb carbon dioxide and release oxygen into the air. Without the forests, the quality of our air would suffer considerably. The roots of the trees in the forest also prevent soil erosion. In contrast, areas that have been stripped of trees often lose valuable topsoil after heavy rainfalls. They may also experience flooding if there is no forest to absorb the water. In fact, forests serve as filters for rainwater. The rainfall is absorbed into the soil and gradually filters back into the streams and rivers that provide fresh groundwater.

3. THREATS TO THE FORESTS

Economic development and population growth are the biggest threats to the forests. Representatives of the timber industry often disagree with conservationists about forest management. Growing and harvesting techniques that are efficient for the timber industry are not always in the best interest of the forests. Natural, undisturbed forests are made up of a variety of trees of different ages. Such diversity serves as a protection. As the older trees mature, their seeds will regenerate the forest before they die out. Insects and diseases that are deadly to one species of tree will not wipe out everything in a diversified forest.

Logging practices such as clear-cutting and tree farming may be cheaper, but they do not guarantee the survival of the forest. If an area is clear-cut, all the trees are cut down at once. It is much faster and cheaper, because the loggers don't have to cut selectively. Nor do the workers need to maneuver their equipment around the trees that will be left to grow. What is left, however, after a clear-cut is a barren, ugly piece of land that provides none of the benefits the forest did.

To accommodate population growth, forests have been cleared to make way for farms, housing developments, and industrial complexes. Our industrialized way of life has also contributed to air pollution, a threat to forests as well as to people.

4. FOREST FIRES

Forest fires can be considered both a threat and a benefit to the forests. Humans cause the largest number of forest fires, followed by lightning. Fires that occur naturally actually help the forests follow a natural pattern of regeneration. *Surface fires,* as the name implies, occur at the ground level. They have the positive effects of consuming litter on the forest floor and destroying tree-killing insects. In fact, the seeds of some trees, like the Giant Sequoia, are released only after intense heat. So the continuation of some species depends on fires. Surface fires don't usually kill mature trees, and wildlife can usually escape from them. In fact, forestry managers sometimes start controlled fires as a conservation measure.

Crown fires, on the other hand, burn at the tops of the trees and can be quite devastating. They can move quickly and are very hard to contain. Unlike the surface fires, crown fires do kill mature trees and wildlife. They can also pose a serious threat to nearby populated areas if the fire spreads uncontrollably.

5. CONSERVATION MEASURES

Although the movement to protect and save our forests may seem new, such efforts were begun as long ago as the nineteenth century in Europe. In this country, the U.S. Forest Service began a campaign to make people aware of dangers to the forests in 1944. With Smokey the Bear as a symbol, this effort to prevent forest fires captured the attention of children and their parents.

Pressure from conservationists and legislation have forced some changes in the practices of the lumber and paper industries. Alternative methods of tree harvesting to insure regeneration of the forests are becoming more common. The Endangered Species Act has also helped the forests. As the connection between wildlife and their habitats becomes clear, the need to protect birds and animals also requires that their homes be preserved.

Finally, as we focus on the connection between our daily habits and their consequences for the environment, we find other ways to help the forests. Since much of the wood that is harvested from our forests is used to make paper, our efforts to recycle paper can make a difference to the demand for trees. Recycling paper, using canvas bags or lunch boxes instead of paper, and changing our "throwaway mentality" can affect the paper industry and its forest management.

1. First, consider the passage as a whole. Identify the topic first by asking yourself, "What is the passage about?" Write your answer below.

   _____

   _____

2. Now, try to identify the main idea of the whole passage. Ask yourself, "What does the passage say about the topic?" Write your answer below.

   _____

   _____

3. The next step is to consider the passage one section at a time. The first paragraph serves as an introduction. It provides some interesting information. The main idea of this paragraph seems to be stated fairly clearly in the last two sentences. Notice that the same point is made in both sentences. Only underline it once. Also, there is additional information included in both sentences that is *not* part of the main idea. Do not include these details in your main idea statement. Write the main idea below, and <u>underline</u> it in the passage.

   _____

   _____

Major details support or explain the main idea of the paragraph. There are no major details in the first paragraph, but there are a few minor details. *Minor details* are specific facts that lend interest but are not essential to the passage. Sometimes they are easy to remember because they are unusual or striking. If they were left out, however, the passage would still be clear and understandable. Without them, the main idea would have enough support from the major details to be convincing. Professors who favor multiple-choice tests or who like to give quizzes to see if you have read the material may ask you about minor details.

4. There are four minor details in the first section. The first two are listed below. Underline them in the text. Then find the other two minor details, underline them, and write them as the answers to parts *c* and *d*.

   a. Forests provide wood, food, shade, and recreation.

   b. Forests make up one-third of the land area of the lower forty-eight states.

   c. _____

   d. _____

5. The second section deals with more specific ideas than the first. Write the main idea of this paragraph. You may use the heading as the basis for your main idea sentence. _____

   _____

6. In the second section, *all* of the details support the main idea. They are all major details. There are three major details that tell why forests are valuable. (You may identify or combine them differently and come up with four reasons, and that's okay.) Underline them in the text and write them below.

   a. _____

   b. _____

   c. _____

The third section contains examples of major and minor details. Think of the progression from main idea to major detail to minor detail as a movement from the general to the specific. The main idea is fairly broad and the minor details are quite narrow.

Main Idea: Forests are threatened.
Major Details
economic development　　population growth
Minor Details
timber industry harvest techniques　　clearing for land development
logging practices　　air pollution
clear-cutting

7. Underline or highlight the main idea, major details, and minor details in section 3.

8. Now do the same thing in section 4. Underline or highlight and write below the main idea, major details, and minor details.

   a. **Main Idea:** _____

   b. *Major Details*

      1. _____   2. _____

   c. *Minor Details*

      1. _____   4. _____

      2. _____   5. _____

      3. _____   6. _____

9. The fifth and final section makes several points, so it is difficult to identify a single main idea. Use the heading as the heart of your main idea sentence, and try to make a connection between the past and the present. Since the main idea is not stated in the paragraph, you cannot underline or highlight it. Write it below.

   _____

   _____

10. In this section, we can consider the main idea of each paragraph as a major detail. The more specific points in each paragraph are the minor details. They have been identified for the first paragraph below. Underline or highlight them in the text.

    a. Major detail: Conservation measures began a long time ago.

    b. Minor details:

       1. Efforts to preserve forests began in nineteenth-century Europe.

       2. The U.S. Forest Service started a campaign in 1944.

       3. Smokey the Bear was the symbol of the "prevent forest fires" campaign.

11. For the last two paragraphs in section 5, identify the major and minor details, underline or highlight them in the text, and write them below.

    a. Major detail: _____

    b. Minor details:

       1. _____

       2. _____

    c. Major detail: _____

    d. Minor details:

       1. _____

       2. _____

Tell why forests are important and what we should do to protect them.

_____

_____

_____

_____

_____

SKILL DEVELOPMENT: OUTLINING AND MAPPING

Outlining and mapping are strategies that help you organize what you read. Most students prefer one method or the other, depending on how they learn. Outlining is a verbal organizational tool; mapping is a visual tool. Whichever you choose, remember its purpose is to help you understand what you are reading.

Outlining is usually a culminating activity; that is, something you do _after_ you have finished reading the material. (Some students prefer to outline _as_ they read.) You have already learned the preliminary steps, and you should be practicing them on a regular basis. After you read, return to the beginning of the passage to underline the main idea, major details, and any minor details you think you should remember. The outlining strategy allows you to organize information in a meaningful way by grouping related ideas. As a visual tool, it helps you see the relative importance of the points the author has made. For example, a main idea will probably appear as a major heading in your outline. A minor detail will be indented and positioned below its related major point. Some students who learned how to outline in elementary or high school have abandoned it because they can't keep the numbers and letters straight. Don't worry about the format. An outline is for _your_ benefit, and the only practical rule is that it make sense to you. An outline is not a substitute for the actual passage. It is, however, an excellent review tool. Presumably, you read the passage carefully before you completed the outline. Later on, if you want to review the material, the outline alone may be sufficient to refresh your memory.

In the passage that follows, the important points have already been underlined; the outline format has also been organized and partially completed. As you finish the outline, observe how the organization reflects the importance of the points that are made. You will also see how to structure and select information. This exercise works well as a small-group activity. With your instructor's permission,

EXERCISE 6

Organizing Details into Outline Form

work with a partner or a small group of fellow students to complete the outline.

This passage is from The Nature Conservancy's annual report. This group is dedicated to promoting environmental concerns. Through its activities and publications, the Conservancy hopes to make people aware of environmental issues and to effect changes that will benefit our environment. The annual report describes new developments, progress, and problems, and includes some information about the Conservancy's goals and predictions.

ANNUAL REPORT OF THE NATURE CONSERVANCY—1993

by Frank O'Donnell

Many utilities are receiving direct financial benefits from a proactive environmental stance: energy conservation. It's a dramatic change in attitude. Some power company officials jeered when President Jimmy Carter put on a sweater to preach energy conservation. But the Edison Electric Institute (EEI), the trade group representing most of the nation's investor-owned utilities, notes there are now more than 2,000 utility-sponsored energy-efficiency programs—up from 134 such efforts in 1977. That's the equivalent of 42 power plants, each big enough to power a city the size of Richmond, Virginia. EEI predicts peak demand reductions will more than double by the year 2000.

Among the power companies investing in conservation is Pacific Gas and Electric Company (PG&E), which serves most of northern California. In 1990, the power company announced that it would integrate environmental considerations into all aspects of its business.

Since then, PG&E has devised more than 40 programs aimed at educating customers on the soundness of energy-efficient investments and, in many cases, providing rebates or other financial incentives to carry them out. Some key programs include improvements in lighting efficiency, heating, and industrial processes.

Pacific Gas and Electric is aiming to reduce the growth for electricity demand in its service area by 75 percent in the next decade. The power company projects this approach will save consumers billions of dollars and prevent about 18 million tons of carbon dioxide emissions.

On the East Coast, the New England Electric System has adopted an aggressive policy to conserve energy. Working in conjunction with environmental organizations such as the Conservation Law Foundation, New England Electric has designed programs for commercial, industrial, and residential customers to reduce its peak demand by more than 300 megawatts—saving 750,000 barrels of oil and preventing 385,000 tons of carbon dioxide from going into the atmosphere.

In one of its power-saving programs, the utility is offering design assistance and financial incentives to help companies construct more energy-efficient buildings. Even though the programs cost the utility more than $80 million in 1991, John Rowe, New England Electric's president and chairman, believes they are good for the utility's bottom line. "They are substantially cheaper than new generation and transmission facilities," Rowe says.

New England Electric, like PG&E, is cooperating with the Environmental Protection Agency's (EPA), "Green Lights" program—an initiative to promote energy-efficient lighting. More than 640 firms (including the Conservancy) are enrolled in the voluntary EPA effort, which offers technical support to persuade companies to upgrade their lighting systems within five years.

"One of the things we're trying to prove is that the market works," says EPA's Susan Bullard. She predicts "Green Lights" could ultimately prompt a reduction of more than 132 million pounds of carbon dioxide—equal to the emissions of 44 million automobiles—while reducing energy expenses for companies.

"The savings are enormous and the payback relatively quick," says Bullard. "We've already saved 92.3 million kilowatt hours, and $6.1 million in electricity bills."

Although environmentalists have long clamored for recycling programs, the market for recycled materials has been relatively limited. But that may soon change thanks to an initiative by the "Buy Recycled Business Alliance," a consortium of 25 major corporations including Sears Roebuck & Company, DuPont, the Coca-Cola Company, and Waste Management Incorporated. In September 1992 the firm announced a program to pump up the demand for recycled products.

The companies are urging their own suppliers to provide them with higher volumes of recycled raw materials and greater recycled content in finished goods. Sears, for example, is pressing its 7,500 suppliers to put products in packaging made with at least 25 percent recycled material.

"Our intent is to show that most recycled products perform as well or better than virgin products," says Sears' Keith Trice. Sears projects that its policy will save the company $5 million annually. "We are well on our way to achieving that goal," says Sears' Perry Chlan.

But recycling alone can't solve the solid waste problem. Companies also need to cut down on the amount of packaging and other waste they generate. One firm that appears to be reaping benefits from waste reduction is the McDonalds Corporation. In 1991, the fast-food giant teamed up with the Environmental Defense Fund (EDF) and devised a strategy to trim its solid-waste output by half. A company spokeswoman says the company has not yet calculated its specific dollar savings, "but we see a long-term benefit for us, and for the environment."

EDF's Jackie Prince agrees there will eventually be "tangible environmental benefits from a company taking a hard look at its operations with a new eye towards the environment."

Another firm that is working to reduce waste is The Proctor & Gamble Company. Among other actions, the firm is using post-consumer recycled cardboard in more than 90 percent of its packaging of laundry and cleaning goods.

Not every company has responded to calls by environmentalists and government watchdogs to curb pollution and reduce waste. In May 1991, the governors of seven northeastern states wrote to the heads of more than 200 major corporations, urging them to voluntarily reduce packaging materials. Twenty-nine companies accepted the challenge.

"They've found that they're not only reducing their wastes but reducing their own costs," says Chip Foley of the Coalition of Northeastern

Governors. But Foley notes that <u>more than 170 companies either refused or ignored the governors</u>.

As you think about the passage you have just read, you should realize that the topic has to do with ways to help the environment. The passage is divided into two subtopics: energy conservation and recycling/packaging. Begin to visualize your outline with the topic centered at the top and the two subheadings below it.

Environmentally Sound Measures

or

Annual Report of the Nature Conservancy

I. Energy Conservation

II. Recycling and Efficient Packaging

In a real outline, of course, you would leave enough space to add major and minor details. We will expand this one a section at a time. Then we will put all of the sections together into a complete outline form.

1. Look over the section that deals with Energy Conservation. Identify the national organization that represents utilities, and write its name next to *A*. Then identify the two utility companies that are mentioned with examples of their energy-saving measures. Write their names next to *B* and *C*. Finally, identify the EPA program with which the two electric companies are cooperating and write that name next to *D*.

   I. Energy Conservation

      A. _____

      B. _____

      C. _____

      D. _____

2. Now look at the details that tell what progress the EEI has reported. Write three of those details below.

      A. Edison Electric Institute (EEI)

         1. _____

         2. _____

         3. _____

3. Look at the section of the text that deals with the accomplishments of the first electric company mentioned. Select four details you would like to include in this section of the outline. Your choices may be different from those of your fellow students. You may wish to discuss why you chose the details you did.

      B. Pacific Gas and Electric Company (PG&E)

         1. _____

         2. _____

         3. _____

         4. _____

4. Follow the same procedure for the second electric company.

    C. _____

       1. _____

       2. _____

       3. _____

5. In the section that tells about the EPA program, identify four important details.

    D. _____

       1. _____

       2. _____

       3. _____

       4. _____

6. Now see if you can complete the portion of the outline that covers the section on recycling and efficient packaging.

    II. Recycling and Efficient Packaging

    A. _____

       1. _____

       2. _____

       3. _____

       4. _____

    B. _____

       1. _____

       2. _____

       3. _____

       4. _____

Compare your outline with a fellow student's work. Have you selected the same material to include? You may find some differences in the details each of you chose and the way you expressed them. Essentially, though, they should be similar.

As you look over the outline, it should help you see the organization of the material. Your outline includes only the important points, so it can also help you as a study guide. In addition, most students find that the exercise of completing the outline helps them remember the material.

WRITING EXERCISE

In recent years, energy conservation, recycling, and efficient packaging have received more attention than in the past. Some progress has been made, but we still have a long way to go. On the basis of the preceding article and your own experience, write a short essay on one of these three areas. Tell what progress you have observed or read about and what you think needs to be done.

_____

_____

_____

_____

_____

_____

EXERCISE 7

Mapping as a Visual Organizational Tool

Mapping is an alternative organizing strategy. Instead of using letters and numbers as in outlining, the information is presented in boxes or circles that are placed on the page to show the relationship. Mapping performs most of the same functions as outlining, but the presentation is more visual. Most students prefer one method or the other. Students who classify themselves as visual learners (rather than as verbal learners) often prefer mapping.

College students usually know if they are visual or verbal learners. If you are not sure what your preference is, think about the way you like to receive information. If a friend directed you to her house, would you prefer a list of verbal directions? For example, should she tell you to travel on the West Side Road for 2.5 miles, and turn left just after the yellow house with the pink flamingo on the lawn? Or, would you rather have her draw you a map with roads and streets and arrows indicating which way to turn? When you are assembling something—a gas grill, a doll house, or a computer table—how do you like the instructions to be presented? Do you prefer a list telling you what to do, step by step, or pictures and diagrams that show you how to proceed? Finally, when you read textbooks, do you prefer the charts, diagrams, and illustrations to the text? Would you rather read the information in paragraph form or follow a visual presentation?

If you prefer a drawn map, diagrammed instructions, and visual aids in textbooks, you are probably a *visual learner*. If you prefer directions and instructions explained in words, and you like textbook information in paragraph form, you are probably a *verbal learner*. If your preference varies according to the material and the situation, you are a versatile learner, comfortable with either style. Even if you have a strong preference for visual or verbal learning, you will have to handle both as a college student. Some authors present information in both ways, but others include information only in one form.

In this exercise, you will read about the problem of radioactive waste disposal. After a brief introduction providing background information, the author presents the information in a list format, an organizational pattern that you will be learning more about in the next exercise. Six methods of radioactive waste disposal are described. This selection is more suited to mapping than outlining. Rather than having relationships to one another, each method is more directly related to the central or main topic. Instead of developing a single topic by establishing the main idea and expanding it with details and examples, the author briefly discusses one method and then moves on to the next.

Before you read, reflect on what you know about nuclear power. Do you have any information or opinions about its benefits and disadvantages? This selection is focusing on one aspect of nuclear power: waste disposal. If you read another selection, you may find a very different point of view. In this passage, concentrate on the proposed disposal methods.

THE RADIOACTIVE WASTE DISPOSAL PROBLEM

About 50 years ago, many scientists believed that nuclear power would be the answer to our energy needs. At one time, it was believed that nuclear power plants would provide between 20% and 25% of the world's supplemental energy by the end of the century. In fact, by 1991, the figure was only about 5%. Nuclear power plants are so controversial that they are being retired faster than new ones are being built. Our reliance on nuclear power for electricity will probably drop in the next 15 years. Some of the problems faced by the nuclear industry include high building costs, frequent problems with equipment, poor management, overproduction of electricity in some areas, and lack of public acceptance based on mistrust and safety concerns.

One of the most serious problems, though, is waste disposal. Nuclear power plants produce radioactive wastes that give off radiation for a long time. Excessive or long-term exposure to radiation can cause soil and water contamination, as well as serious health hazards. Therefore, disposal of such wastes poses serious concerns. In addition to power plants, the United States has maintained nuclear weapons plants since the mid 1940's. Although the threat of nuclear war has decreased in the past few years, we are still faced with the problem of waste material. Also, nuclear facilities themselves are contaminated. A nuclear power or weapons plant cannot be dismantled or torn down in the same way an old factory can. Most of the radioactivity decays within 50 years, but it takes 3 million years for an abandoned plant to become no more radioactive than its original uranium fuel.

Excerpts from *Living in the Environment,* 7th ed., by G. Tyler Miller, Jr. (Belmont, Calif.: Wadsworth, 1992), pp. 486, 493, 496–497.

From the 1940s to 1970, most low-level radioactive waste produced in the United States was dumped in the ocean in steel drums. Since 1970, low-level radioactive wastes from military activities have been buried at government-run landfills. Three of these have been closed because of leakage.

Low-level waste materials from commercial nuclear power plants, hospitals, universities, industries and other producers are put in steel drums and shipped to regional landfills run by federal and state governments. By 1990, three of the six commercial landfills had been closed because of radioactive contamination of ground water and nearby property.

CASE STUDY: WHAT CAN WE DO WITH HIGH-LEVEL, LONG-LIVED RADIOACTIVE WASTE?

Some scientists believe that the long-term safe storage or disposal of high-level radioactive wastes is technically impossible. Others disagree, pointing out that it is impossible to *show* that any method will work for 240,000 years of fail-safe storage. The following are some of the proposed methods and their possible drawbacks:

1. *Bury it deep underground.* Nuclear power plants use fuel rods that need to be replaced every three to four years. After they cool in pools of water at the plant site for several years, they are packaged and buried deep underground. They are usually buried in a salt or granite formation that is earthquake resistant and waterproof.

   Some geologists question the idea of burying nuclear wastes. They argue that the drilling and tunnelling to build the repository might cause water leakage and weaken resistance to earthquakes. They also believe scientists cannot make predictions about earthquakes and underground water paths 240,000 years into the future.

2. *Shoot it into space or into the sun.* Costs would be very high. A launch accident, like the explosion of the space shuttle *Challenger,* could occur. Such an accident could disperse high-level radioactive wastes over large areas of the earth's surface.

3. *Bury it under the Antarctic ice sheets of the Greenland ice caps.* The long-term stability of the ice sheets is not known. They could be destabilized by heat from the wastes, and retrieval of the wastes would be difficult or impossible if the method failed.

4. *Dump it into the deep ocean.* Wastes could eventually be spewed out somewhere else by volcanic activity. Waste containers might leak and contaminate the ocean before being carried downward. Retrieval would be impossible if the method did not work.

5. *Change it into harmless, or less harmful, isotopes.* At this time, there is no way to do this. Even if a method were developed, costs would probably be extremely high. As a result of this process, toxic materials and low-level, but very long-lived, radioactive wastes would be produced. These, then, would have to be disposed of safely.

6. *Use it in shielded batteries to run small electric generators.* Researchers claim that a wastebasket-size battery using spent fuel can still produce electricity. In fact, it could produce enough electricity to run 5 homes for 28 years at half the current price. However, leakage could contaminate homes and communities. Dispersing high-level waste throughout the country would probably be politically unacceptable. Besides, this method would only use a small portion of the nuclear waste.

To organize the information about radioactive waste disposal in map form, you must decide if there is any particular way you think you should group the methods. You may decide that each is unique and deserves equal attention. Or you may decide to group two methods that seem similar. Think of your topic as the central point, and place it in the center of your map. Then surround the topic with the subtopics—in this case, the methods. You may also want to make your boxes or circles large enough to include a brief description or drawback for each method. As with outlining, mapping is a study strategy that should work for *you*. If you have a particular method or arrangement that works, stick with it. There is no *wrong* way to map. The only requirement is that your map should organize the material in a way that is meaningful for you. The following map is based on the information at the beginning of the passage.

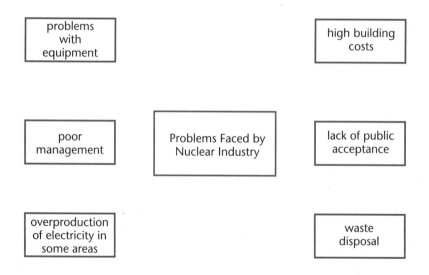

Now complete a map that shows the methods of disposal as discussed in the selection.

```
┌──────────┐                    ┌──────────┐
│          │                    │          │
└──────────┘                    └──────────┘

┌──────────┐   ┌──────────────┐  ┌──────────┐
│          │   │  Methods of  │  │          │
└──────────┘   │   Disposal   │  └──────────┘
               └──────────────┘
┌──────────┐                    ┌──────────┐
│          │                    │          │
└──────────┘                    └──────────┘
```

WRITING EXERCISE

Disposal of radioactive waste is a serious problem. Tell which of the six methods you would recommend and why.

_____

_____

_____

_____

_____

SKILL DEVELOPMENT: IDENTIFYING ORGANIZATIONAL PATTERNS

In this section we are going to explore two organizational patterns: the list pattern and the process description pattern.

EXERCISE 8

Identifying the List Pattern

The *list pattern* is the most straightforward organizational pattern. It is a suitable way to organize information from many different fields. For example, the causes of a war may be listed in a history passage. A list of the symptoms of a disease may be found in a nursing manual. Penalties for crimes may be listed in a criminal justice book. The items in a list may be arranged in order of importance, or they may all be considered equally important. Occasionally, the author will save the most important item for last.

There are key words to look for when you are trying to identify the list pattern. The author may use words—*first, second, third*—or numbers. Other key words or phrases include *first of all, next, then, at the end, finally.* Notice that all of these words seem to indicate a sequence or order. They alert the careful reader to look for items in a series. They also tell when the author is beginning a new point. In this sense, they can be considered *transitional words,* since they indicate a transition or movement from one point to another. In passages where the author uses words rather than numbers to organize the list, thorough readers will often pencil in numbers each time they come to the next item in the list.

Authors who present their information in list form are organizing it for their readers. An outline or map is easy to create from a list. In this exercise you will read a selection whose paragraphs illustrate the list pattern. The first sample shows how to identify the list items in a paragraph and how to organize them into outline or map form. Then you will be asked to do a map on your own.

WHAT TO DO ABOUT GARBAGE

1

Since cities have existed, garbage has always posed a problem for them. Rural areas, with smaller populations, generate less garbage and seem to have fewer disposal problems. In urban areas, however, there is less open space. Many people living close to one another produce a great deal of garbage that has to go somewhere. In previous centuries, city residents thought nothing of tossing their garbage out the window into the street. This practice had to be stopped for two reasons. First of all, it created a very unhealthy environment to live in a city whose streets were filled with garbage. Secondly, as horse-drawn carriages and, later, trucks and automobiles appeared, the streets had to be clear for them to get through.

2

Although garbage is a never-ending problem for cities, we have much better methods now for collecting and disposing of it. City officials and residents have realized how important it is to keep city streets clean. Between 1899 and 1905 about 85% of American cities with populations of more than 25,000 were using mechanical sweeping devices as supplements or replacements for hand sweeping. Soon more than 55% of the smaller cities and towns had followed the larger cities' lead.

3

Companies created machines for every purpose, every street material, every climate, every city size. There were mechanical brooms for general sweeping, squeegee cleaners that sprinkled and scraped the pavements, vacuum cleaners that sucked dirt into large canisters or bags, machines that swept and disinfected the streets at the same time, and flushers that washed dirt into gutters and sewers. Someone even invented a machine that swept over the street and exposed it to temperatures up to 1000 degrees F., presumably to bake or burn up dirt and germs. As you can imagine, many of these machines were expensive and very similar. Their

From *Garbage in the Cities: Refuse, Reform, and the Environment,* by Martin V. Melosi (Chicago: Dorsey Press, 1981), pp. 141, 143, 147.

claims of what they could do had to be tested by trial and error. In some cases, cities kept some of these companies in business as they went through the expensive process of trying to find new solutions for their street-cleaning problems.

4

Another method to cut down on trash in the streets is to try to discourage littering. Reformers joined in the cause with cleanup campaigns and other publicity efforts. Some municipal authorities experimented with various new programs. In Washington, D.C., the police were told to strictly enforce laws against littering. For a while, arrests of violators increased, and fines increased. The mayor of New Haven, Connecticut, encouraged the police and the public-work crews to help reduce litter. He offered prizes to school children for the best essays on the importance of maintaining a clean urban environment. Boston and other cities tried to curb littering by installing more trash barrels in the public parks and on street corners. They also doubled their efforts to educate the public about the evils of littering. No ready solutions were forthcoming, however. Although some progress has been made, littering continues to be a problem for most cities.

The author gives a brief list in the first paragraph. You probably noticed the key words, *first of all* and *secondly*. An outline of this selection could look like this:

A. Tossing garbage out the window

1. unhealthy environment

2. streets impassable

The second paragraph introduces the mechanical street-sweeping machines that replaced people with hand brooms. The third and fourth paragraphs provide more information. Go back to paragraph 3 and number the items you would include in a list of important details. Then compare your numbered details with the ones found in the following outline and map.

STREET-CLEANING DEVICES

---

1. mechanical brooms

2. squeegee cleaners

3. vacuum cleaners

4. disinfecting sweepers

5. flushers

mechanical brooms	squeegee cleaners	vacuum cleaners

Street-Cleaning Devices

flushers		disinfecting sweepers

Now create your list and map based on paragraph 4.

METHODS TO DISCOURAGE LITTERING

1. _____

2. _____

3. _____

4. _____

5. _____

Methods to Discourage Littering

Explain why garbage is a serious problem for cities, and recommend one method to improve the situation.

_____

_____

_____

_____

_____

_____

EXERCISE 9

Identifying the Process Description Pattern

The *process description pattern* is an organizational tool that leads the reader through an explanation or sequence. It is used to trace or follow a path or development. For example, if you want to know how the digestive system works, you might refer to a process description in your biology text. The explanation would probably trace the sequence of food from the time you put it into your mouth until it is thoroughly digested. Or a business or economics text might describe the process that led up to the savings and loan crisis. The discussion might begin with the removal of regulations that restricted what banks could do. A description of some of the unwise actions some banks took might follow. Finally, a description of the impact of the consequences on the American taxpayers as the federal government bailed out many of these institutions would complete the process.

There is some similarity between the process description and the list pattern. Both may use key words like *first, second, third, then, next, finally.* Both may also mention details in order or sequence. The process description pattern tends to be more complicated and to provide more in the way of explanation. It tells *how* or *why* something happened and *shows* how one thing leads to another.

In the exercise that follows, you will read about flooding. As you read, look for information that tells you about the process the river undergoes as it floods its banks. Note the sequence of events, and think about how you could describe them in a map format. As in the previous exercise, one part of the selection will be used as a sample to show you how to identify the process description pattern and how to outline or map it. Then you will be asked to do the same activities for another portion of the selection.

FLOODING: A NATURAL CALAMITY

1

In past centuries, humans have respected nature and its unpredictability. As we have advanced technologically, we have increased our ability to predict and somewhat control the natural order of things. At times, though, nature reminds us of our vulnerability and her power as we are faced with volcanic eruptions, earthquakes, and floods.

2

During the summer of 1993, rain fell in the midwest for forty-nine days. The Mississippi, a giant of rivers, overflowed its banks, covering 15 million acres of farmland in eight states. In some places, the river's waters extended nine miles beyond its usual banks. The flooding destroyed crops and property, resulted in deaths, eliminated river traffic, and caused billions of dollars in damage.

3

Historically, farmers expected floods and droughts and considered the related expenses as part of their overall budget. In earlier centuries, after a serious flood, townspeople would move to higher ground to avoid a repeat experience. Today, people tend to rebuild in the same spots and wonder how to better control nature. About 7 million people live directly along the river's banks, and many of them are found near the area where the Missouri and the Mississippi rivers come together.

4

What has persuaded people to put their lives and properties in danger by living and working so close to such a powerful river? Farmers have been lured by the thick black soil found in the Mississippi River's flood plain. Great cities like New Orleans and St. Louis have grown up around river ports to which goods and people could easily be transported. As devastating as floods are, they occur infrequently enough for people to forget about their devastation. Until the summer of 1993, the Mississippi's last great flood had occurred in 1973, long enough ago to be a distant memory.

5

After the flood of 1927, the federal government began a levee project. A levee is an artificial embankment that keeps a river from overflowing its banks. In effect, farmers pile up dirt mounds that narrow the course of the river and expose some of the surrounding land. Although many of these levees are privately built and maintained, the government has been committed to helping out when they need to be rebuilt or repaired. Dams and reservoirs also have been used to try to alter the course of the river to suit the needs of humans. The water that has been contained has been used for recreation and irrigation. Obviously, in a flood situation like the one that occurred in 1993, no devices or systems created by people could contain or alter the tremendous force of the river.

6

As a result of the flooding disaster, ecologists, engineers, and farmers are examining the situation to decide on a course for the future. Farmers argue that the levees are beneficial in that the water level would have been much higher without them. The farmers would like to see the levees rebuilt so they can reclaim their flooded farmlands. Some ecologists feel that the levees actually increase the floodwater level and question whether they should be rebuilt. The river, ecologists say, is the center of an ecosystem including the banks, floodplain, and valleys that must be considered as a whole. They believe that people should adapt to the natural course of the river, rather than trying to change the river to suit their wishes.

7

To claim rich farmland, the river has been confined to an artificially narrow path, and farms have been established right along the new river banks. During periods of heavy rains, there is nowhere for the excess rainwater to go. It has no opportunity to drain into the soil as it would if the river were its normal size rather than a narrow channel. As a result, the river goes faster and travels where it wishes. With such force and volume, the water washes over the levees and onto the soil they were built to protect. Some say the river reclaims its old places, creating ponds and marshes that once existed.

8

Although the loss of human life and destruction of property is devastating, environmentalists point out that flooding, like forest fires, is part of a natural cycle of renewal. Some of the benefits of flooding are significant. As the river currents grow strong and the channels widen, the water lifts topsoil from the banks. The waters carry nutrients downstream and deposit their richness and new soil in new areas. The heavy rains also cleanse and flush the river water. As some of the pollution is diluted or eliminated, the water becomes more attractive to spawning fish. Certainly, the people whose lives have been drastically disrupted by the flooding take little comfort from the long-term benefits of a flood. But we should all realize and respect nature's wisdom.

Few passages follow one organizational pattern throughout the text. The passage you have just read is no exception. There are two paragraphs at the end of the text that are good examples of the process description pattern. Can you decide which ones they are? Perhaps you also noticed that some paragraphs at the beginning of the passage illustrate the list pattern. Which ones do you think they are?

Notice the overall structure of the passage. In paragraph 1, the author introduces the general topic of nature's power. In paragraph 2, we learn specific information about the flood of 1993 in the form of a list of details. Paragraph 3 contrasts the past and present attitudes toward flooding. Paragraph 4 explains why people choose to live in a floodplain. Paragraph 5 tells how this has been possible. In paragraph 6, we learn about the controversy surrounding flood control. Paragraphs 7 and 8 follow the process description pattern, as they tell us what happens when a river overflows its banks. In paragraph 7, the emphasis is on the consequences of artificially containing a river. In paragraph 8, the natural course of events is described.

The following map illustrates the process description pattern found in paragraph 7.

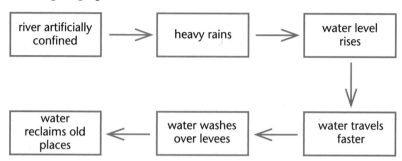

Now create a map illustrating the process description pattern in paragraph 8.

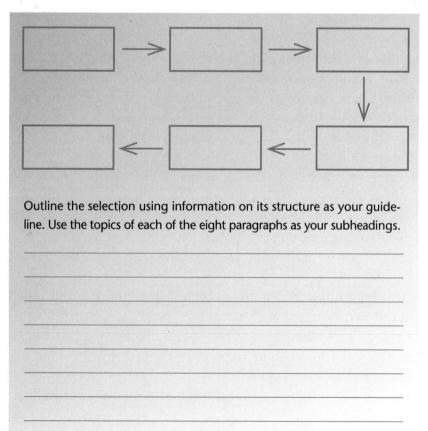

Outline the selection using information on its structure as your guideline. Use the topics of each of the eight paragraphs as your subheadings.

_____

_____

_____

_____

_____

_____

_____

_____

WRITING EXERCISE

Discuss the benefits and disadvantages of trying to artificially control the course of a river. Tell what policy you think should be followed.

_____

_____

_____

_____

_____

_____

SELECTION 1

A challenge that faces all of us who are interested in environmental quality is what to do with our garbage. Americans have developed a "throwaway" attitude that causes us to generate an enormous quantity of solid waste—that is, garbage or trash. Our country is so large that, in the past, dumping garbage away from population centers was acceptable. Advertising that emphasizes convenience over ecology has also contributed to this mentality. For example, take-out food packaged in disposable containers and lightweight plastic soda bottles are more convenient than ecologically sound.

Our attitude toward our environment is changing, however. The rising costs of disposing of large quantities of solid waste have added an economic consideration. Moreover, awareness that our health and safety may be at risk because of unsound disposal methods encourages us to examine the solid waste issue.

Before you begin to read, think about how much garbage you produce in a week. Think about the trash cans you see in the cafeteria, at work, or in a restaurant. Are you familiar with the recycling or composting programs in your community? Do you use them? Do others? Think about whether garbage disposal is a problem in your community.

The following selection presents information on how much solid waste Americans generate, what is done with it, and what it costs. The author discusses the advantages and disadvantages of various methods of disposal, and recommends practical suggestions for adopting a low-waste approach.

As you read the selection, underline details that are clearly important, such as definitions of terms and main ideas. As you answer the questions, underline or highlight the sections of the text where you found the answers. After you finish reading, you will be using your underlining as a guide to outline the selection. Notice the author's organization of the material so that you can organize it similarly in your outline. Your reading will be guided by a directive at the beginning of each section and guide questions after each section to increase and check your comprehension.

Read the first section to find out how much garbage we produce.

WHAT CAN WE DO ABOUT ALL THIS GARBAGE?

SOLID WASTE PRODUCTION

Although the United States represents only 4.5 percent of the world's population, we produce 33 percent of the world's solid waste. Solid waste, what we often refer to as trash or garbage, is any unwanted material that is not a liquid or gas. Americans generate 11 billion tons of it each year.

Here are some figures to help you realize the quantities we are dealing with.

• U.S consumers throw away enough aluminum to rebuild the country's airline fleet every three months.

• We throw away enough glass bottles to fill the World Trade Towers (1350 ft.) every two weeks.

• The tires that are thrown away each year could encircle the earth three times.

• Americans throw away enough disposable plates and cups to serve a meal to everyone in the world six times a year.

• If the 2 billion disposable razors, 600 million ball-point pens, and 350 million disposable lighters that are thrown away each year were lined up end to end, they would reach to the moon and back.

• Each hour, Americans throw away 2.5 million plastic bottles.

As incredible as these quantities are, they represent only 1.5 percent of the total mass of solid waste produced as garbage. The remaining 98.5 percent is produced indirectly through production of the products that we use. Mining and gas operations account for 75 percent of the total, agriculture for 13 percent, industry for 9.5 percent, and sewage sludge for 1 percent.

Mining waste is typically left piled up near the site of the mine. Such waste can pollute the air, surface, and ground water. Industrial waste usually takes the form of scrap metal, plastics, paper, ash, and sludge. It is usually disposed of at the plant site by burying or burning it.

What is known as municipal solid waste is what members of American households throw away. As mentioned before, it represents 1.5 percent of the country's total solid waste. Unfortunately, more than half of what the typical American throws away as garbage is paper, paperboard, and yard waste. All of these are potentially renewable; that is, they could be used again through a recycling or composting program. Instead of recycling or composting 59 percent of the solid waste we produce, Americans recycle or compost a mere 13 percent. The remaining 87 percent of our trash is hauled away to be burned or dumped at a cost of $6 billion per year.

Adapted from *Living in the Environment*, by G. Tyler Miller, Jr., pp. 519–538.

Answer the following questions based on your reading.

1. What is the main idea of this section? _____

   _____

2. What is solid waste? _____

   _____

3. How does the United States compare to the rest of the world as a producer of solid waste? _____

   _____

   _____

4. Which example of materials that we throw away did you find most remarkable? _____

   _____

   _____

5. What proportion of the solid waste produced comes directly from U.S. households? _____

   _____

6. What industries produce the largest quantities of solid waste? _____

   _____

7. How much of our household garbage is potentially renewable through composting or recycling? _____

   _____

Read the next section to learn about landfills.

LANDFILLS

If a society adopts a "throwaway" approach to waste management, the philosophy is to produce the waste and figure out what to do with it *later*. In the past, town dumps were the places to deposit all kinds of wastes. As land became scarce and the dangers of uncontrolled dumping became apparent, the practice had to change. Today, there are strict regulations about the way sanitary landfills are built and what can be dumped there. Unfortunately, we continue to suffer from the problems caused by unsound dumping practices years ago.

In the United States, 75 percent of our solid waste is deposited in sanitary landfills. This compares with a figure of 16 percent in Japan. Japan is a much smaller country than the United States with a much denser population. Apparently, the Japanese feel that using precious land as a garbage dump is foolish, and they have developed other approaches to waste management. In the past, in the United States, one of the most common garbage disposal methods was to dig a hole, dump the trash in, and cover it up. Today's regulations require that a sanitary landfill be lined with clay or plastic to prevent leakage. The trash is spread in thin layers, compacted, and covered with clay or plastic foam. The area is also vented to prevent the build-up of dangerous gases. Sanitary landfills have the advantages of a quick start-up and relatively low-cost maintenance. After a landfill is filled, it can also be graded, seeded, and used as a park or other recreation area.

There are serious problems associated with landfills, though. Because of the traffic, noise, and dust, few people want landfills built in their communities. There are also places, such as Long Island, New York, with such high water tables, that cannot safely accommodate landfills. In a 1990 study, 67 percent of the 356 California landfills tested emitted at least one of ten toxic gases. The Environmental Protection Agency has also included 249 unlined landfills on its list of Superfund hazardous-waste sites that must be cleaned up. In addition to the absence of linings in older landfills, the nature of the waste they contain is also troubling. Until 1980, it was legal to dump any amount of hazardous waste into a municipal landfill. Even today, households and companies that generate less than 1.2 metric tons of hazardous waste are permitted to use municipal landfills.

In five to ten years, half of the existing landfills will be filled and closed. Few new ones are being built to take their places. In fact, heavily populated areas that have been sending their waste elsewhere are finding that this practice may no longer be possible. The city of Philadelphia, for example, has no landfill and ships its waste to seven other states. Many states that have accepted waste from populous states like New York and New Jersey are beginning to refuse to continue. The waste in landfills also biodegrades at a very slow rate. Newspapers deposited in landfills thirty to forty years ago can still be readable. Hot dogs, carrots, and chickens can take ten years to decompose. Plastics can take decades. With all of these problems associated with landfills, it seems obvious that we need to seek alternative methods of dealing with our solid waste.

Answer the following questions based on your reading and on your own experience.

8. What is the main idea of this section? _____

_____

9. How does a sanitary landfill differ from an old-fashioned dump? _____

_____

10. What are three advantages to landfills as a waste-management approach?

    a. _____

    b. _____

    c. _____

11. Tell what you think is the most serious drawback to landfills and why. _____

_____

_____

LOW-WASTE APPROACH

In contrast to the waste-management approach that encourages dealing with waste *after* it is produced, the *low-waste approach* attempts to reduce the production of solid waste. In addition, the low-waste approach

Read the next section to learn about the low-waste approach.

emphasizes composting, recycling, and reusing materials. The first step in this approach is teaching children and adults to be aware of the solid waste problem and to abandon the "throwaway" attitude. Studies have shown that separation of garbage into compostable, recyclable, and reusable categories can significantly reduce the amount of trash that needs to be hauled away to landfills or incinerators. Environmentalists have set a goal of a 60 percent recycling rate as achievable and one that would make a significant difference. Recycling means collecting and reprocessing a resource so it can be made into new products. An example is collecting aluminum cans, melting them down, and using the aluminum to make new cans or other aluminum products. A pilot study conducted with 100 families in East Hampton, New York resulted in an 84 percent rate.

Seattle, the U.S. city with the highest recycling rate, has achieved 39 percent and has set a goal of 60 percent by 1998. In contrast, New York City only recycles at a 6 percent rate, and Tucson, Arizona at 0.02 percent. Ten smaller communities have attained even higher rates than Seattle. Berlin Township, New Jersey, recycled 57 percent of its solid waste in 1988. Although more than twenty-nine states have set recycling goals ranging from 15 to 46 percent, currently more than half of the states in the country recycle less than 5 percent of their municipal solid waste.

Answer the following questions based on your reading and on your own experience.

12. What is the main idea of this section? _____
_____

13. How does the low-waste approach differ from the waste-management approach? _____
_____

14. How are we doing in terms of recycling in this country? _____
_____

15. Do you recycle? If you do, tell what and how. _____
_____

Read the next section to learn about reuse and waste reduction.

REUSE AND WASTE REDUCTION

The most effective way to handle our garbage problem is to create less of it. Although beverage container deposit bills are a step in the right direction, an even more effective reuse plan would be to return to refillable glass bottles. Whereas plastic bottles are collected, redeemed for deposit, and recycled, glass bottles could be collected, washed, and refilled by bottling companies. Only ten states in the country have beverage container deposit laws, an effective method to discourage littering. Refillable glass bottles, though, would save money and energy as well as cutting down on litter.

Other practices that help us reuse rather than throw away are lunch boxes and thermos bottles instead of paper bags and beverage boxes or cans. Cloth napkins and reusable baskets or canvas bags would also eliminate the need for plastic or paper bags.

Reducing unnecessary waste of nonrenewable mineral resources, plastics, and paper can extend supplies even more dramatically than recycling and reuse. Manufacturers can conserve resources by using less material and redesigning processes and products. Lighter cars, for example, save nonfuel mineral resources as well as energy. Solid-state electronic devices and microwave transmissions greatly reduce materials requirements. Optical fibers drastically reduce the demand for copper wire in telephone transmission lines. Manufacturers have reduced the weight of some of their packaging bottles and cartons by 10 percent to 30 percent.

Unnecessary packaging, which makes up 50 percent of the volume and 32 percent of the weight of U.S. garbage, can be eliminated, saving money for manufacturers and consumers. One dollar of every eleven spent for groceries in the United States pays for packaging. U.S. consumers spend more on food packaging annually than all the revenue received by farmers.

Another low-waste approach is to make products that last longer. The economies of the United States and other industrial countries are built on the principle of planned obsolescence. If products wear out or break, people will buy more things to stimulate the economy and raise short-term profits. That can eventually lead to economic and environmental grief, though. Manufacturers should design products that are easy to reuse, recycle, and repair. All engineering and design students should be taught how to do this as a major part of their education. Today, many items are intentionally designed to make repair, reuse, or recycling impossible or too expensive. Manufacturers should adopt the principle of modular design, which allows circuits in computers, television sets, and other electronic devices to be replaced easily without replacing the entire item. We also need to develop manufacturing industries that would disassemble, repair, and reassemble used and broken items.

Answer the following questions based on your reading.

16. What is the main idea of this section? _____

_____

17. Why are glass bottles preferable to plastic beverage containers? _____

_____

18. Give some examples of how manufacturers can reduce waste.

   a. _____

   b. _____

19. How does the low-waste approach differ from the throwaway mentality? _____

_____

Read the last section to learn how to bring about changes in solid waste disposal.

Greatly increased recycling and reuse in the United States could be accomplished through the following measures:

Enact a national beverage container law.

Require that all beverage containers have standard sizes so any bottler can refill bottles produced by other manufacturers.

Ban disposable plastic items and disposable metal, glass, and plastic beverage containers.

Tax manufacturers on the amount of waste they generate.

Include a waste disposal fee in the price of all disposable items (especially batteries, tires, cars, and appliances).

Provide economic incentives for recycling waste oil, plastics, tires, and chlorofluorocarbons used as coolants in refrigerators and air conditioners.

Require labeling of products made with recycled materials and show the percentage used.

Give sales tax reductions for products made with recycled products.

Guarantee a large market for recycled items by encouraging governments to purchase a certain percentage of recycled materials.

Use advertising and education to discourage the throwaway mentality.

Require consumers to separate household waste or give them financial incentives for recycling.

Encourage municipal and backyard composting by banning the disposal of yard wastes in landfills.

Issue no permits for landfills or incinerators until a community or state has achieved a 60 percent recycling rate.

20. Do you think the author has a particular point of view about the environmental issues he discusses? If you believe there is a great deal of opinion included in the selection, do you think it is supported by facts? Support your answers.

   _____

   _____

   _____

   _____

   _____

21. Use the section headings, your underlined details, and your answers to the questions to map each section or outline the entire passage.

WRITING EXERCISE

Write a plan for your school or community to adopt to reduce waste. Be specific about your goal, time frame, and recommendations.

_____

_____

_____

_____

_____

SELECTION 2

Various groups have proposed energy taxes for different purposes. Environmentalists advocate them to encourage people to save energy. Others see them as a source of income. Energy taxes are generally unpopular with politicians and the taxpayers who elect them. The selection that follows gives you some background information about the use and misuse of energy in the United States. It then considers energy taxes as one way to improve our situation ecologically and economically.

Before you begin to read, think about your energy use. How do you heat your home? Does your car burn a lot of gasoline each week? Are you conscious of using energy wisely, or do you take it for granted? How do you feel about taxing energy?

As you read, underline or highlight the obviously important points. As you find answers to the guide questions, underline or highlight those portions of the text as well. After you finish reading, you will be asked to create a map that illustrates the different types of energy taxes.

Read the first section to learn about energy use in the United States.

ENERGY TAXES: A WAY TO INCREASE EFFICIENCY AND RAISE REVENUE?

The United States is the world's biggest user of energy. As the fourth most populous nation, we use 25 percent of the world's commercial energy. We also waste more energy than any other country in the world. Most of our commercial energy comes from burning oil, coal, and natural gas. All of these are <u>nonrenewable energy sources</u>. That means, once they are gone, we cannot replace them. The law of conservation of energy tells us that energy can't be created or destroyed. It is merely changed from one form to another. This sounds like an ideal situation, but it isn't as simple as it seems. When we use energy in one form, it is changed into a lower-level form of energy. For example, when you turn on a light, the light bulb turns electrical energy into light. It also produces heat, though, which is given off into the atmosphere and can't be used again. So, although the energy is <u>transformed</u> and not destroyed, it is no longer usable.

Answer the following questions based on your reading.

1. What is the main idea of this section? _____

   _____

2. What is the meaning of the word *transformed*? _____

   _____

3. How does energy use in the United States compare to energy use in other countries? _____

   _____

4. What does the term *nonrenewable energy source* mean? _____

   _____

Read the next section to learn about oil as an energy source.

OIL

Oil is a very popular fuel, both in the United States and in other countries. It is relatively cheap, is easily transported, yields high energy, and can be used in many ways. There are also disadvantages to oil. The *Exxon Valdez* oil spill off the coast of Alaska reminded us that oil spill and leakage can be disastrous to the environment. Burning oil also releases carbon dioxide, a contributor to global warming, into the environment.

The chief disadvantage to oil as an energy source, though, is that it is destined to run out. Five nations have two-thirds of the world's oil reserves; all are located in the Middle East. The United States has only 4 percent of the world's reserves. We should have learned a lesson about dependence on foreign oil in the 1970s, but the difficulties of those years seem to have been forgotten. The oil scarcity at that time was probably caused by a combination of factors. The economy had expanded rapidly and demand for oil surpassed the production rate. Countries that belonged to OPEC, an organization that regulates the production and price of oil, worked cooperatively to control the amount of oil available and the price. Finally, in 1979, the revolution in Iran further limited access to oil. Drivers in the United States spent hours in line to purchase what was essentially <u>rationed</u> gasoline. Motorists who spent hours waiting in line at filling stations on designated days regretted owning gas-guzzling cars. The crisis passed, though, and Americans abandoned their carpools and other energy-saving strategies and returned to their old ways. Between 1973 and 1985, the fuel efficiency of American-made cars improved dramatically. Since then, however, the auto manufacturers have paid little attention to further development. The American taste for large cars and the low oil prices of the 1980s have provided no incentive for developing fuel-efficient cars. The realization that little of the world's affordable crude oil will be left by the middle of the next century, though, *should* provide a powerful incentive.

Answer the following questions based on your reading.

5. What is the main idea of this section? _____

_____

6. What is the meaning of the word *rationed*? _____

_____

7. What are the advantages of oil as an energy source? _____

_____

8. What are its disadvantages? _____

_____

NATURAL GAS

As a fuel, natural gas has some advantages over oil. Although the United States has only 6 percent of the world's reserves, 95 percent of the natural gas we use comes from <u>domestic</u> sources. The other 5 percent comes via pipeline from Canada. Natural gas burns hotter and produces less air pollution than oil does. It is also relatively cheap. One disadvantage is that it must be converted to a liquid for shipping, a process that can be dangerous and expensive.

Natural gas, too, is a nonrenewable energy source. Once it is gone, there is no more. Although estimates of how long our natural gas supply will last are not promising, there may be untapped, unconventional

Read the next section to learn about natural gas as an energy source.

sources. Coal seams, shale rocks, and other underground sources may provide us with quantities of natural gas that will last longer than the resources we now have available. Research support is needed to investigate these possibilities.

Answer the following questions based on your reading.

9. What is the main idea of this section? _____
   _____

10. What is the meaning of the word *domestic*? _____
    _____

11. What are the advantages of natural gas? _____
    _____

12. What are its disadvantages? _____
    _____

Read the next section to learn about energy policies.

ENERGY POLICIES

We have become extremely dependent on nonrenewable energy sources. Consider how much energy—in the form of electricity, gasoline, and fuel oil—each of us consumes in a week. We take it for granted that we are able to fill up the gas tanks of our cars, raise the temperature of our homes by turning a dial, and refrigerate the food we buy at well-supplied grocery stores. Our comfortable way of life seems less secure when we reflect on two points. Most of the oil we use comes from other countries. And, in the next century, the world's supply of oil, natural gas, and coal will be severely <u>depleted</u>, if not used up.

A national energy policy should reflect the current and future needs of its citizens. Historically, the U.S. approach has been to keep energy prices artificially low. Tax breaks and other federal subsidies, funding for energy research and development have benefited energy industries. Price controls have benefited consumers, and low prices have encouraged them to use more energy. For example, public transportation is underused at times when gasoline prices are low. Commuters are willing to pay for the convenience of driving their own cars to work, if the price isn't too high. There are advantages to an energy policy that keeps prices artificially low. It encourages the development of those resources that are treated favorably. It can also reduce inflation and protect consumers from dramatic price increases. The disadvantages of such a policy are significant, though. Cheap energy prices encourage waste and the depletion of resources. They also discourage research and development of alternative energy sources, such as solar and wind power.

European energy policies take a very different approach. In Europe, energy prices are kept artificially high through taxes. For example, in the United States, drivers have paid approximately $0.14 per gallon in federal taxes, Europeans are used to paying about $2.00 per gallon, and the Japanese pay $1.75. One of the advantages of this policy is that it encourages energy efficiency. In fact, Europeans use about half as much energy per person as Americans do. Countries with high-energy prices are usually less dependent on imported energy. They are also more successful at conserving the limited future supply of energy resources. There are disadvantages to this approach, also. High energy prices contribute to inflation and may discourage economic growth. They may also impose a heavy economic burden on the poor.

Answer the following questions based on your reading.

13. What is the main idea of this section? _____

_____

14. What is the meaning of the word *depleted*? _____

_____

15. How has the U.S. energy policy differed from the European approach? _____

_____

16. Which type of energy policy do you favor? Explain why. _____

_____

ENERGY TAXES

Energy taxes have been politically unpopular for a long time. Americans have become accustomed to cheap energy prices and resent attempts to raise prices at the gas pump or in their electric and oil bills. For many years, environmentalists have been advocating an energy tax to promote conservation. Ironically, the incentive to recommend an energy tax now is an economic one. Politicians and economists have finally realized that our national <u>deficit</u> must be reduced. As a nation, we can't continue to borrow money at the rate we have been. High interest payments and the burden of debt for future generations make deficit reduction a priority. One source of revenue that has been considered is a *gasoline tax*. A one-cent tax on gasoline would generate one billion dollars in revenue. A gas tax increase would not be difficult to put into effect, and it might reduce consumption, and therefore pollution. Such a tax is still unpopular, though. Regions that rely heavily on cars rather than public transportation and trucking businesses would be hit particularly hard.

Another proposal is to *tax imported oil*. Presumably, domestic oil producers would also raise their prices to match the cost of the imported oil. As a result, consumers would pay higher prices regardless of the source of their oil. The prime advantage of this tax is that it would help reduce our dependence on foreign oil. It might also help small, domestic oil companies that have been unable to compete with the low prices of imported oil. Areas of the country that depend on imported oil for heating would suffer, whereas the oil-producing states would benefit. There is also a question about whether the United States could impose such a fee that was not negotiated in our existing foreign trade agreements.

Read the next section to learn about the types of energy taxes that have been proposed.

Environmentalists favor *broad-based* energy taxes. They differ from the gasoline tax and oil import fee in that all forms of energy are taxed. Energy producers and big customers like utility companies would be most affected. Presumably, they would pass on their added costs to consumers. One proposal is to tax energy on the fuel's carbon content. The prime target of this tax is coal. The biggest advantage would be realized in the decrease of energy use, thereby reducing the carbon dioxide that is released into the atmosphere. Scientists who are concerned about global warming see this as a distinct advantage. Coal-mining states, the steel industry, the automobile industry, and manufacturers who rely on coal-fired electricity would suffer with this tax.

Another broad-based energy tax is a sales tax. With this type of tax, all forms of energy would be taxed at the wholesale level. The energy producers would pay the tax and pass the increase along to their customers. Americans would pay higher electric and gasoline bills. Oil and gas producers and environmentalists argue that the coal industry would benefit unfairly from this approach. Since coal is a cheaper fuel, the taxes paid on it would also be lower. Rather than reducing the use of coal—the biggest carbon dioxide producer—the sales tax might actually encourage more reliance on coal.

A BTU tax is based on the amount of heat a fuel can produce. The British thermal unit (BTU) is a measure of the quantity of heat required to raise the temperature of water. Since coal has a high BTU content in relation to its price, this tax would cost the coal industry more than a sales tax and less than a carbon tax. The BTU tax would raise prices for consumers, but it should lower pollution. Some people believe this is the fairest of the options in that it raises revenue, taxes all types of fuel, and promotes pollution control.

Regardless of the economic and environmental arguments in favor of energy taxes, they still meet strong resistance. Labor leaders, oil companies, and most American citizens are not in favor of energy taxes. Senators and representatives from states that would be most affected lobby hard against taxing energy. Some politicians resist any type of new tax at all. Their constituents are not eager to pay more taxes, either. Continuing an energy policy, though, that encourages us to use up and waste our energy resources will eventually lead to disaster.

Answer the following questions based on your reading and on your own thinking.

17. What is the main idea of this section? _____

_____

18. What is the meaning of the word *deficit*, as used in the passage? _____

_____

19. Create a map to illustrate the different types of energy taxes.

20. Do you favor an energy tax? Tell which kind and explain why. _____

_____

Describe the type of energy policy you think the United States should follow. Include a broad philosophy statement and some specific examples.

WRITING EXERCISE

_____

_____

_____

_____

_____

_____

SELECTION 3

Read the first section to learn about a disastrous oil spill.

Environmental disasters occurred long before human beings appeared on the earth. There is geological evidence of floods, volcanic eruptions, and drought. In modern times, however, people have caused many of our "environmental disasters."

The selection that follows describes several recent environmental disasters. Before you begin to read, try to recall an environmental disaster—a hurricane, a flood, or a forest fire—you have experienced or have read or heard about. Think about its causes and the lessons people learned from the experience. As you read, try to understand what caused these disasters and how they might have been avoided. Look for similarities and differences among them. Underline or highlight the obviously important details. As you find answers to the guide questions, underline or highlight those points in the text as well. After you finish reading, you will be asked to map or outline portions of the text.

ENVIRONMENTAL DISASTERS

THE *EXXON VALDEZ* OIL SPILL

One of the best sources of oil for the United States is found in Alaska's North Slope near Prudhoe Bay. Since relatively few people live in Alaska, but many live in the lower forty-eight states, the oil is transported over long distances. First, it is carried by tanker to the Alaskan port of Valdez. Then it is shipped by tanker to the west coast of the United States. In the early 1970s, when this source of oil became important, environmentalists warned of the dangers of this form of transport. Shipping oil through <u>treacherous</u> waters with submerged reefs, icebergs, and violent storms is a risky business. The suggestion that Alaskan oil be transported by pipeline over land, though, was not popular with oil company representatives. They argued that such a pipeline would be expensive and would take too long to build. At the time, the Secretary of the Interior urged that all oil tankers be double-hulled as an added protection against spills and leakage. Eventually, pressure from the oil companies successfully eliminated this requirement. Alyaska, a company formed by seven oil companies with interests in Alaskan oil, assured government officials that the risk of a spill was small. If an accident occurred, they promised, experienced cleanup crews with sophisticated equipment would be on the scene in five hours.

On March 29, 1989, the *Exxon Valdez,* a tanker more than 300 yards long, carrying a $20 million oil cargo, veered off course in a ten-mile-wide channel in Prince Edward Sound. The tanker hit rocks on a submerged reef, and, through its punctured hull, released 11 million gallons of oil. In 1990, an administrative law judge found the captain of the ship guilty of drinking before starting the voyage. At a critical time, he left the bridge and turned over the ship to an exhausted and inexperienced third

Adapted from *Living in the Environment,* by G. Tyler Miller, Jr., pp. 342, 490–92, 561, 616–617, 639.

mate. Since 1984, the captain had been arrested for drunk driving three times and had lost his license to drive a car. The Exxon Corporation, though, entrusted him with transporting precious cargo through dangerous waters.

The promise of a swift and efficient cleanup operation did not materialize. The oil slick killed 580,000 birds (including 144 bald eagles), over 5,000 sea otters, 30 seals, 22 whales, and countless numbers of fish. On the shoreline, 3,200 miles were slicked with oil. Although Exxon mounted a $2 billion cleanup program, the losses, as well as the expense, are extraordinary. Only 3 percent to 4 percent of the oil spilled was recovered. The high-pressure water used to clean the beaches killed many coastal plants and animals. The beach cleanup crews and equipment consumed three times the amount of oil that was spilled. Exxon shipped 30,000 tons of oil-contaminated solid waste to a landfill in Oregon. Cleanup costs, fines, and settlements of lawsuits may raise the price tag to $4 billion. The environmental destruction is impossible to calculate.

Answer the following questions based on your reading and your own knowledge.

1. What is the main idea of this section? _____

2. What is the meaning of the word *treacherous*, as it is used in the passage? _____

3. What caused the oil spill? _____

4. How could it have been avoided? _____

5. What measures would you suggest to prevent a repeat of this incident? _____

LOVE CANAL

Between 1942 and 1953, Hooker Chemicals and Plastics Corporation dumped almost 22,000 tons of toxic and cancer-causing wastes. Most of them were in steel drums that were deposited into an old excavation site known as Love Canal, named after its builder, William Love. In 1953, the company covered the site with clay and topsoil and sold the site to the Niagara Falls school board for one dollar. The deed that the chemical company transferred to the New York school district specified that Hooker would bear no future liability for personal or property damages for the dump's contents. An elementary school, playing fields, and a development with over 900 homes were built on the site.

In 1976, Love Canal area residents complained about chemical smells. Children playing in the canal experienced chemical burns. By 1977, chemicals leaking from the <u>corroding</u> steel drums showed up in storm

Read the next section to learn about an environmental disaster caused by improperly dumping chemicals.

sewers, gardens, and basements. An informal health survey among the residents revealed a high incidence of birth defects, miscarriages, assorted cancers, and nerve, kidney, and respiratory disorders. When state officials surveyed the situation, they, too, documented a higher than average miscarriage rate. They also found air, water, soil, and basements contaminated with toxic and carcinogenic chemicals.

By 1978, the state had closed the school and permanently relocated the 238 families nearest the dump. A fence was constructed around the dump. In 1980, after continuing protests from the remaining 711 families, President Carter declared Love Canal a federal disaster area and had them all relocated. Forty-five families remained, either unwilling or unable to sell their houses to the state and move. In 1983, former Love Canal residents settled out of court with Occidental Chemical Corporation (the company that had bought Hooker Chemicals in 1968), the City of Niagara Falls, and the school board. Payments ranged from $2,000 to $400,000 on claims for a variety of problems including persistent rashes, cancer, and mental retardation. Lawsuits are still pending against Occidental for the cleanup costs and punitive damages.

Eventually, the dump site was covered with a clay cap and surrounded by a drain system that pumps leaking wastes to a new treatment plant. By 1990, the total cost of cleanup and relocation reached $250 million. The Environmental Protection Agency (EPA) renamed the area Black Creek Village and proposed the sale of over 200 abandoned houses at a price 20 percent below the market value. Environmentalists and community groups remain extremely wary about the safety of such a plan.

The Love Canal tragedy is a reminder that we can't really "throw anything away" and that wastes don't stay put. Preventing pollution is safer and cheaper than trying to clean it up later.

Answer the following questions based on your reading and on your own knowledge.

6. What is the main idea of this section? _____

_____

7. What is the meaning of the word *corroding,* as used in the passage? _____

_____

8. What caused the Love Canal disaster? _____

_____

9. How could it have been prevented? _____

_____

10. What measures would you suggest to avoid a repeat of the incident? _____

_____

AGENT ORANGE

Agent Orange is a mixture of herbicides—chemicals that kill plants or prevent them from growing. Between 1962 and 1970, during the Vietnam War, it was used extensively. Agent Orange was sprayed on swamps and forests to <u>defoliate</u> the area. The elimination of leaves, trees, and other plant growth improved visibility so the U.S. fighting forces could see their targets more easily.

The EPA has banned 2,4,5-T, one of the two chemicals that make up Agent Orange, since 1985. The other, 2,4-D, is still the third most widely used pesticide in the United States.

About 35,000 Vietnam veterans have filed claims for disabilities allegedly caused by exposure to Agent Orange. The Veterans Administration and chemical manufacturers deny any connection between the herbicide and the medical disorders. They claim that the problems are caused by post-Vietnam stress syndrome. In 1984, the companies making Agent Orange agreed to a $180 million out-of-court settlement with some 9,300 Vietnam veterans. But the companies admitted no guilt or connection between the disorders and the herbicide.

Several studies have been conducted to determine if Agent Orange causes medical problems. The results, though, are conflicting. In 1988, one study provided evidence linking many of the veterans' health problems to a highly toxic substance formed during the manufacture of 2,4,5-T. In 1989, National Cancer Institute scientists studied Nebraska farmers who mixed or applied 2,4-D. They reported as much as a three-fold increase in non-Hodgkin's lymphoma, a rare, fatal cancer, among this group. In 1990, the Centers for Disease Control found no evidence linking Agent Orange to an increased risk of this disease. Other scientists have criticized this study for being incomplete. Studies by the Air Force and Veterans Affairs Department conducted in 1991 also found little, if any, health impact on Vietnam veterans exposed to Agent Orange. In 1990, however, an independent scientific review of 285 studies of the effects of Agent Orange on humans concluded differently. It found that there is a significant statistical association between exposure to the herbicide Agent Orange and various cancers, serious skin disorders, and liver disorders.

Read the next section to learn about another chemically caused problem.

Answer the following questions based on your reading and on your own knowledge.

11. What is the main idea of this section? _____

_____

12. What is the meaning of the word *defoliate,* as it is used in the passage? _____

_____

13. Do you think the herbicide Agent Orange caused problems? Support your answer. _____

_____

_____

14. Why do you think we need herbicides? How should they be regulated? _____

_____

_____

Read the last section to learn about a nuclear accident.

THREE MILE ISLAND

In 1979, the Three Mile Island nuclear plant in Pennsylvania suffered the worst accident in the history of U.S. commercial nuclear power. One of two reactors lost its coolant water because of a series of mechanical failures and human operator errors. Such a series of events was not <u>anticipated</u> in the safety studies that had been done on the plant.

As a result of the accident, the reactor's core became partially uncovered, 70 percent of it was damaged, and 50 percent of it melted and fell to the bottom of the reactor. Unknown amounts of ionizing radiation escaped into the atmosphere. No one has died as a result of the accident, but 144,000 people were evacuated. The long-term effects will remain unknown for some time.

Initial construction costs for the reactor totaled $700 million, but partial cleanup costs for the damaged reactor will reach more than $1 billion. Taxpayers' money contributed $187 million to the cleanup operation. In addition, the plant owners have paid $25 million in damages to more than 2,000 people. When the partial cleanup is finished, the plant will be sealed. Some radioactive debris will be left in the plant for twenty to ninety years.

Answer the following questions based on your reading and on your own knowledge.

15. What is the main idea of this section? _____

_____

16. What is the meaning of the word *anticipated,* as used in the passage? _____

_____

17. What caused the problem at Three Mile Island? _____

_____

18. How could it have been prevented? _____

_____

19. What measures would you suggest to avoid a repeat of the accident? _____

_____

_____

20. Outline or map the selection below.

Tell what the environmental disasters in this section have in common. Discuss what you think should be done to prevent future disasters.

WRITING EXERCISE

_____

_____

_____

_____

_____

Read the first section to learn the reasons we should be concerned about wild species.

In addition to the air, land, and water resources around us, our environment includes the plants and wildlife that share "our" world. People living in urban or suburban communities may feel removed and disconnected from "the natural world." However, human beings are part of a global ecosystem, where one species depends, directly or indirectly, on another.

The following selection is about endangered species. You will learn why they are threatened and what can be done about the situation. You will also learn why it is important to all of us to protect wild species of plants and animals. Before you read, think about what you may have read or heard about endangered species. Can you recall a situation in which environmentalists were at odds with industry representatives who wanted to cut timber or build a road through the habitat of an endangered species? Have you experienced people treating plants or animals with a lack of respect?

As you read, underline or highlight the obviously important points. As you answer the questions after each section, underline or highlight the portions of the text where you found the answers. After you finish reading, you will be asked to map or outline the selection.

ENDANGERED SPECIES

Sooner or later, all species become extinct, but people have become a primary factor in the premature extinction of an increasing number of species. Every day, at least 11 and probably 100 species become extinct because of our activities.

WHY PRESERVE WILD PLANT AND ANIMAL SPECIES?

Why Not Let Them Die? Species <u>extinction</u> over earth's long history is a natural occurrence, so why should we be concerned about losing a few more? Does it make any difference that the California condor, the black rhinoceros, or some plant in a tropical forest becomes extinct because of our activities? The answer is yes for a number of reasons.

Economic and Medical Importance. Wild species that are actually or <u>potentially</u> useful to people are called *wildlife resources*. They are potentially renewable resources, if not driven to extinction by our activities.

Most of the plants that supply 90 percent of the world's food today were domesticated from wild plants found in the tropics. Existing wild plant species will be needed by agricultural scientists and genetic engineers to develop new crop <u>strains</u>, and many of them may become important sources of food. Wild animal species are a largely <u>untapped</u> source of food. Wild plants and plants <u>domesticated</u> from wild species are also important sources of rubber, oils, dyes, fiber, paper, lumber, and other important products.

Adapted from *Living in the Environment*, by G. Tyler Miller, Jr., pp. 410–431.

About 75 percent of the world's population relies on plants or plant extracts as sources of medicine. Roughly half the prescription and non-prescription drugs used in the world, and 25 percent of those used in the United States today have active ingredients extracted from wild organisms. Worldwide, medicines from wild species are worth $40 million a year. Only about 5,000 of the world's estimated 250,000 plant species have been studied thoroughly for their possible medical uses.

Many wild animal species are used to test drugs, vaccines, chemical toxicity, and surgical procedures to increase our understanding of human health and disease. Elephants under stress are used to study the causes of heart disease. The nine-banded armadillo is being used to study leprosy and to prepare a vaccine for that disease. Mice, rats, chimpanzees, and rhesus monkeys are used to test for possible cancer-causing agents and toxic chemicals. However, animal rights and welfare advocates are protesting the use of animals in medical and biological research and teaching.

Aesthetic and Recreational Importance. Wild plants and animals are a source of beauty, wonder, joy, and recreational pleasure for large numbers of people. Wild *game species* provide recreation in the form of hunting and fishing. Each year, almost 50 percent of the American population participate in bird watching, photography, and other nondestructive forms of outdoor recreational activities involving wildlife.

Wildlife tourism, sometimes called ecotourism, is important to the economy of some countries, such as Kenya and Tanzania. One wildlife economist estimated that one male lion living seven years in Kenya leads to $515,000 of expenditures by tourists. If the lion were killed for its skin, it would be worth only about $1,000. However, too many visitors to favorite ecotour spots can damage ecosystems and disrupt species. Environmentalists call for strict guidelines governing tours to sensitive areas.

Scientific and Ecological Importance. Each species has scientific value because it can help scientists understand how life has evolved and will continue to evolve on this planet. Wild species also perform vital ecosystem services. They supply us and other species with food from the soil and the sea, recycle nutrients essential to agriculture, and help produce and maintain fertile soil. They also produce and maintain oxygen and other gases in the atmosphere, moderate Earth's climate, help regulate water supplies, and store solar energy as chemical energy in food, wood, and fossil fuels. Moreover, they detoxify poisonous substances, decompose organic wastes, control potential crop pests and carriers of disease, and make up a vast gene pool of biological diversity from which we and other species can draw.

Ethical Importance. So far, the reasons given for preserving wildlife are based on the usefulness of wild species as resources for people. Many ecologists believe that wild species will continue to disappear at an alarming rate until we replace this *human-centered (anthropocentric)* view of wildlife and the environment with either a *life-centered (biocentric)* view or an *ecosystem-centered (ecocentric)* view.

According to the biocentric world view, each wild species has an in-herent right to exist equal to that of any other species. Some distinguish between the survival rights of plants and animals. The poet Alan Watts once commented that he was a vegetarian "because cows scream louder than carrots."

The ecocentric world view stresses the importance of preserving entire ecosystems rather than focusing only on individual species. It recognizes that saving wildlife means saving the places where they live.

Answer the following questions based on your reading and on your thinking.

1. What is the main idea of this section? _____

   _____

2. List, map, or outline the reasons wild species of plants and animals should be preserved.

3. Tell which world view you agree with and explain why. _____

   _____

4. Define the following words as they are used in the passage:

   a. *extinction:* _____

   b. *potentially:* _____

   c. *strains:* _____

   d. *untapped:* _____

   e. *domesticated:* _____

   f. *inherent:* _____

Read the next section to learn about extinction.

HOW SPECIES BECOME DEPLETED AND EXTINCT

The Rise and Fall of Species. Extinction is a natural process. As the planet's surface and climate have changed over its 4.6 billion years of existence, species have disappeared and new ones have evolved to take their places. Throughout earth's history, about 450 million species have probably existed. Today, there are roughly 40 to 80 million species on earth. That means that about 370 million to 420 million of the planet's species have become extinct or have evolved into new species. The rise and fall of species has not been smooth. There have been several periods of <u>mass</u> extinctions, and others when the diversity of life has increased and spread.

Extinction of Species Today. Imagine you are driving on an interstate highway at a high speed. You notice that your two passengers are passing the time by using wrenches and screwdrivers to remove various bolts, screws, and parts of your car on a random basis and are throwing them out the window. How long will it be before they remove enough parts to cause a crash or a breakdown?

Past extinctions took place slowly enough to allow new forms of life to arise. This began changing about 40,000 years ago when the latest version of our species came on the scene. Since agriculture began, about 10,000 years ago, the rate of species extinction has increased sharply as human settlements have expanded worldwide. Now we are the primary force in a new mass extinction.

There are three important differences between the present mass extinction and those in the past:

1. The present "extinction spasm" is being brought about by us—the first one to be caused by a single species.

2. The current wildlife <u>holocaust</u> is taking place in only a few decades rather than over millions of years. Such rapid extinction cannot be balanced by new or adapted species because it takes between 2,000 and 100,000 years for new species to evolve.

3. Plant species are disappearing as rapidly as animal species, thus threatening many animal species as they lose their food supplies.

Answer the following questions based on your reading.

5. What is the main idea of this section? _____

_____

6. Why weren't the extinctions that occurred centuries ago a problem? _____

_____

7. How does extinction today differ from what went on in the past?

a. _____

b. _____

c. _____

8. Define the following words:

a. *mass:* _____

b. *holocaust:* _____

Endangered and Threatened Species Today. Species heading toward extinction can be classified as either endangered or threatened. An *endangered species* is one having so few individual survivors that the species could soon become extinct over all or most of its natural range. Examples are the white rhinoceros in Africa, the California condor in the United States, the giant panda in central China, the snow leopard in central Asia, and the rare swallowtail butterfly.

Read the next section to learn why certain species are endangered.

A *threatened species* is still <u>abundant</u> in its natural range but is declining in numbers and likely to become endangered. Examples are the bald eagle and the grizzly bear.

Many wild species are not in danger of extinction, but their populations have been sharply reduced locally or regionally. Because such number losses are occurring much faster and more frequently than extinctions, they may be a better sign of the condition of wildlife and entire ecosystems. They can serve as early warnings so that we can prevent species extinction rather than respond mostly to emergencies.

Habitat Loss and Disturbance. The greatest threat to most wild species is destruction, <u>fragmentation</u>, and degradation of their habitats. Such <u>disruption</u> of natural communities threatens wild species by destroying migration routes, breeding areas, and food sources. Deforestation, especially of tropical forests, is the greatest offender, followed by destruction of coral reefs and wetlands and plowing of grasslands.

In the United States, tall grass–prairies have been reduced by 98 percent, virgin forests by 98 percent, wetlands by 50 percent, and overall forest cover by 33 percent.

Many rare and threatened plant and animal species live in <u>vulnerable</u>, specialized habitats, such as on islands or as single trees in tropical forests. About 10 percent of the world's bird species have a range of only one island. Hawaii accounts for two-thirds of the species that became extinct in the 1980s. It is fast becoming the world capital of biological extinction because of increasing population and development.

Commercial Hunting and Poaching. There are three main types of hunting: subsistence, sport, and commercial. The killing of animals to provide enough food for survival is called *subsistence hunting. Sport hunting* is the hunting of animals for recreation and in some cases for food. *Commercial hunting* involves killing animals for profit from sale of their furs or other parts. Illegal commercial hunting or fishing is called *poaching*.

Today, subsistence hunting has declined sharply because there are not many hunting-and-gathering societies left in the world. Sport hunting is closely regulated in most countries and, therefore, rarely endangers game species. No animal in the United States, for instance, has become extinct or endangered because of regulated sport hunting.

In the past, legal and illegal commercial hunting has led to the extinction or near extinction of many animal species, such as the American bison. This continues today. It's not surprising that Bengal tigers face extinction. A coat made from their fur sells for $100,000 in Tokyo. A mountain gorilla is worth $150,000; an ocelot skin, $40,000; rhinoceros horn, up to $28,600. Even if the poacher is caught, the economic <u>incentive</u> far outweighs the risk of paying a small fine and the much smaller risk of serving time in jail.

Predator and Pest Control. Extinction or near extinction can occur when people attempt to <u>exterminate</u> pest and predator species that compete with humans for food and game. Fruit farmers exterminated the Carolina parakeet in the United States around 1914 because it fed on fruit crops.

As animal habitats have shrunk, farmers have killed large numbers of African elephants to keep them from trampling and eating food crops. Since 1929, ranchers and government agencies have poisoned prairie dogs because horses and cattle sometimes step into the burrows and break their legs. This poisoning has killed 99 percent of the prairie dog population in North America. It has also led to the near extinction of the black-footed ferret which preyed on the prairie dog.

Pets and Decorative Plants. Each year, large numbers of threatened and endangered animal species are smuggled into the United States, Great Britain, Germany, and other countries. Most are sold as pets.

Some species of exotic plants, especially orchids and cacti, are also endangered because they are gathered, often illegally. They are then sold to collectors and used to decorate houses, offices, and landscapes. A collector may pay $5,000 for a single rare orchid.

Pollution and Climate Change. Toxic chemicals degrade wildlife habitats, including wildlife refuges, and kill some plants and animals. Slowly degradable pesticides, especially DDT and dieldrin, have caused populations of some bird species to decline.

Wildlife in even the best-protected and best-managed wildlife reserves throughout the world may be depleted in a few decades because of climactic change caused by projected global warming.

Introduction of Alien Species. As people travel around the world, they sometimes pick up plants and animals intentionally or accidentally and introduce them to new geographical regions. Many of these alien species have provided food, game, and beauty and have helped control pests in their new environment.

Some alien species, however, have no natural predators and competitors in their new habitats. That allows them to dominate their new ecosystem and reduce the populations of many native species. Eventually, such alien species can cause the extinction of native species.

One example of an alien species is the kudzu vine, brought in from Japan. In the 1930s, it was planted in many areas of the Southeast to help control soil erosion. It does control erosion, but it is so prolific and hard to kill that it spreads rapidly and covers hills, trees, houses, roadsides, stream banks, utility poles, patches of forest, and anything else in its path.

Population Growth, Affluence, and Poverty. As the human population grows, it occupies more land and clears and degrades more land to supply food, fuel, timber, and other resources.

Increasing affluence leads to greatly increased average resource use per person. People with more money build bigger houses on larger lots and buy more things that use up natural resources. On the other end of the economic scale, poverty is an underlying cause of wildlife reduction and extinction. In less-developed countries, the combination of rapid population growth and poverty push the poor to cut forests, grow crops on marginal land, and poach endangered animals.

General Characteristics of Extinction-Prone Species. Some species have natural traits that make them more vulnerable than others to premature extinction. One trait that affects the survival of species under different environmental conditions is their reproductive strategy.

Each animal species has a critical population density and size, below which survival may be impossible because males and females have a hard time finding each other. Once the population reaches its critical size, it continues to decline, even if the species is protected, because its death rate exceeds its birth rate. The remaining small population can easily be wiped out by fire, landslide, flood, or disease.

Answer the following questions based on your reading.

9. What is the main idea of this section? _____

_____

10. What is the difference between an *endangered species* and a *threatened species?* _____

_____

11. Define the following words as they are used in the passage:

a. *abundant:* _____

b. *fragmentation:* _____

c. *disruption:* _____

d. *vulnerable:* _____

e. *incentive:* _____

f. *exterminate:* _____

12. Map or outline the reasons species become endangered.

13. Write a paragraph explaining one of the reasons species become endangered.

_____

_____

_____

_____

_____

PROTECTING WILD SPECIES FROM EXTINCTION

Methods for Protecting and Managing Wildlife. There are three basic approaches to wildlife conservation and management.

1. *The species approach.* Protect endangered species by identifying them, giving them legal protection, preserving and managing their critical habits, propagating species in captivity, and reintroducing species in suitable habitats.

2. *The ecosystem approach.* Preserve balanced populations of species in their native habitats, establish legally protected wilderness areas and wildlife reserves, and eliminate alien species from an area.

3. *The wildlife management approach.* Manage species, mostly game species, for sustained yield by using laws to regulate hunting, establishing harvest quotas, developing population management plans, and using international treaties to protect migrating game species, such as waterfowl.

THE ENDANGERED SPECIES ACT

The Endangered Species Act of 1973 is one of the world's toughest environmental laws. This act makes it illegal for the United States to import or to carry on trade in any product made from an endangered or threatened species unless it is used for an approved scientific purpose or to <u>enhance</u> the survival of the species.

To make control more effective, all commercial shipments of wildlife and wildlife products must enter or leave the country through one of the nine designated ports, but many illegal shipments of wildlife slip by. The sixty Fish and Wildlife Service inspectors are able to physically examine only about one-fourth of the 90,000 shipments that enter and leave the United States each year. Permits have been falsified, and some government inspectors have been bribed. Even if caught, many violators are not prosecuted, and convicted violators often pay only a small fine.

The law also provides protection for endangered and threatened species in the United States and abroad. It authorizes the National Marine Fisheries Service (NMFS) to identify and list endangered and threatened marine species. The Fish and Wildlife Service (FWS) identifies and lists all other endangered and threatened species. These species cannot be hunted, killed, collected, or injured in the United States.

Any decision by either agency to add or remove a species from the list must be based only on biological grounds, without economic considerations. The act also prohibits federal agencies from carrying out, funding, or authorizing projects that would <u>jeopardize</u> an endangered or threatened species or destroy or modify its critical habitat—the land, air, and water necessary for its survival.

Between 1970 and 1990, the number of species found only in the United States that have been placed on the official endangered list increased from 92 to 592. Also on the list are 508 species found in other parts of the world.

Once a species is listed as endangered or threatened in the United States, the FWS or the NMFS is supposed to prepare a plan to help it recover. However, because of a lack of funds, recovery plans have been

Read the next section to learn about different approaches to protecting wild species.

Read the next section to learn about the Endangered Species Act. Try to decide which of the three approaches it exemplifies.

developed and approved for only about 51 percent of those native to the United States. Half of those plans exist only on paper. Only a handful of species have recovered sufficiently to be removed from protection.

The current annual federal budget for endangered species is $8.4 million—equal to the cost of about twenty-five Army bulldozers. This helps explain why it will take the Fish and Wildlife Service fifty years to evaluate the 3,600 species now under consideration for listing. Many species will probably disappear before they can be protected, as did 34 species in the 1980s.

Answer the following questions on the basis of your reading and your own thinking.

14. What is the main idea of this section? _____

_____

15. Which protection approach do you think the Endangered Species Act exemplifies? _____

_____

16. Define the following words according to the way they are used in the passage:

   a. *enhance:* _____

   b. *jeopardize:* _____

17. According to the Endangered Species Act, what do you think would be the outcome of the situations described below?

   a. The owner of a private zoo in Illinois would like to import a snow leopard, an endangered species, from central Asia to become his prime exhibit. _____

   _____

   _____

   b. A developer in Texas wants to fill in some wetlands where whooping cranes graze to build a golf course. _____

   _____

   c. A researcher who is investigating the habitat of rare hyacinth macaws—Brazilian parrots—wants to import one of the birds to continue her studies. _____

   _____

   _____

   d. The Los Angeles Zoo is the site of a captive breeding program for the endangered California condor.

   _____

   e. While hunting for geese, a hunter shot a bald eagle. He claims it was accidental. _____

   _____

   f. A tourist from Pennsylvania digs up a black lace cactus, an endangered plant, and gives it to her neighbor who watered the grass during her absence. _____

   _____

g. Medical researchers use the armadillo to study leprosy in hopes of developing a vaccine against the disease. _____

_____

h. A landscape architect wants to import a symphonia, an endangered plant found on the island of Madagascar, to use in her exhibit at the New York Flower Show. _____

_____

i. Officials of a northwestern paper company would like to cut trees on their own land where the endangered spotted owl lives. _____

_____

j. A fur dealer wants to import coats made from Bengal tiger skin to sell to his customers. _____

_____

18. Would you like to see the Endangered Species Act maintained, eliminated, weakened, strengthened, or more heavily funded? Explain why. _____

_____

_____

Explain why it is in our best interest to protect wild plants and animals. Tell what you think is the best way to go about it.

WRITING EXERCISE

_____

_____

_____

_____

_____

_____

Civil Rights

I n the United States, we believe that all people have certain basic rights that should be honored and protected. Often we take our civil rights for granted, assuming that we will be treated fairly and offered the same opportunities as everyone else. Although we realize that our civil rights are protected by the Constitution and other laws, we probably don't spend much time thinking about our rights and liberties until they are violated. Some countries, however, extend no legal protection to an individual's rights and freedoms. When discrimination, exploitation, and abuse occur, the victims have no recourse.

As you work on the civil rights theme, you will learn some related vocabulary. You will also explore the rights guaranteed by the Constitution and learn how these protections developed. This theme will be treated historically; you will learn about rights that were guaranteed *or* denied to groups or to individuals in this country. You will also read about law and politics as they relate to civil rights and about the effects of the civil rights movement on our society.

THEME FOCUS

TOPIC: CIVIL RIGHTS

ASSOCIATED VOCABULARY

SKILLS: MULTIPLE MEANINGS OF WORDS
FIGURATIVE LANGUAGE
MAKING INFERENCES
DRAWING CONCLUSIONS
MAKING JUDGMENTS
PARAPHRASING
CHRONOLOGICAL OR SEQUENTIAL
ORGANIZATIONAL PATTERN

SKILL DEVELOPMENT: EXPANDING YOUR VOCABULARY

This section helps you extend your vocabulary. First, you will be introduced to vocabulary that is relevant to the civil rights theme. Next, you will explore the multiple meanings that familiar words may have. And, last, you will learn to distinguish between literal and figurative language.

Exercise 1
Words in Context

The underlined words in these sentences appear in the passages you will read in this section of your text. They are presented in context here to help you figure out their meanings. Write the meaning of the underlined word after each sentence.

1. For President Johnson to push civil rights <u>legislation</u> through Congress meant overcoming strong Southern opposition to any change in the laws. _____

2. Because of widespread racial <u>prejudice</u>, even the free blacks in the North suffered from the hostility of white society. _____

3. At one time, all Southern cities had strict <u>segregation</u> policies that restricted the activities of African Americans. _____

4. At times, racial identity and <u>ethnicity</u> are sources of pride, but they may also target individuals who belong to a particular group as outsiders. _____

5. Although most universities pride themselves on recruiting minority students, several <u>elite</u> institutions with reputations for academic excellence were charged with maintaining quotas against Asian American students. _____

6. The Civil Rights Act of the 1960s did not end <u>discrimination</u> entirely, but it strengthened voting rights, outlawed segregation in public facilities, increased the federal role in desegregation cases, and empowered the Civil Rights Commission. _____

7. In 1960, many African American students saw the sit-in as a protest movement that provided them with a personal opportunity in their own community, to stand up and reject <u>submission</u> to unjust laws and regulations. _____

8. President Truman tried to please Southern blacks with executive orders prohibiting discrimination in federal employment and <u>desegregating</u> the armed forces. _____

9. In the 1980s, for a variety of reasons, less than one-half of the <u>eligible</u> African Americans voted in elections. _____

_____

10. National leaders, at times, persuade the nation that the <u>status quo</u> is acceptable, rather than encouraging change. _____

_____

11. After federal agents <u>infiltrated</u> white supremacist groups to learn about their activities, the Justice Department used the information to file charges against 150 activists. _____

_____

12. Students staged sit-ins to pressure officials to recruit minority students and faculty members, and to <u>rescind</u> tuition hikes. _____

_____

13. Since the 1960s, <u>civil disobedience</u>, a tactic where the protester expects to be arrested and puts up no resistance, has been used by a variety of groups. _____

_____

14. In 1619, twenty blacks were brought to Jamestown, Virginia and sold by the Dutch ship master as <u>indentured servants</u>, who had to work off the cost of their passage and purchase. _____

_____

15. At the end of the seventeenth century, the growth of <u>plantation</u> agriculture increased the demand for slaves to farm these individually owned large tracts of land. _____

_____

16. In the 1700s, to eliminate competition, white tradesmen in several Northern cities attempted to have blacks legally <u>barred</u> from doing certain kinds of skilled labor. _____

_____

17. As he tried to point out the unfairness of prejudice, President Johnson said, "We must overcome the crippling legacy of <u>bigotry</u> and injustice." _____

_____

18. In the 1840s, black <u>abolitionists</u> met at conventions to discuss reasons and strategies to eliminate slavery.

_____

19. Although the <u>Emancipation</u> Proclamation took effect in January 1863, the remaining slaves were not freed until the Thirteenth Amendment was ratified in December 1865. _____

_____

20. A <u>suffrage</u> restriction in Mississippi required each applicant to vote to interpret a portion of the state constitution. The intention was to eliminate blacks from the voting lists. _____

_____

Exercise 2
Definitions

Match the words in column A with their definitions in column B.

PART I	
COLUMN A	COLUMN B
____ 1. legislation	a. traits, background, or association common to a group of people
____ 2. rescind	b. to revoke; to annul; or to invalidate
____ 3. civil disobedience	c. the right to vote
____ 4. ethnicity	d. the refusal to obey certain laws in order to effect change; characterized by nonviolent tactics
____ 5. infiltrate	e. to eliminate racial or other segregation
____ 6. discrimination	f. the act of making laws; a body of laws enacted
____ 7. bar	g. to block; to prevent; or to hinder
____ 8. desegregate	h. to move into an organization secretly and with hostile intentions
____ 9. abolitionist	i. one who believes in the principle of eliminating slavery
____ 10. suffrage	j. action or policies based on prejudice or partiality

PART 2

COLUMN A	COLUMN B
_____ 1. elite	a. a person bound to work for another for a specific time
_____ 2. prejudice	b. the choice or best of a group
_____ 3. segregation	c. the act of freeing, particularly from slavery
_____ 4. indentured servant	d. the practice of separating or isolating people or groups
_____ 5. plantation	e. the existing state or condition
_____ 6. submission	f. a large farm or estate
_____ 7. bigotry	g. the act of yielding to another's power or authority
_____ 8. eligible	h. meeting the stipulated requirements
_____ 9. emancipation	i. extreme intolerance of people or beliefs different from one's own
_____ 10. status quo	j. an unfavorable opinion formed without knowledge

Exercise 3
Multiple Meanings

You have practiced using the context to help define unfamiliar words. Efficient readers also need to realize that familiar words may be used in different ways. Many words have *multiple meanings;* that is, they take on different definitions according to their context.

For example, consider the word *side.* Read the following sentences and define the word *side* as it is used in each one.

1. Write on both <u>sides</u> of the paper. _____

2. Whose <u>side</u> are you on in this argument? _____

3. Put the box on its <u>side</u> so it doesn't tip over. _____

4. The maid of honor stood at the bride's <u>side</u> during the ceremony. _____

5. She inherited her curly, red hair from her mother's <u>side</u> of the family. _____

6. The challenger stood nervously on the far <u>side</u> of the tennis court. _____

Although the word *side* was already familiar, you had to consider how it was used in each sentence to choose the correct meaning. Many other English words also have multiple meanings. You can find these meanings in the dictionary, or you can use context clues to help you figure them out. Flexible readers are always ready to adjust their thinking about the meaning of a word to suit the way it is used.

In the exercise that follows, you will read pairs of sentences that use the same word in a different way. Read both sentences. Then write two definitions for each underlined word, according to the way it is used in each sentence. For example, for the series of sentences using the word *side,* you might write the following definitions for the first two sentences: the surface of a flat object, or one of two opposing points of view.

1. a. The habitat of the blue heron colony was <u>degraded</u> as developers cleared the land of trees to make way for a shopping mall. _____

    _____

    b. The African American man felt <u>degraded</u> as the waiter served every white customer in the restaurant before coming to his table. _____

    _____

2. a. Arturo's <u>discriminating</u> taste in antique jewelry led to his career as a costume consultant. _____

    _____

    b. <u>Discriminating</u> against job applicants on the basis of race or sex is illegal. _____

    _____

3. a. At the scene of the accident, the rescue workers were encouraged as the victim regained <u>consciousness</u>.

    _____

    b. <u>Consciousness</u> raising was an important first step for the civil rights movement and the women's movement, as the leaders tried to get their members to see the issues clearly. _____

    _____

4. a. Before purchasing her new sound system, Felicia asked for a <u>demonstration</u> of the compact disc player.

    _____

    b. The <u>demonstration</u> remained peaceful despite hostile remarks from the crowd as the marchers approached city hall. _____

    _____

5. a. To make the curtains and slipcovers, the tailor ordered fifteen yards of the cotton print <u>material</u>.

    _____

    b. Individuals who are committed to a cause often sacrifice <u>material</u> possessions for their idealism. They give their volunteer activities precedence over their income-producing jobs. _____

    _____

6. a. Lobbyists—individuals who are paid by special interest groups—try to <u>court</u> the favor of elected officials who have some influence over policy that will affect them. _____

    _____

b. The Supreme <u>Court</u> played a significant role in the civil rights movement, since its decisions clearly determined that racial discrimination is unconstitutional. _____

_____

7. a. After the <u>submission</u> of photocopies of a birth certificate and social security card, the new teacher had completed all of the eligibility requirements for the job. _____

_____

b. Rebellions by the slaves often began when they tired of constant <u>submission</u> to the unreasonable demands of cruel masters. _____

_____

8. a. When the psychology professor announced the date of her guest lecturer's visit, she invited students from other classes to <u>sit in</u> as well. _____

_____

b. Lunch counter <u>sit-ins</u> where blacks demanded service at "white-only" restaurants were an effective tool at the beginning of the civil rights movement. _____

_____

9. a. After an elaborate and filling dinner, the group stopped at the <u>bar</u> for one last drink before heading home. _____

_____

b. Attempts to <u>bar</u> blacks from voting in Southern states were common for some time after the end of the Civil War. _____

_____

10. a. The senior class planned a ten-mile <u>hike</u> through the woods, followed by swimming in the lake and a picnic. _____

_____

b. People who live in inner-city neighborhoods often suffer from the price <u>hike</u> imposed by supermarket chains on stores in high-crime areas. _____

_____

Language is a powerful tool that is used for communication, education, persuasion, explanation, and countless other purposes. You have learned that words may convey different meanings according to their context and that other influences can affect the interpretation of a word. For example, a person's body language and tone of voice may provide as many clues to his or her intention as the words themselves. *Figurative language* applies to the broad, interpretive use of words. In some cases, words may be used as symbols or may take on completely different meanings. If you look up a word in the dictionary, you find its *literal meaning;* that is, what the word itself means. For example, if you look up the word *goo,* you will learn that

Exercise 4

Figurative Language

it means "a wet, sticky substance." It would be appropriate to describe a chocolate dessert as *gooey*. In other words, the dessert feels and tastes wet and sticky. You may also use the adjective *gooey* in a figurative sense. A romance novel or an excessively sentimental movie might prompt you to say, "That's too *gooey* for my taste." Of course, you didn't mean that the book or movie was wet and sticky. You used the *figurative meaning,* or *connotation,* of the word. The connotative or figurative use of the word *gooey* is broadly related to its *literal meaning.* A *gooey* dessert is often *too* sweet or messy, and a *gooey* story may also create that impression.

Phrases or groups of words can also be used in a figurative way. *Idioms,* expressions that are commonly used by native speakers of a language, often confuse nonnative speakers. For example, a student of English as a second language would be confused by the following idiomatic expressions:

I am so hungry that I could eat a horse.

I thought I would die when I saw my ex-boyfriend at the party.

Linda said she would kill for that dress.

Certainly, you don't expect the first speaker to eat horsemeat or the second to call for a doctor. That is because you know the figurative meaning of the idioms or phrases. However, nonnative English speakers do not have the same experience with the language. They may try to use the literal meaning of each word and plan to restrain Linda, for fear of what she may do.

Fiction writers and poets tend to use figurative language more than textbook authors do. Since figurative language lends itself to more interpretation, it requires more interaction between reader and writer. It also allows readers more freedom in creating their own meanings for words. Martin Luther King, Jr., used figurative language in most of his speeches to convey images and symbols that described the plight of his people and that touched the hearts of his listeners. Consider the following quotations from his "I Have a Dream" speech, delivered from the steps of the Lincoln Memorial in Washington, D.C., in 1963.

I have a dream that right there in Alabama little black boys and black girls will be able to join hands with little white boys and little white girls as sisters and brothers.

When we allow freedom to ring—when we let it ring from every city and every hamlet, from every state and every city, we will be able to speed up that day when all of God's children, black men and white men, Jews and Gentiles, Protestants and Catholics, will be able to join hands and sing in the words of the old Negro spiritual, "Free at last, Free at last, Great God a-mighty. We are free at last."

King uses the imagery of joining hands to convey the ideas of equality and respect. It doesn't matter if God's children literally or actually join hands. What matters is that each group considers the others as equals. Similarly, the expression *let freedom ring* doesn't refer to ringing bells, except in a symbolic way. King's point is that the idea of freedom must be spread throughout the nation.

In this exercise, you will read two poems written by Langston Hughes, a fine American poet who lived between 1902 and 1967. Notice how he uses ordinary words to represent broad ideas and situations. For the first section of "I, Too," the figurative language will be described. Then the guide questions will help you interpret the rest of the poem.

I, Too

I, too, sing America.

I am the darker brother.
They send me to eat in the kitchen
When company comes,
But I laugh,
And eat well,
And grow strong.

Notice the word *too* used in the title and in the first line. It is almost like a charge to white readers to notice him. He, *too*, celebrates (*sing*) America. He is an American, *too;* don't forget about him. "I am the darker brother." The term *brother* indicates equality, and *darker,* of course, refers to skin color. "They send me to eat in the kitchen when company comes." This is as an example and a symbol of second-class treatment. Literally, blacks are not invited to the dining rooms of whites. Figuratively, they are discriminated against in many ways. The image of being sent to the kitchen may also represent housing discrimination, inferior educational opportunities, or job discrimination. The last three lines of this stanza describe the poet's reaction to such treatment. "But I laugh, and eat well, and grow strong." In other words, you can't beat me or keep me down. The poet, too, may represent all African Americans.

Consider the rest of the poem and use the guide questions that follow to help you interpret it.

Tomorrow,
I'll be at the table
When company comes.
Nobody'll dare
Say to me,
"Eat in the kitchen,"
Then.

Besides,
They'll see how beautiful I am
And be ashamed—

I, too, am America.

1. What are the literal and figurative meanings of *tomorrow*? _____
_____
_____

2. What does being "at the table when company comes" represent? _____
_____

3. Why will nobody dare say, "Eat in the kitchen"? _____
_____

4. What could "how beautiful I am" represent, in its broadest sense? _____
_____
_____

5. Who are they? _____

6. What will they be ashamed of? _____
_____

7. What does "I, too, am America" mean? _____
_____

The next poem is also by Langston Hughes. As you read it, pay attention to his use of the imagery of black and white. The guide questions that follow will help you interpret the figurative language.

DREAM VARIATIONS

To fling my arms wide
In some place of the sun,
To whirl and to dance
Till the white day is done.

———————
From *Selected Poems*, by Langston Hughes.

Then rest at cool evening
Beneath a cool tree
While night comes on gently,
    Dark like me—
That is my dream!

To fling my arms wide
In the face of the sun,
Dance! Whirl! Whirl!
Till the quick day is done.
Rest at pale evening . . .
A tall, slim tree . . .
Night coming tenderly
    Black like me.

8. What is the *mood* or feeling in this poem? What words create the impression? _____

_____

_____

9. What do you think the phrase *white day* refers to? _____

_____

10. Why do you think the narrator identifies with night? _____

_____

_____

The two poems you have just read were written several decades ago. Are they appropriate today as when they were written? Do you think figurative language helps poetry maintain its timeliness?

Writing Exercise

_____

_____

_____

_____

_____

SKILL DEVELOPMENT: MAKING INFERENCES

Locating details and identifying facts in reading passages test the reader's comprehension on a literal level. He or she answers questions and provides information of the *who, where, when,* and sometimes *what* variety. If you read a selection from your history textbook that discussed the adoption of the U.S. Constitution, you would probably be able to tell when it was adopted, how many people signed it, and who they were. You can *find* this information in the text. However, if you limit yourself to the facts and details in your reading, you will miss important information and perhaps the richness of the author's message.

To make an inference means to:

- read between the lines,

- use the author's hints and suggestions,

- draw from your own experience,

- draw a conclusion, or

- make a judgment.

We make inferences from sources other than the printed page every day. For example, if you arrive home to be greeted by stony silence and a scowling face, you may infer that your roommate is upset or angry. If you ask someone to go out with you four times and she's always busy, you may infer that she is not interested. If you observe a conversation between a coach and player during which the coach smiles and pats the player on the back, you may infer that the coach is pleased. If your professor returns an exam with a grade of 55 percent and says, "You did a great job on this one!" you may infer that she is being sarcastic. In these examples, you are drawing inferences from observing facial expressions, behaviors, gestures, and tones of voice. By adding that information to what you already know about human nature and your own experiences in similar situations, you can draw a conclusion or make an inference.

Unfortunately, when we read, we do not have the benefit of additional clues like tone of voice or gestures to help us in our interpretations. We have to rely on the text and our own thinking to make inferences from the printed page.

Exercise 5

Making Inferences

Each of the following sentences contains a small amount of information. Read each one carefully to see if you can make an inference about the topic. An example is provided to get you started.

> A Federal judge ordered the Clinton administration to provide better medical care to Haitian refugees with AIDS who were being held at the naval base at Guantanamo Bay, Cuba, either by improving conditions there or by evacuating them within ten days.

Before you begin to make inferences, take note of the information that is *given*. What do you know from the sentence?

1. You know that Haitian refugees were being held at the American naval base in Cuba.

2. You know that at least some of these refugees have AIDS.

3. You know that a judge has ordered improved medical care or removal of the refugees.

What can you infer about the medical care the refugees are now receiving?

> If a judge ordered improvement, the medical care the refugees were receiving must have been inadequate or unacceptable.

The sentence did not specifically say that the medical care at the naval base is inferior, but we can infer that it is because of the judge's order.

In the following sentences, identify the information given. Then draw an inference according to the instructions.

1. Mahmud Abohalima, a suspect in the World Trade Center bombing, was arrested in Egypt and flown back to the United States to stand trial.

   a. What information is given in the sentence? _____

   _____

   b. What can you infer about an agreement between Egypt and the United States regarding criminals?

   _____

2. New York is the only state where infants can stay with their incarcerated mothers in a prison nursery until their first birthday, or for eighteen months if their mothers will be paroled within that time.

   a. What information is given? _____

   _____

   b. What can you infer about the meaning of the word *incarcerated*? (If you already knew the meaning, you didn't need to make that inference.) _____

   _____

   c. What can you infer about other states' policies about babies in prison? _____

   _____

   _____

   d. What can you infer about what will happen to a nine-month old child whose mother's sentence does not permit parole for five years? _____

   _____

   _____

3. A decision by an administrative law judge in Washington significantly weakened the government's ability to penalize companies whose workers develop repetitive stress injuries. The judge threw out a fine imposed by OSHA (the Occupational Safety and Health Administration) because there was no federal standard dealing with repetitive stress. (*Hint:* Repetitive stress syndrome is caused by performing the same or similar motions over and over, for long periods without rest. It can cause pain and numbness in the arms and hands. A computer operator, for example, may experience such injuries.)

   a. What information is given about the decision? _____

   _____

b. What can you infer about what OSHA does? _____

_____

c. What can you infer about the rules by which OSHA makes its decisions about penalties?

_____

d. Which group do you think would be pleased by the judge's ruling—the workers or the employers?

_____

4. Defendants who are unable to speak the "language of the court" (English in the United States) are assisted by court interpreters. In such cases, Spanish-speaking defendants and English-speaking judges must address each other *through* the court interpreter. Thus, defendants and judges *cannot* address one another directly to clarify their points or provide examples.

a. What information is given about non-English speakers? _____

_____

b. What can you infer about the difference between the courtroom experience of a Spanish-speaking defendant and that of an English-speaking one? _____

_____

c. What advice would you give to a Spanish-speaking defendant? _____

_____

5. Persons with disabilities are attempting to change the view of themselves as helpless, as victims, or as merely sick. One disabled man reported, "People do not consider me, they consider the chair first. I was in a store with my purchases on my lap and money on my lap. The clerk looked at my companion and said, 'Cash or charge?'"

a. What information is given about the incident? _____

_____

b. What can you infer about the store clerk's attitude toward the disabled? _____

_____

c. What can you infer about the disabled person's feelings? _____

_____

Exercise 6

Contrasting Facts and Inferences

Many passages include facts, details, *and* the opportunity to make inferences. Careful readers are able to locate the information provided and use their own thinking skills to expand on this information. Conclusions and judgments are appropriate reading responses. However, they must be based on the text, and the reader should realize the difference between stated facts and inferences.

The following passage is an excerpt from a history text. The topic is the Bill of Rights. After you read it, underline the facts.

THE BILL OF RIGHTS

A subject on which the Constitution was almost silent was "liberty"—all those rights that individuals have *against* governments. This question was fiercely debated during the ratification process, and the Federalists responded by promising to add amendments spelling out the rights of citizens under the new government. The result of this promise was a series of amendments—twelve at first, but reduced to ten—that came quickly to be known as the Bill of Rights.

The task of drawing up the amendments fell to James Madison. He sifted through a large number of recommendations, some proposing as many as forty different provisions. He also worked through precedents in the state constitutions, particularly the Declaration of Rights adopted in Virginia in the first year of the Revolution. Finally, Madison boiled the proposals down to seventeen. The Senate dropped five of these, and what finally emerged were the first ten amendments to the Constitution. They contained the now familiar guarantees of freedom of speech, press, religion, assembly, trial by jury, the right to bear arms, and so forth, plus a general amendment stressing that the federal government had *only* those powers explicitly granted in the Constitution.

You should be able to find the answers to the first group of questions in your underlined material. All of these questions are testing your comprehension on a literal, factual level.

1. On what subject was the original Constitution silent? _____

2. When was this question debated? _____

3. How was the problem resolved? _____

_____

4. Who drew up the amendments? _____

5. How many amendments are included in the Bill of Rights? _____

6. Name two freedoms guaranteed by the Bill of Rights. _____

_____

Now that you have a grasp of the factual information contained in the passage, here are some questions that ask you to respond to the material on an inferential level. You will be given some clues to help your thinking.

Excerpt from *The Pursuit of Liberty: A History of the American People,* vol. 1, 2nd ed., by R. Jackson Wilson et al. (Belmont, Calif.: Wadsworth, 1990), p. 231.

7. Why was the Bill of Rights needed? (*Hint:* You will probably want to include some mention of "liberty.")

_____

_____

8. How did the Framers of the Constitution feel about the role of the federal government? (*Hint:* Notice the italicized words in the first and last paragraphs.) _____

_____

_____

9. The number of amendments was reduced from a possible forty to ten. How do you think Madison made his decisions about what to include? (*Hints:* How would you make this type of decision? Consider the freedoms that were mentioned.) _____

_____

_____

10. Do you think the Bill of Rights improved the Constitution? Why? (You shouldn't need a hint for this one.)

_____

_____

Exercise 7
Drawing Conclusions

Proficient readers are comfortable dealing with information on an inferential level, as well as on a literal one. In addition to the facts that the author lays out, they use the larger context of the passage and their own experiences to *draw conclusions*. Some readers are reluctant to draw conclusions because they are afraid they won't be able to *prove* their points. While it is true that the passage won't contain *the* answer to an *inferential* question, it should provide supporting material.

For example, consider three of the nine points included in the program of the National Association for the Advancement of Colored People (NAACP) adopted in 1919.

A vote for every Negro man and woman on the same terms as for white men and women.

Defense against lynching and burning at the hands of mobs.

Equal right to the use of public parks, libraries, and other community services for which they are taxed.

Although there is no description of the type of discrimination African Americans faced in 1919, we can easily draw conclusions about what went on. We can conclude that they faced problems as voters, as victims of violence, and as users of community services. The program does not list grievances, but we can conclude that blacks were denied the right to vote. We can *support* this conclusion with the phrase *on the same terms*. It implies that prospective African

Americans voters had not been treated the same way as white voters. If this had not been the case, the NAACP wouldn't have stated it as an organizational aim. Similarly, blacks must have been lynched and burned, or the NAACP wouldn't see the need to seek defense against such actions. Finally, we can conclude that African Americans paid taxes as whites did but did not receive the same services, and that blacks were denied access to libraries and parks. We see *support* for this conclusion in the phrase *equal right to the use of.* From our own knowledge, we may *infer* that African Americans may not have been completely excluded from the parks, but they may have been restricted to a certain area. Perhaps they were only allowed to use the libraries on certain days or in particular locations. Any of these examples would illustrate that blacks did not have *equal use* of public services.

In the exercise that follows, you will read some information about the life and career of Martin Luther King, Jr., the leader of the civil rights movement. You will be asked to draw conclusions from the information provided and from your own knowledge.

Read the first section to learn about Martin Luther King's educational background.

King was a new resident of Montgomery, Alabama, in 1955. He had arrived there just one year earlier. With a new Ph.D. and his wife, Coretta, he answered a call from the Dexter Avenue Baptist Church. King had grown up in Atlanta, where his father was a prominent minister at the Ebenezer Baptist Church. His mother was the daughter of Ebenezer's previous minister.

King entered public school and then switched to the private laboratory school at Atlanta University. From there he attended Atlanta's only black high school, Booker T. Washington. He skipped ninth grade and graduated at the age of fifteen. Like his father before him, he went on to Morehouse College. During this period he began to think seriously about the ministry. He began preaching at the age of seventeen and shortly thereafter became assistant pastor at Ebenezer.

Excerpt from *Afro-American History, Primary Sources,* 2nd ed., by Thomas R. Frazier (Belmont, Calif.: Wadsworth, The Dorsey Press, 1988), pp. 213–214. "The Task for the Future—A Program for 1919," *Report of the National Association for the Advancement of Colored People for the Years 1917 and 1918* (New York, 1919), pp. 76–80.

The following questions ask you to draw conclusions based on your reading and on your own knowledge.

1. a. What kind of student was King? _____

   b. Which specific facts support your conclusion? _____

   _____

2. a. What can you conclude about his family background? _____

   _____

   b. Which facts support your answer? _____

   _____

3. What can you conclude about the educational opportunities for blacks if Atlanta had only one black high school? _____

4. a. What can you conclude about King's ability as a preacher? _____

   _____

   b. Which facts support your answer? _____

   _____

Read the next section to learn what and where King studied.

At this point, King's career diverged from his father's. Martin Luther King, Sr.'s experience had always been limited to the black community and to the black educational institutions of Atlanta. Young King wanted a deeper, wider, more committed education. Thus in 1948 he enrolled at Crozier Theological Seminary in Chester, Pennsylvania, a predominantly white school. During his three years there, he also attended philosophy courses at the University of Pennsylvania.

In his studies, King immersed himself in the social philosophy of Marx, Hegel, and other Europeans, and in the writings of the American Protestant theologian Reinhold Niebuhr. He avidly studied the Social Gospel, an earlier theological movement that stressed working for social justice. He read deeply the writings of Mahatma Ghandi, the pacifist leader of the Indian revolution against British colonial rule. King interwove ideas from these sources into the fabric of his experience. His developing philosophy brought together his understanding of the economic exploitation of his race, his admiration for nonviolent tactics, and the traditions of Southern black religion as he had experienced them.

Adapted from *The Pursuit of Liberty,* vol. 1, by R. Jackson Wilson et al., pp. 986–987.

As you answer the following questions, base your conclusions on what you have read and on your own knowledge.

5. Why do you think Martin Luther King, Jr., thought he would receive a broader education at the schools he chose? _____

_____

6. What does the phrase *social justice* mean to you, and why do you think King was interested in it? _____

_____

7. What comparisons do you see between the Indian revolution against British colonial rule and the situation African Americans in the United States faced in the 1950s? _____

_____

_____

8. The authors use figurative language to describe King's developing philosophy. What do you think they mean by the phrase *interwove ideas from these sources into the fabric of his experience*? _____

_____

9. What do you think the phrase *the economic exploitation of his race* means? (*Hint:* Think about the situation blacks faced in the 1950s. Compare their economic status with that of whites.) _____

_____

10. What do you think *nonviolent tactics* means? _____

_____

Read the next section to learn something about King's personal life.

While working for his doctorate in philosophy at Boston University, King met a young woman. Coretta Scott was studying at the New England Conservatory of Music. He decided immediately that this was the woman he wanted to marry. After their first meeting, he said to her abruptly: "You have everything I have ever wanted in a wife."

For Coretta, the decision was difficult. As her affection for King grew, she was torn. Should she give up a promising career in music and marry a Baptist minister? She finally consented, and the couple wed in June 1953. Coretta joined the Baptist church and put aside her career. In 1954 the Kings accepted the call from the church in Montgomery. Within a year, King, only twenty-six years old, had become the leader of a bus boycott that initiated the modern civil rights movement.

As you answer the following questions, base your conclusions on what you have read and on your own knowledge.

11. Why do you think the decision to marry was more difficult for Coretta than for King? Do you think a young woman would face the same dilemma today? Explain why. _____

_____

_____

12. Why do you think Coretta joined the Baptist church? _____

_____

Writing Exercise

Based on what you have read, why do you think Martin Luther King, Jr., was suited to be the leader of the modern civil rights movement? Discuss his qualifications.

_____

_____

_____

_____

_____

Exercise 8
Making Judgments

We all *make judgments* in our daily activities. They may be as insignificant as deciding whether to buy a new T-shirt or as important as choosing a college. Judgments are not usually right or wrong, but good judgments are usually wiser, better, and more supportable than poor ones. In reading, too, readers' judgments are based on their own interpretation, but they must be supported in the text. You may bring your own interpretation to the text, but it should be in keeping with what the author has been saying.

For example, if you had been working long hours as a server in a small restaurant for minimal wages and limited tips, and you weren't satisfied with the job, you would probably prefer another position. If you were offered a job in a larger, more prestigious restaurant at higher pay, your good judgment would probably tell you to take the new job. Of course, you may decide to stay at the original place for numerous reasons: convenience, family business, friends. However, based on the information provided, most people would say the best judgment would be to accept the new job offer.

Readers who make judgments when they read usually appreciate the text more than those who do not. Using inferential thinking will help you get more out of the text. You can use your own experience and knowledge to enhance the information in the text.

In the exercise that follows, you will read about the history of slavery in the United States. You will be asked questions that require you to make judgments about what you read. Complete this exercise with a partner in class so you can combine your background knowledge and experiences. Base your answer on what you read *and* on your own knowledge, experience, and thinking.

1. In 1619, the first black inhabitants of the English colonies were brought to Jamestown, Virginia. The twenty blacks were sold by the master of the ship into indentured servitude. In the beginning, it seems that no clear-cut distinction was made between black and white indentured servants, but by 1640, a clear difference in treatment had emerged.

   a. What judgment can you make about when slavery started in the United States and why blacks were treated differently from whites? _____

   _____

2. Black slavery grew slowly in the South until the end of the seventeenth century. The rapid growth of plantation agriculture and the opening up of the slave trade led to a large increase in the number of Africans imported to the English colonies.

   a. Why do you think the growth of plantation agriculture led to an increase in the number of slaves?

   _____

3. During the seventeenth century, laws prohibited slaves from owning property, carrying weapons, or traveling without a pass. _____

   a. Why do you think such laws were passed? Who do you think passed them? _____

   _____

   _____

4. Slaves were not usually allowed to serve in the military, but during the Revolutionary War, a shortage of troops in the Continental Army led to their acceptance.

   a. What conclusion can you draw about the role of blacks in the military? _____

   _____

   _____

5. The ideas of "natural rights" as expressed in the Declaration of Independence were popular during and after the American Revolution. In the North, there was little interest in continuing slavery. The Great Compromise at the Constitutional Convention, however, established a legal basis for slavery. It was agreed that five slaves would be considered the equivalent of three free persons in determining representation in Congress.

   a. Where do you think the support for slavery came from? _____

   _____

Adapted from *Afro-American History,* by Thomas R. Frazier, pp. 24, 25, 112, 113.

b. Why was it significant that slavery was mentioned in the Constitution? _____

_____

6. Free blacks began to organize in the 1770s. Groups of blacks brought their complaints to such groups as the Boston Town Selectmen and the Massachusetts legislature.

a. What can you conclude about the legal rights of blacks? Do you think they differed from the North to the South? _____

_____

7. By the end of the seventeenth century, several private schools had been established for black children, but there were no public schools for blacks.

a. What can you conclude about the educational opportunities for blacks? Why do you think they were so limited? _____

_____

_____

8. At the beginning of the Civil War, blacks had two major goals: to get into the fight and to see that all blacks were freed.

a. Why do you think it was important for blacks to participate in the fighting? _____

_____

_____

9. At first, the War Department wanted no black soldiers. They were not considered brave enough or trustworthy with weapons. In July 1862, realizing the manpower necessary to continue the war, Congress passed a bill authorizing the use of black troops.

a. What similarity do you see between the role of blacks in the Revolutionary and Civil wars? _____

_____

10. Lincoln issued the Emancipation Proclamation in 1863. His intention was to free the slaves in rebel territories. He believed that it would be easier for whites if the freed slaves left the country.

a. What can you conclude about Lincoln's commitment to blacks? _____

_____

_____

SKILL DEVELOPMENT: PARAPHRASING

Paraphrasing, stating someone else's ideas in your own words, is very useful. It allows you to check your comprehension or explain a concept to someone else. Students who merely repeat the words they read in their texts or hear in class may not truly understand what they are saying. The goal of paraphrasing is to state the ideas as clearly, simply, and briefly as possible. You want to use words that are familiar to you so the meaning is clear. Paraphrasing sentences is much like picking out the main idea.

In Theme 1, Exercise 6, "Sentence Restatements," you identified the main idea of each sentence and then stated it more simply. This exercise is very similar. You want to clarify the point of each sentence and express it simply. The sentences come from two texts. The first is a history text. Before you begin, review the following example.

> Black suffrage might be essential for any real freedom for the ex-slaves, but it also seemed essential for keeping the Republicans in power. In fact, it was not until the Republicans began to lose power in the North in 1870 that they passed the Fifteenth Amendment, granting suffrage to African-American males in the North and South. (vol. 1, p. 552)

To understand this pair of sentences, you must know the meaning of *suffrage*. It is critical to understanding the whole idea. From the vocabulary exercise at the beginning of this theme, you should remember that suffrage means the right to vote. From your own experience, you should know that people who vote have a voice in government through their representatives. You can also assume that slaves had no vote, no representatives, and no voice in government. By inference from the first sentence, you can conclude that freedom from slavery did not automatically bring with it the right to vote. The first sentence also tells that the Republican Party would benefit if blacks voted (it seemed essential for keeping the Republicans in power). The second sentence reinforces that notion and supports it with specific facts: (1) blacks got the vote when Republicans started to lose, and (2) the Fifteenth Amendment granted blacks the right to vote.

To *paraphrase* these two sentences, pick out the most important information and state it simply. Here is one way:

> Blacks got the right to vote in 1870 when the 15th Amendment was passed by Republicans, who hoped the blacks would vote for them.

Paraphrase the following sentences. First, define any critical words or phrases. Second, try to understand the main point. Finally, state the idea as simply as possible. When you finish paraphrasing all of the sentences, compare your answers with those of a fellow student. (If your instructor approves, you may wish to work with a partner from the beginning.)

Exercise 9
Paraphrasing Sentences

1. The Fourteenth Amendment contained the basic features of the Civil Rights Act of 1866 that President Andrew Johnson had vetoed. It also reduced the power of those who had ruled the old South by keeping from public office anyone who had ever sworn to be loyal to the Constitution and then participated in a rebellion. (vol. 1, p. 552) (*Hint:* The main point deals with the Fourteenth Amendment, *not* the Civil Rights Act.) _____

_____

_____

2. In order to gain support, the civil rights movement had raised the expectations of every black American, and, inevitably, these expectations were frustrated. (vol. 2, p. 1060) _____

_____

_____

3. As a result of mass migration from the rural South during and after World War II, the black population in northeastern cities more than doubled between 1950 and 1970 while the white population actually fell in the same areas. (vol. 2, p. 1060) _____

_____

_____

4. Since blacks were a minority of the American population, the strategy of nonviolence depended ultimately on some form of national action—inspired either by agreement with the goals of integration or by fear of the social disorder that might result from violent confrontation. (vol. 2, p. 991) _____

_____

_____

5. Former President Reagan appointed a Civil Rights Commission with several members openly hostile to previous federal attempts to reverse patterns of discrimination. (vol. 2, p. 1171)_____

_____

_____

The next five sentences to paraphrase come from a book about social movements, including the civil rights movement. Before you begin to paraphrase the sentences, review the following example.

In 1954, although the Supreme Court issued its landmark decision, *Brown* v. *Board of Education,* it proposed gradual change and assigned local southern authorities the responsibility for drawing desegregation plans and federal judges the power to determine the pace of progress. (p. 144)

To understand this sentence, it is very helpful to know that the court case declared the "separate but equal" school philosophy unconstitutional. Your hints are "landmark decision" and "education." The word *although* indicates the shift or contrast between "landmark

Excerpts from *The Pursuit of Liberty,* vols. 1 and 2, 2nd ed., by R. Jackson Wilson et al. (Belmont, Calif.: 1990).

decision" and "gradual change." So, even though the Supreme Court said that separate schools for blacks and whites were not allowed anymore, they didn't expect things to change immediately. The second part of the sentence tells that the "local southern authorities" were put in charge of desegregation plans. We can *infer* that the local authorities were the people who established the separate schools to begin with. They probably would not be too eager to integrate them. We also learn that federal judges get to decide if these plans are coming along quickly enough.

To paraphrase this sentence, pick out the most important information and state it simply. Here is one way:

> As a result of the *Brown* v. *Board of Education* case, the Supreme Court expected the schools to be desegregated gradually.

Paraphrase the following sentences. First, define critical words or phrases. Second, try to understand the main point. Finally, state the idea as simply as possible. When you finish paraphrasing all the sentences, compare your answers with those of a fellow student.

6. Through tactics ranging from lobbying and voting efforts to parades, boycotts, sit-ins, demonstrations, threats, and violence, activists attempt to mobilize sufficient resources to prod decision makers toward change. (p. 3) _____

_____

_____

7. On 1 February 1960, when four black college students sat down at a segregated lunch counter in Greensboro, North Carolina, their action was not impulsive. (p. 147) _____

_____

_____

8. Students occupied the front ranks of the sit-in offensive because they were willing, and less at risk than others in the black community. (p. 148) _____

_____

_____

9. In 1968, the National Advisory Commission on Civil Disorders warned: "Our nation is moving toward two societies, one black and one white—separate and unequal." (p. 166) _____

_____

_____

10. Civil rights accomplishments may be less far-reaching and more precarious than assumed. (p. 166)

_____

_____

Excerpts from *Grassroots Resistance: Social Movements in Twentieth Century America* by Robert A. Goldberg (Belmont, Calif.: Wadsworth, 1991), pp. 1, 144, 147, 148, 166.

Exercise 10
Paraphrasing Paragraphs

As you can imagine, paraphrasing paragraphs is much like paraphrasing sentences. The difference is in the quantity of information or the length of the text. In one way, paraphrasing paragraphs is harder because you have to deal with more information. However, a longer piece does provide more context. After working through the entire first and second themes of this book, you should realize that the more you know or learn about a particular topic, the easier it is to understand additional information on the same topic. In this exercise, you will be working with larger text units—paragraphs—and they all deal with the same topic. Each paragraph provides some data about the situations African Americans faced from the 1840s to the present. They are arranged in *chronological,* or time, *order,* which should help you organize the information. They all come from the same source, so you should become familiar with the author's style.

Since you will be reading paragraphs, and not just sentences, underline the important points before you begin to paraphrase. Before you attempt to paraphrase the paragraphs, review the following example.

> In the 1840s, the convention movement provided a major outlet for abolitionist thought. Although many leading blacks were active in the predominantly white antislavery organizations, it was widely felt that there were some things black people should deal with among themselves. Henry Highland Garnet addressed a convention in Buffalo in 1843. His call for the violent overthrow of the slave masters by the slaves marked a turning point in the development of the movement. Although the assembled delegates rejected a resolution supporting the address by one vote, subsequent conventions treated the question of violence with much more sympathy. By 1854, in fact, violence was being openly advocated. [p. 103]

The important points have been underlined for you. You can put those key words and phrases into sentences to explain the point simply. Here is one way to paraphrase this paragraph:

> In the 1840s and 1850s, some white abolitionists advocated violence to end slavery.

Here is another acceptable paraphrase:

> Henry Highland Garnet's address to a Buffalo convention in 1843 introduced the idea of violence to the abolitionist movement.

Underline the important points in the following paragraphs. Then use those key words and phrases in sentences that explain the

Excerpts from *Afro-American History,* by Thomas R. Frazier.

points simply. Compare your paraphrases with those of a fellow
student.

1. After the Civil War ended, several proposals were made for providing each freedman with "forty acres and a mule," so that he might make a start toward real freedom. As different parts of the South became liberated, however, various federal plans prevented the freedmen from getting land. Before the assassination of Lincoln, there was a possibility that land would be confiscated from plantation owners who had supported the Southern war effort and distributed among the former slaves. For the most part, though, the land policy of the Union, even before the end of the war, seemed just another form of slavery. Instead of being given land of their own, the freedmen were required to sign labor contracts with Northern adventurers to whom the former plantations had been leased in order to provide money for federal troops. Many of these Northerners were more interested in making money than in aiding the freedmen, and the former slaves often worked as hard as they had in the past at ridiculously low wages. [pp. 113–114]

_____

_____

_____

2. The years from 1877 to 1900 were a period of renewed victimization for the black population of the United States, both North and South. The Republican Party, which had guaranteed black political freedom, withdrew its support in 1877 under President Rutherford B. Hayes and gave the white South the freedom to deal with the black population as it saw fit. Abandoned by the federal government and without Northern support, the blacks of the South lost whatever little political power they had. What was worse, they were forced to support political policies that were clearly not in their own interests. [p. 162]

_____

_____

_____

3. When the Reconstruction period ended, the hostility of local white authorities caused black people to look to the federal government for legal aid. At that time, the Civil Rights Act of 1875 was in effect. It provided for protection against segregation in transportation and public accommodations. The blacks had every reason to expect federal support. The Supreme Court, however, struck the struggle for equal rights several near-fatal blows. The first came in 1883. The Court declared the Civil Rights Act of 1875 unconstitutional on the grounds that the Fourteenth Amendment did not prohibit discrimination by individuals. Later, in 1896, the Court issued the _Plessy_ v. _Ferguson_ decision. It ruled that "separate but equal" facilities were permissible and that states could use police power to enforce segregation law. Shortly thereafter, it ruled that states could limit the right to vote in any way that was not explicitly based on race, color, or previous condition of servitude. [pp. 163–164] (_Hint:_ Focus on the consequences for blacks of the Supreme Court decisions.) _____

_____

_____

_____

4. Founded in 1910, the National Association for the Advancement of Colored People (NAACP) very quickly clarified its task. It would concern itself with the problem of achieving first-class citizenship for black people. Rather than "bogging down" in questions of "social equality," it would work for what it called "public equality." Though concerned with the problem of racial prejudice, the Association concentrated

on trying to provide equal protection for blacks under the Constitution. [p. 213] (*Hint:* Focus on the difference between "social equality" and "public equality.") _____

_____

_____

_____

5. Desegregation cases were filed in South Carolina, Kansas, Virginia, and Delaware. The cases eventually reached the Supreme Court, grouped together under the designation *Brown* v. *Board of Education of Topeka, Kansas.* The court, in a unanimous decision issued in May 1954, ruled that segregated schools were unconstitutional under the Fourteenth Amendment. They found that they were inherently unequal and deprived black children of equal protection of the laws. In its ruling, the Court gave the following explanation: "Segregation of white and colored children in public schools has a detrimental effect upon the colored children. The impact is greater when it has the sanction of law; for the policy of separating the races is usually interpreted as denoting the inferiority of the Negro group." [p. 317] (*Hint:* Try to simplify the language of the Supreme Court ruling.) _____

_____

_____

_____

6. It first appeared that Little Rock, Arkansas, would deal with the Supreme Court decision on school desegregation as did many moderate cities outside the Deep South. Nine black students had been selected to attend the formerly all-white Central High School in the fall of 1957. Then Governor Faubus of Arkansas, previously considered a racial moderate, called out the state-controlled National Guard to prevent the black students from entering Central High. This resulted in a clash between the federal and state powers that reached dimensions unknown since 1877. Faubus' use of armed force to prevent the carrying out of a federal order required President Eisenhower to use federal troops to force the desegregation of the Little Rock school. The black students attended the school under guard for the 1957–58 school year. The Governor closed all the Little Rock high schools the next year rather than permit them to open on a desegregated basis. [p. 324] _____

_____

_____

_____

7. The tactic of massive nonviolent direct action appeared on the scene of American race relations with the Montgomery, Alabama, bus boycott of 1955. Rosa Parks, a black woman, decided not to stand up when ordered to give her seat to a white person on a Montgomery bus, thus breaking city law. She was arrested, and the nonviolent civil rights movement was on. For more than a year blacks refused to ride the buses in an attempt to bring about a slight change in the seating arrangement on public transportation. As a result of the boycott, they were subjected to intimidation, arrest, and economic consequences of various sorts. On November 13, 1956, the Supreme Court ruled that bus segregation violated the Constitution. The Montgomery boycott was declared ended. After the decision that finally forced a change in Southern customs, several black churches were bombed. [p. 340] _____

_____

_____

_____

8. As the use of the boycott technique spread, an event occurred that changed all the rules and tactics of the protest movements. On February 1, 1960, four black college students "sat in" at a lunch counter in a Woolworth store in Greensboro, North Carolina. For some reason, this act provided the spark that set off the dynamite of Southern race relations. Within a matter of weeks, tens of thousands of students all over the South were engaged in sit-in campaigns. The number of arrests and violent acts of retaliation by whites soared. It has been estimated that at least 20,000 persons were arrested as a result of participating in nonviolent demonstrations in the South between 1960 and 1963. [p. 341] _____

_____

_____

_____

9. After Freedom Summer of 1964, the focus of the movement for the liberation of black people began to shift from the South to the urban ghettoes of the North and West. Legal battles were won, but it became apparent that these victories had little relevance to the masses of black people. Many blacks remained stuck in poverty and fear generated by helplessness before the economic and political power of the white community. The nonviolent direct action campaigns had desegregated lunch counters and public facilities. These gains seemed insignificant, though, compared to the demands of real freedom. Militant young blacks were particularly discouraged. The murderers of civil rights workers went free, and racism was revealed as an attitude built into the institutions of American society. [p. 374] _____

_____

_____

_____

10. This paragraph comes from *"Cries of Harlem," Youth in the Ghetto,* by HARYOU-ACT (New York, 1964), p. 314ff. It contains revealing statements from a young ghetto resident.

—No, you have to survive. You have to survive, if you don't . . . Well, I'll say if you don't have the proper education that you should have, and you go *downtown* and work, they don't pay you any money worthwhile. You can work all your life and never have anything, and you will always be in debt. So you take to the streets, you understand? You take to the streets and try to make it in the street, you know what you have; out here in the street you try to make it. All right. Being out in the street takes your mind off all these problems. You have no time to think about things because you're trying to make some money. So this is why I'm not up to par on different organizations. I don't belong to any, but perhaps I should. But I haven't taken the time to see or to try to figure it out. I've been trying to make it so hard and trying to keep a piece of money. I'm trying not to work like a dog to get it, and being treated any sort of way to get it. How to make another buck enters your mind. As far as bettering the community, this never enters your mind because it seems to me, well, I'm using my opinions—to me the white man has it locked up. The black man is progressing, but slowly. The only solution I see to it, I mean, if you are actually going to be here awhile, you have to stay healthy and not die. [p. 377]

_____

_____

_____

SKILL DEVELOPMENT: IDENTIFYING ORGANIZATIONAL PATTERNS

The *chronological* or *sequential pattern* gives information in time order. You will find this pattern used in history texts and other passages that tell about events in the order they happened. A recounting of your day's activities is an example of a chronological or sequential pattern: "Yesterday, I got up, ate breakfast, drove to school, went to my first class, and spent an hour in the student center. Then I went to my next class, ate lunch, studied for an hour, and drove to work. I worked until 9:30, returned home, watched a little TV, and went to bed." A description of the plot of a novel, movie, or television program could also be a chronological or sequential paragraph. An agenda for a meeting lists items for discussion chronologically. In many cases, a chronological passage will mention specific dates or times. A health professional, for example, would record information on a patient's chart in chronological order. A physician would like to see the patient's temperature reading on Thursday recorded *before* Friday's temperature reading.

The topic of this unit, civil rights, offers many examples of chronological or sequential passages. In particular, the history of the civil rights movement is usually described chronologically. The development of the movement is easier to understand if it is taught in the order that events actually happened.

You will see some similarities between the chronological pattern and the list and process description patterns. The key words are often similar: *first, second, third; in the beginning, then, next, finally.* Sequential events are often listed, or a history may be described in terms of its development. The primary distinction between the chronological pattern and the others is that it always uses *time order.*

Exercise 11

Identifying the Chronological or Sequential Pattern

The exercise that follows consists of paragraphs written in chronological or sequential order. You will be asked to identify the steps or events in order. Before you begin, review the following example. This paragraph describes some important events in the African American struggle for equal educational opportunities.

> For a hundred years before the end of the Second World War, black people struggled with the courts of America over their children's education. In 1849, the courts of Massachusetts ruled that black children could be excluded from white schools if a black school was available. In reaction to this decision, the Massachusetts legislature passed an act desegregating the schools in 1855. Charles Sumner was a senator from Massachusetts who had been involved on the side of the blacks in the Massachusetts court case. He tried unsuccessfully to get a provision for desegregating the schools in the Civil Rights Act of 1875. (This act was

later declared unconstitutional by the Supreme Court in 1883.) When the principle of "separate but equal" was set up in the case *Plessy* v. *Ferguson* in 1896, it was, of course, applied to education as well as to transportation and public accommodation. (*Afro-American History,* by Thomas R. Frazier, p. 316.)

The clues that tell you this is a chronological passage include the first sentence. The key phrases are *for a hundred years* and *before.* The dates are another clue. Notice that their order is sequential, indicating that the events are listed in the order they happened. You might organize the information in this way:

1. Massachusetts court excluded blacks from white schools.

2. Massachusetts passed a law desegregating schools.

3. Civil Rights Act of 1875 did *not* provide for desegregated schools.

4. Civil Rights Act of 1875 declared unconstitutional.

5. Supreme Court set up "separate but equal" principle & applied it to schools.

The next two chronological passages also deal with equal education for African Americans. After you read them, list the important points in the order they are described.

1. Desegregation cases were filed in South Carolina, Kansas, Virginia, and Delaware. The cases eventually reached the Supreme Court, grouped together under the title, *Brown* v. *Board of Education of Topeka, Kansas.* The Court issued a unanimous decision in May 1954. It ruled that segregated schools were unconstitutional under the Fourteenth Amendment. It found that they were inherently unequal and deprived black children of equal protection of the laws. In its ruling, the Court noted that: "the lawful separation of the races is usually interpreted as denoting the inferiority of the Negro group." Compliance with this decision began in the fall of 1954 when a few large cities and scattered towns in three states started school desegregation. By 1955, the Court vaguely ordered the states to proceed with desegregation "with all deliberate speed." In 1956, the Southern Manifesto of 1956 was signed by 19 U.S. senators and 81 members of the House of Representatives. It praised "those states which have declared the intention to resist forced integration by any lawful means." (From *Afro-American History,* by Thomas R. Frazier, p. 317.)

   a. _____

   b. _____

   c. _____

   d. _____

   e. _____

2. In the fall of 1958, desegregation came to a virtual standstill. The South threatened to close its public schools rather than give into the Court ruling. Public schools were actually shut down in Little Rock, Arkansas, and in certain counties in Virginia during the 1958–59 school year. By 1959, however, the South had given in to some extent. The number of black children in formerly white schools began to creep

upward. In 1963, after nine years of school desegregation, 9.2 percent of the black children in public schools in the South attended classes with whites. Only Alabama, Mississippi, and South Carolina had completely segregated systems at the end of the 1962–63 school year. After 1963–64, only Mississippi held out, and it was soon to give way. (*Afro-American History,* by Thomas R. Frazier, p. 317.)

a. _____

b. _____

c. _____

d. _____

e. _____

The following chronological passages deal with the social and political consequences of the civil rights movement. Look for the important points, and write them in sequence below each passage.

3. After World War II, politicians became increasingly sensitive to the position of the black community voting power. In 1948, President Harry Truman's reelection bid was in jeopardy. To improve his chances, Truman courted Northern blacks with executive orders prohibiting discrimination in federal employment and desegregating the armed forces. Blacks gave Truman 80 percent of their votes and were an important group in the Democratic coalition. Republican Dwight Eisenhower's victories in 1952 and 1956 confirmed Democratic judgment about black political power. Securing enough votes to win Virginia, Florida, Texas, and Louisiana, the Republican party broke the democratic hold on the "solid South." Eisenhower, at the same time, appealed to blacks by pressing integration of the armed forces and public facilities in Washington, D.C. Blacks responded, delivering 40 percent of their votes to the president in 1956, a gain of 20 percent over 1952. With their eyes on the 1960 presidential election, both parties backed passage of civil rights legislation in 1957 and 1960. (*Grassroots Resistance,* by Robert A. Goldberg, p. 144.)

a. _____

b. _____

c. _____

d. _____

4. The extension of civil rights was not initiated by government act. Civil rights were won through a long and bitter struggle of people determined to seize the rights of citizenship. Deprived of political and business opportunities for a century, bright young black men and women turned to the black church to express their hopes, energies, and dreams. This was particularly true in the segregated South. But during the 1950s many blacks began to find the restrictions of racial separation intolerable. A young scholar, Martin Luther King, Jr., returned from Boston University to take up the ministry of Dexter Avenue Baptist Church in 1954. At first, he had no hint that a nationwide civil rights movement would soon swirl around him. He had no way of knowing that his name would be linked with the great march on Washington of 1963 that would help open the floodgates of integration. (*The Pursuit of Liberty,* vol. 1, by R. Jackson Wilson et al., p. 982.)

a. _____

b. _____

c. _____

d. _____

5. In the spring of 1963, Martin Luther King, Jr., and the Southern Christian Leadership Conference (SCLC) planned to lead demonstrations in Birmingham, Alabama. That segregated city, with its record of police brutality to blacks, had become a symbol of resistance to integration. The civil rights organizers planned to launch Project C (for confrontation) during Easter week to disrupt the season's sales. They hoped to force economic leaders in the city to negotiate with integrationists. B—day (the first day of protest) had to be postponed until April 3 to avoid disrupting the local mayoral election. During the first few days, demonstrations and sit-ins occurred without serious incident. Then, on April 10, a local judge issued an injunction prohibiting all further demonstrations. King decided to break the law and suffer the consequences. On April 12, Good Friday, King and several volunteers set out on an illegal protest march. The public safety commissioner, T. E. ("Bull") Connor, arrested King and held him in solitary confinement. He was allowed no calls or visitors. When Mrs. King heard nothing from her husband, she was advised by one of Birmingham's leaders to call President Kennedy. She finally was able to get through to the president's aide, Pierre Salinger. (*The Pursuit of Liberty,* vol. 1, by R. Jackson Wilson et al., p. 993.)

a. _____

b. _____

c. _____

d. _____

6. In Northern cities during the mid 1960s, no visible progress toward either racial equality or improved living standards was seen. Mass migration from the rural South during and after World War II more than doubled the black population in northeastern cities between 1950 and 1970. The white population actually fell in the same areas. Consequently, urban tax bases eroded, and city social services were overburdened. At the same time, discrimination in hiring, poor schools, and inadequate training kept much of the black population unemployed or underemployed. Angry about discriminatory police enforcement and violent incidents, urban ghettoes exploded into rioting in 1964–67 and particularly in 1968. Increasing violence created a split in the civil rights movement that Martin Luther King, Jr., had tried to guide. The charismatic Black Muslim leader, Malcolm X, for example, preached a separatism that appealed to many urban blacks. Malcolm X was assassinated in 1965. His beliefs, though, continued to attract the more radical elements of the Northern ghettos. The first major urban riot occurred in the summer of 1964 in Harlem. Then violence exploded in the Watts section of Los Angeles the following summer. Other cities were struck in 1965–68. By the time Martin Luther King was assassinated in 1968, the violence that resulted came as no surprise. (*The Pursuit of Liberty,* vol. 1, by R. Jackson Wilson et al., p. 1060.)

a. _____

b. _____

c. _____

d. _____

e. _____

The last two passages deal with terminology and identification of racial and ethnic groups. Look for the important points, and write them down in order.

7. The changing terminology of race and ethnic groups was complex. For people of African descent, the question was changeable and complicated. Popularly used terms like *colored* gave way in the 1950s and 1960s to *Negro*. Then, with the explosion of civil rights and cultural pride, the preferred term became *black*, and to a lesser degree, *Afro-American*. By the late 1980s, however, there was another shift to *African-American,* suggesting the mixed cultural identity of every citizen. (*The Pursuit of Liberty,* vol. 1, by R. Jackson Wilson et al., p. 1163.)

   a. _____

   b. _____

   c. _____

   d. _____

8. The U.S. Bureau of the Census defines the Hispanic population on the basis of persons' self-identification of their origins or descent as "Mexican-American," "Chicano," "Mexican," "Puerto Rican," "Cuban," "Central or South-American," or as "Other Spanish." Today more than 20 million Americans select one of these responses when asked. This amounts to more than 8 percent of the total U.S. population. Moreover, the Hispanic-American population grew by 38.9 percent between 1980 and 1989, while the total population grew by only 9.5 percent and the black population grew by 12.7 percent. If current rates of Hispanic immigration and fertility continue, Hispanic-Americans will outnumber black Americans around the year 2015, and fifty years from now about one out of three Americans will be of Hispanic descent. (*Sociology,* 4th ed., by Rodney Stark [Belmont, Calif.: Wadsworth, 1992], p. 310.)

   a. _____

   b. _____

   c. _____

   d. _____

Selection 1

What Are Civil Rights?

Most American citizens take their rights, liberties, and freedoms for granted. Other countries that prohibit people from voting, practicing their religious beliefs, or criticizing the government are difficult to understand. We assume that our elected officials and their employees will serve our interests, and we are shocked to hear or read about abuses of power. Rarely do we think about where these rights come from or what guarantees we have that they will not be taken away. The selection that follows explains the legal basis for our assumption of a right to liberty.

Before you read, think about the rights you possess as a citizen of the United States. Write down five of those rights, and then compare your choices with those of a fellow student.

1. _____

2. _____

3. _____

4. _____

5. _____

As you read, take note of whether the rights you mentioned are guaranteed. Underline the important points, including the rights you mentioned and others that are presented. The guide questions will help you see the relevance of civil rights to particular situations. *All* of the questions are inferential. You will need to use the information provided *plus* your own background knowledge and thinking skills to answer them.

The first immigrant settlers in this country were looking for a place they could settle where they could live their lives as they chose. Freedom of religion was not widespread in Europe. A <u>rigid</u> social class system prevented individuals from moving up the socioeconomic ladder. America appeared to be a land with opportunities and freedoms that the first immigrants desired. Indeed, this impression is still a powerful incentive for people from other countries who want to immigrate to the United States today.

After a period of time as a British colony, Americans began to feel powerless to make their own decisions. They felt that the restrictions, and particularly taxes, that the British imposed on the colonists denied them the freedoms they felt <u>entitled</u> to. The American Revolution began as a demand for a voice in running the colonies, and ended with the founding of an independent nation. The Declaration of Independence states that "all men are created equal," and describes the role of government as guarantor of its citizens' basic rights: life, liberty, and the pursuit of happiness.

Read the first section to learn about the origin of American civil rights.

Answer the following questions based on your reading, on your own knowledge, and on your experience.

1. Why do you think Americans were more concerned with liberty than their European counterparts were?

   _____

2. What do the following words mean as they are used in the passage?

   a. *rigid:* _____

   b. *entitled:* _____

3. Do you think the phrase *all men are created equal* better describes the attitude of people who lived at the time the Declaration of Independence was signed *or* the beliefs of most people today? _____

Read the next section to learn about the specific liberties that the first four amendments guarantee.

After the <u>framers</u> of the Constitution drew up that document, they felt that civil liberties—basic human rights—should be identified and guaranteed. As a result, the first Ten Amendments to the Constitution were written and passed in 1791 as the Bill of Rights. First Amendment rights include freedom of religion, speech, and the press. Individuals are free to worship as they choose or not to worship at all. People are allowed to express their thoughts in spoken or written form without fear of <u>reprisal</u>. Statements can be critical, as long as they are not libelous or scandalous; that is, untrue and damaging to someone else's reputation. This amendment also says citizens have the right to meet in groups ("assemble") and to "petition the government for a redress of grievances." In other words, if citizens believe they have been treated unfairly, they can call a meeting or ask the government to review the situation and take action.

The Second Amendment reads as follows: "A well-regulated Militia, being necessary to the security of a free State, the right of the people to keep and bear arms shall not be infringed." Most people interpret this amendment to mean that the States have the right to maintain an army. Some opponents of gun-control legislation, however, point to this statement as support for their position. They believe that private citizens have a constitutional right to own and carry guns. The Third Amendment protects homeowners from being required to <u>board</u> soldiers. This situation was common at the time of the Revolutionary War but not today.

Amendment IV says that people have the right "to be secure in their persons, houses, papers, and effects against unreasonable searches and seizures." This provision requires specific search warrants that are granted only for probable cause. For example, a drug enforcement officer couldn't randomly search all the houses in a neighborhood. However, if a reliable witness provided evidence that a particular house contained illegal drugs, a search warrant would probably be granted. This amendment also addresses the issue of privacy. Discussions about abortion often include references to the constitutional guarantee of privacy. If citizens are guaranteed privacy, what role, if any, should the government play in medical decisions?

Answer the following questions.

4. What do the first four amendments have in common? _____

_____

5. What do the following words mean as they are used in the passage?

a. *framers:* _____

b. *reprisal:* _____

c. *board:* _____

6. Which of these amendments do you consider most important? Why? _____

_____

The Fifth Amendment says that before a person can be prosecuted for a serious crime, he or she must be indicted (formally accused) by a grand jury. Individuals can only be tried once for the same offense. This is referred to as freedom from double jeopardy. Finally, no one can be forced to give <u>incriminating</u> evidence against himself or herself. You may have heard the expression: "She plans to plead the Fifth Amendment." The actual words used may be something like: "I refuse to answer on the grounds that it may incriminate me." You may not be forced to testify if what you say may worsen your situation or make you appear to be guilty.

Amendment VI guarantees a "speedy and public trial by an <u>impartial</u> jury." Defendants are entitled to know the crimes they are accused of and to face the witnesses against them. Members of the jury should listen to the case with open minds and make their decisions on the basis of the evidence. The assistance of a lawyer is also guaranteed to the defendants. The Seventh Amendment guarantees jury trials in federal civil suits. Apparently, a trial by one's peers is thought to be fairer than a decision by a judge alone. The Eighth Amendment prohibits excessive bail, fines, and cruel and unusual punishment. In other words, individuals can*not* be arrested, held without bail, or remain uninformed about the accusations against them. Neither can they be held in jail indefinitely awaiting trial. The phrase *cruel and unusual punishment* is often used as an argument against capital punishment or a particular method of administering it. For example, states that execute convicted murderers in the electric chair have been accused of using cruel and unusual punishment.

Read the next section to learn about the rights guaranteed to persons accused of crimes.

Answer the following questions.

7. Why do you think the rights of people accused of crimes are important? _____
   _____

8. What do the following words mean as they are used in the passage?

   a. *incriminating:* _____

   b. *impartial:* _____

9. Give an example of how citizens might be abused without the protection of the Sixth, Seventh, or Eighth Amendments. _____
   _____

When we read the language of the Declaration of Independence and the Bill of Rights, it seems <u>inconceivable</u> that for about one hundred years after the American Revolution, blacks in this country enjoyed none of those rights. Even though the philosophy of natural rights and equality were popular, the social and economic situation in the South depended on slavery and <u>perpetuated</u> its existence. Finally, in 1865, during the Civil War, the Thirteenth Amendment abolishing slavery was passed. Three years later, the Fourteenth Amendment was passed. It includes two provisions. The first conveys full civil rights on slaves. The second part prohibits any former federal or state official who had served the Confederacy from becoming a federal official again. This provision had the potential of changing the political power base of the South. Since most southern

Read the next section to learn how amendments to the Constitution finally provided for the rights of African Americans.

white males had served in the Confederate army, few were eligible for public office after the Civil War ended. During this period, known as Reconstruction, a variety of factors caused the continued exploitation and powerlessness of the former slaves.

In 1870, the Fifteenth Amendment gave the ex-slaves the right to vote. It says: "The rights of citizens of the United States to vote shall not be denied or abridged by the United States or by any state on account of race, color or previous condition of servitude." It also empowered Congress to enforce this article. Since only white men had been able to vote up to this time, the right to vote was extended to black men who had been slaves. Neither white nor black women were able to vote until the Nineteenth Amendment extended that right to them in 1920.

In spite of the constitutional guarantees, there were continued efforts in the South to deny blacks the right to vote. One of the methods required potential voters to pay a poll tax, a fee collected at the voting place. Although this appears to discriminate against all poor people who could not afford to pay the tax, its intention was to keep blacks from voting. Wealthy white citizens provided poor whites with the money to pay the tax, perhaps also influencing the way they voted. In 1964, the Twenty-Fourth Amendment outlawed the poll tax in federal elections. Finally, in 1971, the Twenty-Sixth Amendment lowered the voting age from twenty-one to eighteen.

Answer the following questions.

10. Define the following words according to the way they are used in the passage:

   a. *inconceivable:* _____

   b. *perpetuated:* _____

11. Do you think there are any other civil rights that should be protected by the Constitution? _____

12. Which amendment would guarantee the right of the student editor of a college newspaper to criticize the president of the college? _____

13. Which amendment would prohibit the use of confessions made by criminals before seeing a lawyer or being told of their rights? _____

14. Which amendments were necessary to guarantee the right to vote to a nineteen-year-old African American woman? _____

15. Why is a poll tax discriminatory? _____

   _____

Many countries in the world do not have a document comparable to our Bill of Rights. Tell why you think it is an important part of our American heritage.

_____

_____

_____

_____

_____

As you have learned from what you have already read about civil rights, change comes slowly, and attitudes cannot be changed through legislation alone. One aspect of American life that seems relatively egalitarian and racially mixed is sports. Some people think that sports offers opportunities to members of minority groups that are not available anywhere else. Looking back on the history of American sports, however, shows that this was not always the case. At one time, sports teams were as segregated as other parts of society. In most cases, African Americans were not permitted to try out for teams with white players. Although there were limited opportunities for blacks in most sports, the Negro Baseball League did provide a place for talented players to develop their skills and provide entertainment to an appreciative audience. Of course, the facilities and salaries were far inferior to what white teams enjoyed. In fact, Negro team players were often housed in private homes after away games because African Americans were not permitted to stay in hotels. In spite of the hardships, the Negro league attracted and developed some fine players. One such player was Satchel Paige, a star of the Negro Baseball League in the 1930s. Finally, at the end of his career, he was able to play in the National Baseball League.

Selection 2

The Desegregation of Baseball: Branch Rickey and Jackie Robinson

The passage that follows tells about the introduction of Jackie Robinson, the first African American player in the major league. Rather than merely celebrating Robinson's arrival, it offers some perspective on the state of civil rights at the time, provides some of the reasons baseball was integrated, and comments on the comparative situation today.

Before you begin to read, think about what you have learned about civil rights in the 1940s and 1950s. Imagine what segregated sports were like for the players and the fans. Picture what professional team photos of today would look like if all of the African American players were removed.

As you read, underline the points you think are important. The guide questions will ask you to make some inferences and to paraphrase some of what you are reading. Notice also the chronological order in which most of the information is presented.

Read the first section to learn about the status of civil rights fifty years ago and to find out who Branch Rickey was.

Fifty years ago this spring, Martin Luther King, Jr., was beginning high school. Harry S Truman was just a relatively obscure Senator, and Jesse Jackson was 1½ years old. Linda Brown, whose family name would be immortalized 11 years later by a United States Supreme Court decision, had not yet been born. But in downtown Brooklyn, a white midwesterner named Branch Rickey was already <u>plotting</u> a civil rights revolution of enormous magnitude.

In 1943, Mr. Rickey—barely anyone addressed him more familiarly—approached George V. MacLaughlin, president of the Brooklyn Trust Company, with a daring proposal. Mr. Rickey was the president of the Brooklyn Dodgers, a team that was deeply indebted to MacLaughlin's bank.

"Rickey mentioned the possible recruitment of black players," Jules Tygiel wrote in "Baseball's Great Experiment" (Oxford, 1983). "MacLaughlin responded favorably, but added a warning, 'If you find the man who is better than the others, you will beat it. And if you don't, you're sunk.'" With MacLaughlin's support, Rickey presented the issue to the Dodger board of directors. All endorsed the plan, although one owner questioned Rickey's "real motive." The owners then swore to guard the secret, withholding the information even from their own families.

Answer the following questions based on your reading, as well as your own knowledge and thinking. The *inference* questions are indicated.

1. (inf.) On the basis of the information presented in the first paragraph and what you know about the civil rights movement, what were racial relations like fifty years ago? _____

_____

2. Based on your reading in this section, what Supreme Court decision made Linda Brown's last name famous?

_____

3. What is the meaning of the word *plotting* as it is used in the passage? _____

4. (inf.) Why do you think MacLaughlin told Rickey it was important to find a superior black player? _____

_____

5. (inf.) Why do you think the owners promised to keep the secret? _____

_____

_____

Excerpts from "The Unfulfilled Legacy of a Daring Experiment," by Sam Roberts, *The New York Times*, April 5, 1993, p. B3. ©1993 by The New York Times Company. Reprinted by permission.

That season, Dodger scouts began evaluating black players in preparation to sign the first black man in organized baseball in the 20th century. Luck, Mr. Rickey said, is the residue of design. Less than three years later, minor league baseball resumed after the war. At Jersey City's Roosevelt Stadium, the better man whom Mr. Rickey recruited and signed with the Montreal Royals batted in the first inning and broke the color barrier in organized baseball. Jackie Robinson later described himself modestly as "only a principal actor" in Mr. Rickey's drama.

Almost single-handedly, Branch Rickey ignored the skepticism or <u>antagonism</u> of other owners—one of whom even warned that fans would "burn down the Polo Grounds the first time the Dodgers came in there for a Series." Rickey integrated baseball years before President Truman banned segregation in the Armed Forces and the Supreme Court decided that Linda Brown's separate education was unequal. His decision transcended.

Read the next section to learn about Robinson's debut and the opposition Rickey faced.

Answer the following questions.

6. How long did it take to recruit an excellent African American player? _____

7. What does the word *antagonism* mean as it is used in the passage? _____

_____

8. (inf.) What does the expression *broke the color barrier* mean? _____

_____

9. (inf.) Explain Jackie Robinson's comment that he was "only a principal actor" in Mr. Rickey's drama. _____

_____

10. What was the reaction of other owners to Rickey's innovation? _____

_____

11. (inf.) What is the author's estimate of the importance of Rickey's decision? _____

_____

The Reverend Jesse Jackson, national civil rights leader, offered some comments on Jackie Robinson's influence on baseball. "In a fundamental way," Mr. Jackson said the other day, "that experiment helped lay the predicate for the Supreme Court decision.

"My father was a semi-pro baseball player," Mr. Jackson continued. "I was the batboy when Don Newcombe was playing. In my heart of hearts, I was Dodger-bred. When the Dodgers left Brooklyn, some of us in South Carolina cried. And much of my whole sense of social justice can be traced to when Jackie Robinson came through Greenville and couldn't get off the airplane to use the restroom at the airport."

The year 1993 marked the 47th anniversary of Jackie Robinson's <u>debut</u> in Jersey City and the 25th anniversary of Dr. King's assassination. Jesse Jackson marked the Baltimore Orioles season opener with a protest demonstration to remind America that major league baseball still has a long way to go. Despite major progress in breaking the color barrier in upper management, Mr. Rickey's legacy remains unrealized among owners

Read the next section to learn about the impact on society today.

and forgotten even among some players. ("Don't know no Jackie Robinson, man," Vince Coleman of the Mets announced last year.)

"We're not asking for reparations," Mr. Jackson said. "Affirmative action is a conservative remedy for negative action. And there's nothing that moves our culture more toward multiculturalism on a daily basis than the expectation of blacks and whites winning together."

Answer the following questions.

12. (inf.) Explain the significance of Jackie Robinson's trip through Greenville. _____

_____

13. What does the word *debut* mean as it is used in the passage? _____

14. Paraphrase Mr. Jackson's comments about the racial situation in major league baseball today. _____

_____

Read the next section to learn more about Branch Rickey.

Mr. Rickey, a former major league catcher, was skillful at reading and sending signals. He warned fellow team owners that they would be liable for violating the state's fair employment law. He enlisted a Southern voice—Red Barber's—to announce Robinson, which he did without mentioning the player's race. He cautioned blacks against staging what he maintained would be a <u>premature</u> Jackie Robinson recognition day.

What was Mr. Rickey's real motive? It was probably the same that guides the more enlightened team owners today: a mixture of commercialism and morality. Injustice had seared his conscience in 1904 when he was coaching for Ohio Wesleyan University. When the team visited South Bend, Ind., to play Notre Dame, a hotel refused a room to the black first baseman. Four decades later, Mr. Rickey hired another black infielder. He took what the sportswriter Leonard Koppet called "perhaps the most visible single desegregation action ever taken."

Answer the following questions.

15. In what *two* ways does the author use the phrase *reading and sending signals*? _____

_____

_____

16. How does the author use the word *premature* in the passage? _____

_____

17. Why did Branch Rickey desegregate baseball? _____

_____

Read the last section to learn about some impressions of baseball today.

Fred Wilpon, co-owner of the Mets, remembers Mr. Rickey as a man of "intellect and character." "If he were alive today, he would say we haven't done enough yet."

New York Governor Mario Cuomo, a Rickey <u>recruit</u>, agrees that the legacy is incomplete. Mr. Rickey signed Mr. Cuomo to the Pittsburgh

Pirates organization as a college freshman in 1950. "I got a $2000 signing bonus; Mickey Mantle got $1100 the year before." Today, Mr. Cuomo said, "My guess is Rickey would be disturbed that the black athlete may have made it, but the rest of the black community has not made it in the same way.

"He wasn't just interested in making baseball American," Mr. Cuomo said, "but in making America American."

Answer the following questions.

18. (inf.) Why does the author include the sentence about the signing bonuses? _____

_____

19. What does the word *recruit* mean in the passage? _____

_____

20. Paraphrase Governor Cuomo's assessment of Branch Rickey. _____

_____

Discuss the short- and long-term influence of Branch Rickey's actions on baseball and American society.

Writing Exercise

_____

_____

_____

_____

_____

Hispanic-Americans—or Latinos, as some prefer to be called—represent a growing segment of the population. Continued immigration from Spanish-speaking countries as well as the increasing population of Latino groups will further this trend. In areas such as Miami, where large numbers of Latinos live, the Latino influence can be seen in language, food, music, and cultural patterns. As with most immigrant groups, Latinos were attracted to the United States by the promise of social and economic opportunities. And, as other immigrant groups before them, they have experienced discrimination and denial of their civil rights. Read the selection that follows to learn about some of the difficulties and successes experienced by Latinos.

Selection 3

Latinos: A Growing Force in Our Culture

Read the first section to learn about the impact Latinos have had on the United States population.

Although non-Latinos tend to lump them together as Hispanic Americans, Latinos really belong to one of several distinct ethnic groups. In the United States, Mexican Americans, Puerto Ricans, and Cuban Americans share a heritage of language but have distinct cultures. In fact, Puerto Ricans should not be considered part of the <u>immigrant</u> population because they are U.S. citizens, with all the rights and privileges, from the moment of birth.

According to the latest 1990 census data, there are more than 22 million Latinos in the United States. This represents an increase of over 35 percent since 1980, and indicates that 9.5 percent of the total U.S. population is Latino. Moreover, if the current trends continue, within our lifetime, one out of every three Americans will be Latino. Latinos tend to settle in particular areas of the country. Approximately 50 to 75 percent of the Latinos in the United States live in California. This predominantly Mexican American group accounts for more than 25 percent of each state's population. In New York, most Latinos are from Puerto Rico, and they represent 10 percent of the nation's Latinos. Finally, we find a concentration of Latinos in Florida, most of whom are of Cuban descent. In the 1950s and early 1960s, a large group of middle-class Cubans fled their native land to escape the communist Castro regime. Attracted to Florida partially because of its location and climate, they are now well established. In fact, Cuban Americans have the highest educational and income levels of the three groups. In part, this success can be explained by the fact that Cuban Americans are, as a group, older than their Puerto Rican and Mexican American counterparts. As people get older, they tend to earn more money. They also have been in the country for quite a long time and have adapted to it. Finally, many Cuban refugees were professionals with some money, so it was easier for them to begin their careers again. Immigrants who arrive in the United States with little money and no job skills, on the other hand, usually experience great difficulty.

Answer the following questions based on your reading.

1. What three groups of Latinos are mentioned in the selection?
   a. _____
   b. _____
   c. _____
2. What trend do the statistics indicate about the Latino population in the United States? _____
   _____
3. Which immigrant Latino group has been the most successful? Why? _____
   _____

Read the next section to find out what kinds of obstacles Latinos face.

Latinos Face Difficulties

All immigrant groups face obstacles as they try to adapt to their new environment. Typically, the biggest hurdles are language barriers, cultural differences, and lack of job opportunities. New arrivals who can join a group of other immigrants from their home country or area often benefit, as those who have been here longer can sometimes smooth the way for the newcomers. Historically, as long as the immigration rate for a particular group remains high, fluency in the native language will continue. As fewer non-English-speaking immigrants arrive, the switch to English becomes faster and more common. Although there have been charges that Latinos have been more reluctant to learn English than other immigrant groups, there is no evidence to support this. In fact, with the modern emphasis on a global economy and intercultural exchanges, perhaps bilingualism should be a goal for all of our citizens.

As recently as the 1950s, many schools adopted policies to discourage, and even punish, immigrant children for speaking their native language. This "sink or swim" attitude often resulted in tremendous pressure on the children as they struggled to make themselves understood. Also, it often meant that the child's education in science, math, and other subjects was put on hold until he or she became fluent in English. Today, most schools provide English instruction by specially trained teachers of English as a Second Language (ESL) as the children continue to learn other subjects in English.

In areas with a large Latino population, some schools have provided bilingual education for their Spanish-speaking students. Although the goals of this program are admirable, the approach has been highly controversial. Ideally, the bilingual teacher teaches the children in both Spanish and English, selecting the language according to the difficulty of the concept or the child's English proficiency. The goal is to gradually move the child from learning and thinking in Spanish to learning in English. However, the child does not have to wait until his or her English is fluent to continue studying other subjects. Proponents of this approach emphasize the common sense of allowing children to progress at their own pace in developing language skills and the soundness to continue their development in other academic areas. Critics of the program charge that bilingual instruction goes on far too long, actually slowing the child's mastery of English. They fear that the teacher and students will be so comfortable in the Spanish teaching environment that the transition to English will never take place smoothly.

Cultural differences can also cause problems for immigrants. For example, the Latino emphasis on warmth and openness in social situations may lead them to interpret American social gestures as unfriendly, or even hostile. Latino children, who are accustomed to affectionate relationships with adults, may perceive an American teacher's formality as distant and disapproving. Immigrants often miss familiar foods and cultural celebrations that they enjoyed at home. Fortunately, in areas where the Latino population is concentrated, these traditions continue. In some cases, they are even adopted and enjoyed by the non-Latino residents. For example, in Los Angeles, Cinco de Mayo, a traditional Mexican holiday, is celebrated throughout the city. The Feast of the Three Kings, an important religious tradition in Puerto Rico, is now often celebrated in sections of New York City, too.

Answer the following questions based on your reading and thinking.

4. What are some of the obstacles immigrants face? _____
_____

5. What is the difference between ESL and bilingual education? _____
_____

6. Which approach would you recommend? Why? _____
_____

Read the next section to read about discrimination against Latinos.

DISCRIMINATION

All immigrant groups are perceived as possible job rivals of native-born Americans. Latinos are no exception. In fact, for many years, Mexicans have provided a valuable labor source for California agriculture. Growers could not find Americans who were willing to work in the fields for very low wages, so they turned to Mexicans. Many of these migrant workers have been shamefully exploited by their employers as they worked long hours for little money, often under intolerable conditions. In addition to these difficulties, they also often faced discrimination and violence as prejudice against Latinos surfaced.

In 1986, the Immigration Reform and Control Act was passed. Its intention was to cut down on illegal immigration in several ways. First of all, it extended an invitation to immigrants who had been working in this country for several years the opportunity to apply for citizenship. Secondly, it made employers responsible for their hiring practices. In the past, only the illegal workers were penalized; the new law specified fines against the bosses who hired undocumented workers as well. Unfortunately, the threat of sanctions has led some employers to refuse to hire anyone of Latino heritage. As a result, Latinos, who may be legal immigrants or U.S. citizens, have faced job discrimination on the basis of their names, accents, or appearance. Even though this job discrimination is against the law, it is often difficult and costly to prove.

Another controversy Latinos have faced is the issue of language in public documents. There has been a proposal that ballots be printed in Spanish as well as English in areas where the Latino voter turnout is extremely low. Advocates of this suggestion feel it is necessary to provide Spanish speakers with adequate representation in their government. Those who are against it stress the need to emphasize English as the national language and the need for all who live here to learn it. In a courtroom situation, too, a Spanish-speaking individual may not be as well served as an English speaker would be in the same circumstances. Although an interpreter may be provided, the inability of a defendant or witness to communicate directly with a judge or jury increases the chances of misunderstanding.

Answer the following questions based on your reading and thinking.

7. Do you think the intentions of the Immigration Reform and Control Act of 1986 have been realized? Explain. _____

_____

8. Do you favor printing ballots in Spanish and English in predominantly Spanish-speaking areas? Tell why or why not. _____

_____

THE UNITED STATES AS A SALAD BOWL

Read the last section to learn how our perception of the role of immigrants in our country has changed.

In the past, the United States, a nation made up primarily of immigrants, has been referred to as a melting pot. The implication of this term is that, as new groups of people arrive in the country, they lose their differences and become "American." In fact, many immigrants who arrived at the turn of the century took great pride in how quickly they could learn the language, customs, and styles of their new country. They didn't want to be thought of as "foreign." Today, it would be difficult, or perhaps impossible, to define what the term *American* means. We are a nation composed of so many people from such varied places and cultures. When we use the term *salad bowl,* we emphasize the notion that people with differences can exist side by side in harmony. There is no need to give up one's native culture when becoming part of a new one. In fact, one of America's strengths is its diversity and openness to new people and their ideas. Just as the previous immigrant groups have left their marks on our society, we can see the influence Latinos have had, and will continue to have on our culture. For example, we have benefited from the introduction of Spanish words to our language, and music, food, and traditions to our salad bowl.

Answer the following based on your reading and thinking.

9. Explain the difference between thinking of the United States as a *melting pot* or as a *salad bowl.* Which term do you prefer? Why? _____

_____

10. What recommendations would you make to a recent Latino immigrant to make her transition to the United States a bit smoother? _____

_____

Writing Exercise

Latinos are entitled to the same civil rights as anyone else. Yet, they have faced discrimination, at times. From your reading or personal experience, describe one example of discrimination against a Latino.

_____

_____

_____

_____

_____

Selection 4

Civil Rights in an Age of Social Change

The civil rights movement has been identified as an organized attempt to secure for African Americans the rights to which they are legally entitled. Since the 1950s when the movement began, other groups have adopted the language and the activities of the civil rights activists to demand rights for their members as well. The selection that follows explores the continued efforts in the 1990s to secure equal opportunities for African Americans and for members of other groups.

Before you begin to read, think of some examples of discrimination. Perhaps you have heard of situations where people have not received fair treatment because of race, gender, age, disability, or some other feature that may single them out. Maybe you have experienced or observed discriminatory treatment in school. Can you recall a time when you or someone you know was prejudged on the basis of race, sex, ethnic background, or personal appearance? Describe your example:

_____

_____

Read the first section to learn what issues are important to a civil rights organization that has changed with the times.

The National Organization for the Advancement of Colored People (NAACP) continues to be active in civil rights causes more than eighty years after its beginning. The NAACP Legal Defense and Education Fund, which has a separate budget from the rest of the organization, has broadened its role to include attempts to legally halt <u>subtle</u> forms of discrimination. For example, it is handling many environmental cases brought by African American, Latino, Asian, and Native American groups that charge residents of their neighborhoods are <u>disproportionately</u> exposed to toxic wastes. Challenges to college scholarships that are earmarked for black students are being defended by the fund. Its director, Elaine Jones, notes that scholarships for members of other groups (such as alumni children or sons and daughters of the Confederacy) are not being similarly challenged. In addition to the question of whether capital punishment is "cruel and unusual," the fund is also exploring the disproportionate number of men of color awaiting execution on death row.

Answer the following questions based on your reading as well as on your own background knowledge and thinking skills.

1. What role has the NAACP been playing in the 1990s to fulfill its mission? _____

_____

2. What does the word *subtle* mean as it is used in the passage? _____

_____

3. What does the word *disproportionately* mean as it is used in the passage? _____

_____

Asian immigrants to the United States have been generally successful in adjusting to American life. In particular, members of this group place a high value on education. In general, Asian immigrants (with the exception of the Vietnamese) <u>attain</u> higher education levels and earn higher wages than native-born Americans. In certain parts of the country, like California, the Asian population has reached 7 percent. The impact on higher education, though, has been significant. For example, at the University of California at Berkeley, in 1989, one-third of the students were Asian Americans. Native-born white students made up only half of the enrollment. Several colleges and universities were charged with maintaining <u>quotas</u> to limit the enrollment of Asian American students.

Latino immigrants have tended to settle in Florida, Texas, California, and other states. Large numbers of Latinos can influence the food, culture, and language of a particular area. In an effort to accommodate the needs of Latino children and their parents, some school systems introduced bilingual education. This controversial approach to educating children in their own language has sparked much controversy. In some areas of the country, opponents of the growing use of Spanish have tried to pass legislation to declare English the official language of the state. Ordinances banning the use of Spanish in courts, and on ballots and legal documents have been proposed.

Read the next section to learn about other minority groups that may have faced discrimination.

Answer the following questions based on your reading and thinking.

4. What does the word *attain* mean as it is used in the passage? _____

5. What does the word *quota* mean as it is used in the passage? _____

6. To what educational opportunities do you think Asian Americans are entitled? _____

_____

7. What is your position on the use of Spanish in schools, courts, and voting places? _____

_____

Read the next section to learn about other groups that are trying to secure support for their members.

Gay rights activists have been campaigning to end violence and discrimination against homosexuals. They have also been trying to focus attention on support for victims of AIDS, who often face employment and medical discrimination. The AIDS Coalition to Unleash Power (ACTUP) is probably the most <u>confrontational</u> gay rights group. Its members have decided to employ disruptive tactics to call attention to their cause. In New York State, a program intended to identify and treat newborns with AIDS has created a controversy. In an effort to protect privacy, a state law requires written consent and counseling before and after AIDS testing. A positive test for the baby would indicate the mother, too, carries the virus. Testing all newborns would, in effect, be imposing AIDS testing on the mothers without their consent.

Pro-choice and antiabortion groups have adopted some of the tactics of the civil rights movement. Antiabortion activists have used picketing and sit-ins to try to close abortion clinics. In Wichita, Kansas, protesters succeeded in calling attention to their cause by their arrests and court hearings. In the abortion controversy, both sides claim constitutional support. Pro-choice advocates claim that a woman's right to privacy guarantees that medical decisions should be hers alone. Antiabortion groups claim that they are protecting the rights of the unborn.

Since the 1970s, many adult adoptees have organized to try to secure access to their birth records. The American Adoption Congress has argued that keeping information about an individual's identity hidden is discriminatory and a violation of a fundamental right. Opponents say that the biological parents also have rights to privacy.

The American Civil Liberties Union (ACLU) is a group committed to protecting the civil rights of all individuals. Recently, it has taken up the cause of the homeless in Baltimore, Maryland. Merchants who feared the negative effect of homeless people on their businesses hired "public safety guides." The guides and the merchants claim that they are working with shelters and soup kitchens to try to help the homeless. The guides try to direct the homeless to services for them at specific locations that are listed in pamphlets they carry. The homeless say this "assistance" is a form of harassment, and the intention is to get rid of them. They also say they are treated differently from other people. Shoppers who sit down on a park bench are left alone, but the homeless people who do the same are questioned and directed elsewhere. The ACLU believes their rights to travel and assembly, among others, may have been violated.

The notion of civil rights is a complicated one. In addition to guaranteeing the rights and liberties of one individual, the effect on others must be considered as well. The Constitution, particularly its amendments, serves as a guide to the rights we all have. The courts often interpret those rights as they apply to particular situations.

Answer the following questions
based on your reading and thinking.

8. What does the word *confrontational* mean as it is used in the passage? _____

_____

9. What do all of the groups mentioned in this section have in common? _____

_____

10. Do you think an organization like the ACLU is necessary? Explain why or why not. _____

_____

Paraphrase the selection you have just read. You may wish to begin with a sentence like this one: Guaranteeing civil rights is still a concern in the 1990s. Then include three examples that were mentioned in the selection or that you have learned about through other reading or experience. Describe them in your own words.

Writing Exercise

_____

_____

_____

_____

_____

_____

THEME 4

Business

any students begin college with the intention of studying
and pursuing a career in business. Others become intrigued
after an introductory course exposes them to the varied
and interesting aspects of the business world. Business majors who
are interested in mathematics and analysis may be drawn toward
accounting. The psychological aspects of advertising and marketing
offer a different perspective. In this section, you will find a sampling
of topics, including readings on money, consumers, advertising, business ethics, and others. Once again, the vocabulary you will study
and the skills and strategies you will learn will be introduced and
practiced in the context of business.

You will increase your reading efficiency as you learn how to skim
and scan. In addition to the practice you will have in this text, you will
find other applications for these skills in your academic and daily life.
The lessons on taking notes and summarizing will be helpful to you. Although you will learn and practice these skills with business text, you
will be able to apply the same strategies to other subject areas as well.

You may find the reading selections more difficult than the earlier
ones. Since many of you are approaching the end of your formal
reading instruction, it is time to see whether you are truly an independent college reader. The reading strategies you have been practicing throughout the text should enable you to handle the readings in
this section. The guide questions should also be useful.

THEME FOCUS	
TOPIC:	BUSINESS
	RELATED VOCABULARY
SKILLS:	DICTIONARY USE
	PREVIEWING AND REVIEWING
	SKIMMING AND SCANNING
	TAKING NOTES
	SUMMARIZING
	COMPARISON/CONTRAST ORGANIZATIONAL PATTERN
	CAUSE/EFFECT ORGANIZATIONAL PATTERN

SKILL DEVELOPMENT: EXPANDING YOUR VOCABULARY

The exercises in this section expand your vocabulary by introducing you to business-related terms. You will also learn how to use a dictionary.

Exercise 1
Words in Context

The underlined words in the following sentences appear in the passages you will read in this section of your text. They are presented in context here to help you figure out their meanings. Write the meaning of the underlined word after each sentence.

1. Unfortunately, the consumer has few channels to seek <u>redress</u> for wrongs caused by false and misleading information or faulty products. _____

2. During the trial, the attorney for the <u>plaintiff</u> tried to portray the defendant as an individual who had exhibited criminal tendencies since childhood. _____

   _____

3. Food companies have made questionable health claims for cereals that <u>allegedly</u> reduce cholesterol, decrease the risk of heart disease, and help prevent cancer. _____

   _____

4. In 1911, advertising professionals crusaded to "clean up the industry" resulting in the downfall of patent-medicine <u>vendors</u> who often sold their product door-to-door. _____

   _____

5. The most clever copywriters, the best artists, and the most talented graphic designers <u>collaborate</u> over the national advertising campaigns that bombard us. _____

   _____

6. One advertising theory is that by surrounding a product with an unusual environment, the ad can <u>entice</u> the consumer to try it. _____

7. In one television commercial, a husband amazes his wife with the latest <u>innovation</u> in diapers. _____

   _____

8. If <u>inflation</u> becomes acute, the public's confidence in the value of money is shaken and economic chaos may result. _____

9. Most nations, at one time, operated on a <u>barter system</u>, in which a farmer might pay for health care with milk or eggs. Such systems became awkward and obsolete in the modern industrial age. _____

   _____

10. Although they are not legal tender (accepted as payment by law), 90 percent of all money spent in the United States is in the form of <u>checks</u>. _____

11. Investors who buy real estate and diamonds have fewer <u>liquid assets</u> than those who deposit their funds in banks. _____

12. Because a bank may require advance notice before withdrawal, <u>time deposits</u> are not considered part of the money supply. _____

13. The income statement (or profit and loss statement) is an accounting statement that summarizes a company's <u>revenues</u>, costs of goods sold, expenses, and net profit or loss over time. _____ _____

14. The primary concern of <u>consumerism</u> is to ensure the consumer's rights in the process of the exchange of money for goods and services. _____

15. <u>Fraudulent</u> advertising and deceptive packaging that intentionally mislead consumers have been the focus of regulations established by the Federal Trade Commission. _____ _____

16. In the 1990s, money became tight, and advertising agencies blamed the <u>recession</u> for the large cutbacks corporations made in their advertising budgets. _____ _____

17. In 1982, when some Tylenol capsules were discovered to have been tainted with deadly poison, McNeil Consumer Products Company <u>recalled</u> all Tylenol capsules from the market—31 million bottles with a retail value of about $100 million. _____ _____

18. Nestlé has endured many consumer <u>boycotts</u> since the early 1970s as a result of its intense marketing of infant formula in Third World nations, where the lack of sanitation, refrigeration, and education led to serious health problems in infants given the formula. _____ _____

19. <u>Liability</u> issues were hotly debated in court to determine how much Union Carbide had to pay in damages resulting from a deadly gas leak at its plant in Bhopal, India, in 1984. _____ _____

20. In the U.S. economic system, individuals own the means of production, have the freedom to choose their careers and locations, and have the right to profits—the reward of their <u>entrepreneurship</u>. _____ _____

Exercise 2

Definitions

Match the words in column A to their definitions in column B.

PART I	
COLUMN A	COLUMN B
____ 1. redress	a. an economic system where goods and services are traded
____ 2. plaintiff	b. decrease in the value of society's money
____ 3. alleged	c. to work together
____ 4. vendors	d. the setting right of what is morally wrong
____ 5. collaborate	e. something new or different introduced
____ 6. entice	f. one who brings legal action or suit in court
____ 7. innovation	g. claimed or asserted without proof
____ 8. inflation	h. bank depositor's written order to a bank to pay a certain sum to a third party
____ 9. barter	i. to tempt or lure
____ 10. check	j. sellers of goods

PART 2

COLUMN A	COLUMN B
____ 1. liquid asset	a. value that is easily transferred from hand to hand
____ 2. entrepreneurship	b. cash or other items received in exchange for merchandise or services
____ 3. liabilities	c. to join together to refuse to buy products or services as a form of protest
____ 4. consumerism	d. a period of economic decline
____ 5. fraudulent	e. involving deceit or trickery for unfair advantage
____ 6. recession	f. moneys owed; debts or obligations
____ 7. recall	g. movement to protect the consumer's rights
____ 8. boycott	h. sum of money deposited with a bank that cannot be withdrawn by writing a check
____ 9. time deposit	i. the summons by a manufacturer of a product because of a known defect
____ 10. revenues	j. the organization and management of a business by an enterprising individual

You learned about using a textbook glossary when you worked on Theme 2, about the environment. Glossaries and dictionaries are similar in that both list the words in alphabetical order and define them. Dictionaries, however, provide more extensive information. First of all, a dictionary contains many more words than a glossary. The glossary includes a limited number of words that are restricted in some way. It may include only words used in the particular text or only definitions related to a particular subject area.

There are other differences as well. A dictionary provides more information about each word. For each dictionary entry, you will find the word divided into syllables, the pronunciation, the part of speech, multiple meanings, variations of the word's forms, and the etymology. In addition, some dictionaries provide sample sentences, cross references, maps, illustrations, and other helpful information.

In this exercise, you will work with sample entries from *Webster's*

Exercise 3

Dictionary Use

College Dictionary (New York: Random House, 1991). Notice the following features on the sample dictionary page:

1. *Guide words:* The words at the top of the page that indicate the first and last words included on this page. Words in the dictionary are arranged alphabetically, so you can expect to find on this page those words that would alphabetically follow the first guide word but precede the second.

2. *Pronunciation key:* An abbreviated pronunciation key found at the bottom of the page. A complete pronunciation key is located at the beginning of the book, but this one should be sufficient to figure out how to say each word on this page according to the diacritical markings.

3. *Main entry words:* The words listed in boldface that are listed alphabetically and defined on this page. The words are divided with dots placed between syllables. If you are checking the spelling of a word, this is your reference.

4. *Pronunciation:* How the word is usually pronounced. After the entry, the pronunciation is indicated in parentheses. Use the pronunciation key at the bottom of the page as your guide.

5. *Part of speech:* How the word would be used in a sentence, as a verb or noun, for example.

6. *Meanings:* Most common meanings first. Other meanings may follow.

7. *Etymology:* A history of the word, perhaps including the language (usually Latin or Greek) from which it or its parts are derived. Abbreviations are often used for the language; for example, *L* stands for Latin and *GK* for Greek. The letters *O* and *M* before the language letter (as in *OF* for Old French or *ME* for Middle English) tell how long the word has been in use.

After you have completed this exercise, you should be comfortable using other dictionaries as well. All dictionaries do not follow exactly the same format. It is wise to read the introductory information found at the beginning of each dictionary to learn about its particular setup. Essentially all dictionaries include an elaborate pronunciation key at the beginning of the book and a simpler one at the bottom of most pages. You don't need to memorize the pronunciation key or the diacritical pronunciation symbols, because you can easily refer to them at the bottom of the page.

Ven•ice (ven′is), *n.* **1.** Italian, **Venezia.** a seaport in NE Italy, built on numerous small islands in the Lagoon of Venice. 361,722. **2. Gulf of,** the N arm of the Adriatic Sea. **3. Lagoon of,** an inlet of the Gulf of Venice.

ven•in (ven′in, vē′nin), *n.* any of several poisonous substances occurring in snake venom. [VEN(OM) + -IN²]

ven•i•punc•ture (ven′ə pungk′chər, vē′nə-), *n.* the puncture of a vein for surgical or therapeutic purposes or for collecting blood specimens for analysis. [1900–05; < L *vēn(um)* VEIN + -I- + PUNCTURE]

ve•ni•re fa•ci•as (və ni′rē fā′shē as′, -nēr′ē), *n.* **1.** a writ ordering the summoning of a jury. **2.** the panel from which a trial jury is selected. [1400–50; late ME < L: lit., make (someone) come]

ve•ni•re•man (vi ni′rē mən, -nēr′ē-), *n., pl.* **-men.** one summoned under a venire facias. [1770–80, *Amer.*; *venire* (see VENIRE FACIAS) + MAN]

ven•i•son (ven′ə sən, -zən), *n.* the flesh of a deer or similar animal as used for food. [1250–1300; ME < OF *veneison, venaison* < L *vēnātiōnem,* acc. of *vēnātiō* hunting, a hunt = *vēnā(ri)* to hunt + *-tiō* -TION]

Ve•ni•te (vi nī′tē, ve nē′tā), *n.* **1.** the 95th Psalm (94th in the Vulgate and Douay), used as a canticle at matins or morning prayers. **2.** a musical setting of this psalm. [1175–1225; ME < L: come ye; so called from the first word of Vulgate text]

ve•ni, vi•di, vi•ci (wā′nē wē′dē wē′kē; *Eng.* vē′nī vī′dī vī′sī, ven′ē vē′dē vē′chē, -sē), *Latin.* I came, I saw, I conquered.

Ven•lo (ven′lō), *n.* a city in the SE Netherlands. 63,820.

Venn′ di′agram (ven), *n. Math., Logic.* a diagram that uses circles to represent sets and their relationships. [1940–45; after John *Venn* (1834–1923), English logician]

veno-, a combining form representing VEIN: *venography.* [< L *vēn(a)* VEIN + -O-]

ve•nog•ra•phy (vē nog′rə fē), *n.* x-ray examination of a vein or veins following injection of a radiopaque substance. [1925–30]

ve•nol•o•gy (vē nol′ə jē), *n.* PHLEBOLOGY.

ven•om (ven′əm), *n.* **1.** the poisonous fluid that some animals, as certain snakes and spiders, secrete and introduce into the bodies of their victims by biting, stinging, etc. **2.** something suggesting poison in its effect, as malice or jealousy. **3.** *Archaic.* poison in general. [1175–1225; var. of ME *venim* < AF; OF *venim, venin* < VL **venimen,* for L *venēnum* magical herb or potion, poison < **wenes-nom* = **wenes-* desire (see VENERATE, VENUS) + **-nom* n. suffix] **—Syn.** See POISON.

ven•om•ous (ven′ə məs), *adj.* **1.** (of an animal) having a gland or glands for secreting venom; able to inflict a poisonous bite or sting. **2.** full of or containing venom; poisonous. **3.** spiteful; malignant. [1250–1300; ME < AF, OF] **—ven′om•ous•ly,** *adv.* **—ven′om•ous•ness,** *n.*

ve•nous (vē′nəs), *adj.* **1.** of or pertaining to a vein or veins. **2.** having or composed of veins. **3.** pertaining to or designating the oxygen-poor, dark red blood that is carried back to the heart by the veins and by the pulmonary artery. [1620–30; < L *vēnōsus;* see VEIN, -OUS] **—ve′nous•ly,** *adv.* **—ve′nous•ness, ve•nos•i•ty** (vi nos′i tē), *n.*

vent¹ (vent), *n., v.,* **vent•ed, vent•ing.** **—*n.*** **1.** an opening, as in a wall, serving as an outlet for air, fumes, or the like. **2.** an opening at the earth's surface from which volcanic material, as lava or gas, is emitted. **3.** a means of exit or escape; an outlet, as from confinement. **4.** expression; utterance; release: *giving vent to one's emotions.* **5.** the small opening at the breech of a gun by which fire is communicated to the charge. **6.** *Zool.* the external opening of the cloaca. **—*v.t.*** **7.** to give free play or expression to (an emotion). **8.** to relieve through such expression: *to vent one's disappointment.* **9.** to release or discharge (liquid, smoke, etc.). **10.** to furnish or provide with a vent or vents. **—*v.i.*** **11.** to be relieved of pressure or discharged by means of a vent. **12.** (of a marine animal) to rise to the surface of the water to breathe. [1350–1400; ME (v.): to furnish (a vessel) with a vent, by aphesis < OF *aventer, esventer* = *es-* EX-¹ + *-venter,* v. der. of *vent* < L *ventus* WIND¹]

vent² (vent), *n.* a slit in the back or side of a coat, jacket, or other garment, at the bottom part of a seam. [1400–50; late ME *vente;* r. ME *fente* < MF, der. of *fendre* to slit < L *findere* to split]

vent•age (ven′tij), *n.* a small hole or vent, as one of the fingerholes of a flute. [1595–1605]

ven•tail (ven′tāl), *n.* a movable part on the lower front of a medieval helmet. See diag. at ARMOR. [1300–50; ME < MF *ventaille* = *vent* (< L *ventus* WIND¹) + *-aille* -AL²]

ven•ter (ven′tər), *n.* **1.** *Anat., Zool.* **a.** the abdomen or belly. **b.** a bellylike cavity. **c.** a bellylike protuberance. **2.** *Law.* **a.** the womb. **b.** a wife as a source of offspring. [1535–45; < L: belly, womb]

ven•ti•fact (ven′tə fakt′), *n.* a pebble or cobble that has been faceted, grooved, and polished by the erosive action of wind-driven sand. [1911; < L *venti-,* comb. form of *ventus* WIND¹ + (ARTI)FACT]

ven•ti•late (ven′tl āt′), *v.,* **-lat•ed, -lat•ing.** **—*v.t.*** **1.** to provide (a room, mine, etc.) with fresh air in place of air that has been used or contaminated. **2.** (of air or wind) to circulate through or blow on, so as to cool or freshen the air of: *Cool breezes ventilated the house.* **3.** to expose to the action of air or wind: *to ventilate floor timbers.* **4.** to submit (a question, problem, etc.) to open, full examination and discussion. **5.** to give utterance or expression to (an opinion, complaint, etc.). **6.** to furnish with a vent or opening, as for the escape of air or gas. **7. a.** to oxygenate (blood) by exposure to air in the lungs or gills. **b.** to assist the breathing of (a person), as with a respirator. **—*v.i.*** **8.** to give utterance or expression to one's emotions, opinions, etc. [1400–50; late ME < L *ventilātus,* ptp. of *ventilāre* to fan = *vent(us)* WIND¹ + *-ilāre* v. suffix, var. of *-ulāre,* orig. with ders. of nouns ending in *-ulus* -ULE; cf. SPECULATE]

ven•ti•la•tion (ven′tl ā′shən), *n.* **1.** the act of ventilating or the state of being ventilated. **2.** facilities or equipment for providing ventilation. [1425–75; late ME < L] **—ven′ti•la′tive, ven′ti•la•to′ry** (-ə tôr′ē, -tōr′ē), *adj.*

ven•ti•la•tor (ven′tl ā′tər), *n.* **1.** one that ventilates. **2.** a contrivance or opening for replacing foul or stagnant air with fresh air. [1735–45]

ven•tral (ven′trəl), *adj.* **1.** of or pertaining to the venter or belly; abdominal. **2.** situated on or toward the lower, abdominal plane of an animal's body, equivalent to the front in humans. **3.** of or designating the lower or inner surface of a plant structure. [1730–40; < L *ventrālis* = *vent(e)r* VENTER + *-ālis* -AL¹] **—ven′tral•ly,** *adv.*

ventri-, var. of VENTRO-.

ven•tri•cle (ven′tri kəl), *n.* **1.** any of various hollow organs or parts in an animal body. **2.** either of the two lower chambers of the heart that receive blood from the atria and in turn force it into the arteries. See diag. at HEART. **3.** one of a series of connecting cavities of the brain. [1350–1400; ME < L *ventriculus* belly, ventricle. See VENTER, -I-, -CLE¹]

ven•tri•cose (ven′tri kōs′), *adj.* **1.** protuberant on one side. **2.** having a large abdomen. [1750–60; < NL *ventricōsus.* See VENTER, -IC, -OSE¹] **—ven′tri•cos′i•ty** (-kos′i tē), *n.*

ven•tric•u•lar (ven trik′yə lər), *adj.* **1.** of, pertaining to, or of the nature of a ventricle. **2.** of or pertaining to a belly or to something resembling one. [1815–25]

ven•tric•u•lus (ven trik′yə ləs), *n., pl.* **-li** (-lī′). **1.** the enlarged part of the alimentary tract of an insect in which digestion takes place. **2.** GIZZARD (def. 1). [1685–95; < L; see VENTRICLE]

ven•tril•o•quism (ven tril′ə kwiz′əm) also **ven•tril•o•quy** (-kwē), *n.* the art or practice of speaking with little or no lip movement so that the voice does not appear to come from the speaker but from another source. [1790–1800; *ventriloqu(y)* (< ML *ventriloquium* = LL *ventriloqu(us)* a ventriloquist (*ventri-* VENTRI- + *-loquus,* der. of *loqui* to speak) + *-ium* -IUM¹) + -ISM] **—ven′tri•lo′qui•al** (-trə lō′kwē əl), **ven•tril′o•qual,** *adj.* **—ven′tri•lo′qui•al•ly,** *adv.*

ven•tril•o•quist (ven tril′ə kwist), *n.* a person who performs or is skilled in ventriloquism. [1650–60]

ven•tril•o•quize (ven tril′ə kwīz′), *v.i., v.t.,* **-quized, -quiz•ing.** to speak in the manner of a ventriloquist. [1835–45]

ventro- or **ventri-,** a combining form meaning "abdomen": *ventrodorsal.* [comb. form of NL *venter* VENTER; see -O-]

ven•tro•dor•sal (ven′trō dôr′səl), *adj.* of or pertaining to the ventral and dorsal aspects of the body. [1890–95]

ven•tro•lat•er•al (ven′trō lat′ər əl), *adj.* of or pertaining to the ventral and lateral aspects of the body. [1825–35]

Ven•tu•ra (ven to͝or′ə), *n.* a city in SW California, NW of Los Angeles. 88,900. Official name, **San Buenaventura.**

ven•ture (ven′chər), *n., v.,* **-tured, -tur•ing.** **—*n.*** **1.** an undertaking involving risk or uncertainty. **2.** a business enterprise in which something is risked in the hope of profit. **3.** the money or property risked in such an enterprise. **—*v.t.*** **4.** to expose to hazard; risk. **5.** to take the risk of; brave: *to venture a voyage.* **6.** to undertake to express, in spite of possible contradiction or opposition: *to venture a guess.* **—*v.i.*** **7.** to undertake or embark upon a venture: *We ventured deep into the jungle; to venture upon an ambitious program of reform.* **8.** to invest venture capital. **—*Idiom.*** **9. at a venture,** according to chance; at random. [1400–50; late ME, aph. var. of *aventure* ADVENTURE] **—ven′tur•er,** *n.*

ven′ture cap′ital, *n.* funds invested or available for investment in a new business enterprise. Also called **risk capital.** [1940–45] **—ven′ture cap′italism,** *n.* **—ven′ture cap′italist,** *n.*

ven•ture•some (ven′chər səm), *adj.* **1.** having or showing a disposition to undertake ventures; adventurous. **2.** attended with risk; hazardous. [1655–65] **—ven′ture•some•ly,** *adv.* **—ven′ture•some•ness,** *n.*

ven•tu′ri tube′ (ven to͝or′ē), *n.* **1.** a device for measuring fluid flow, consisting of a tube constricted in such a way that a pressure differential is created between the center and the ends. **2.** an alteration in the shape of the throat of a carburetor for controlling the flow of fuel. [after G. B. *Venturi* (1746–1822), Italian physicist whose work led to its invention]

ven•tur•ous (ven′chər əs), *adj.* VENTURESOME. [1555–65] **—ven′tur•ous•ly,** *adv.* **—ven′tur•ous•ness,** *n.*

ven•ue (ven′yo͞o), *n.* **1.** *Law.* **a.** the place of a crime or cause of action. **b.** the county or place where the jury is gathered and the case tried. **c.** the designation of the place where a trial will be held. **2.** the scene or locale of any action or event. [1300–50; ME: an attack < MF: lit., a coming, OF (fem. ptp. of *venir* to come) < VL **venūta,* for L *venta*]

ven•ule (ven′yo͞ol), *n.* **1.** a small vein. **2.** one of the branches of a vein in the wing of an insect. [1840–50; < L *vēnula.* See VEIN, -ULE] **—ven′u•lar** (-yə lər), **ven′u•lose′** (-lōs′), **ven′u•lous** (-ləs), *adj.*

Ve•nus (vē′nəs), *n., pl.* **-us•es.** **1.** an ancient Italian goddess, identified by the Romans with Aphrodite as the goddess of love and beauty. **2.** an exceptionally beautiful woman. **3.** the most brilliant planet, second in order from the sun, having an equatorial diameter of 7521 miles (12,104 km), a mean distance from the sun of 67.2 million miles (108.2 million km), a period of revolution of 224.68 days, and no moons. See table at PLANET. **4.** Also called **Ve′nus fig′ure.** (*sometimes l.c.*) a statuette of a female figure, usu. carved of ivory and typically having exaggerated breasts, belly, or buttocks, often found in Upper Paleolithic cultures from Siberia to France. [< L *Venus,* s. *Vener-* orig. a neut. common n. meaning "physical desire," hence "qualities exciting desire, charm," "a goddess personifying sexual attractiveness"; c. Skt *vanaḥ* desire, akin to WISH; cf. VENERATE, VENOM]

Ve•nus•berg (vē′nəs bûrg′), *n.* a mountain in central Germany in the caverns of which, according to medieval legend, Venus held court.

Ve•nu•si•an (və no͞o′shən, -shē ən, -sē ən, -nyo͞o′-), *adj.* **1.** of or pertaining to the planet Venus. **—*n.*** **2.** a supposed being inhabiting Venus. [1895–1900]

Ve′nus's-fly′trap, *n.* an insectivorous bog plant, *Dionaea muscipula,* of the sundew family, native to the Carolinas, having spiny-edged leaves divided in halves that snap shut when sensitive hairs on their inner surface are touched. [1760–70, *Amer.*]

Venus's-flytrap, *Dionaea muscipula,* height about 1 ft. (0.3 m)

Ve′nus's gir′dle, *n.* an iridescent blue and green comb jelly, *Cestum veneris,* having a ribbon-shaped, gelatinous body.

PRONUNCIATION KEY: act, cāpe, dâre, pärt; set, ēven; if, ice; ox, nō, fôr, oil, bo͝ok, bo͞ot, out; up, ûrge; child; sing; shoe; thin, *th*at; zh in trea*s*ure. ə = *a* in *alone, e* in *item, i* in *easily, o* in *gallop, u* in *circus;* ᵊ in *fire* (fīᵊr), *hour* (ouᵊr).

Webster's College Dictionary (New York: Random House, 1991), p. 1479.

The following questions ask you to find examples of the features that were just described. Write your answers after you refer to the dictionary page.

1. What are the guide words for this page? _____

2. Find the pronunciation key. What symbols would you use to pronounce the word *ventilator*? _____

3. Which of these words would you find on this page: *ventriloquist, vacuum, vicarious, ventral.* Explain why.

   _____

4. What part of speech is the word *venue*? _____

5. How many meanings are given for the word *vent*? Which is the most common? _____

   _____

6. What is the derivation of the word *venison*? What language do its word parts come from, and what do they mean? _____

   _____

7. Which entry is accompanied by an illustration? _____

8. Which definition of the word *venture* would probably be used when discussing business? _____

9. What is the past tense of the word *ventriloquize*? _____

10. If you were studying astronomy, which definition of *Venus* would you probably use? _____

    _____

This exercise is best completed with a partner. If you do not have a partner, try to pronounce the words aloud. Your ear may recognize the words before your eye does. In the left-hand column is a list of words that are spelled phonetically. Try to pronounce them and spell them as best you can. After you write out the word, try to match it with its definition in the second column. You may wish to refer to the pronunciation key found at the bottom of the dictionary page in exercise 3. As an alternative, you may use the pronunciation key in your own dictionary.

Exercise 4

Pronunciation

MATCH	PHONETIC SPELLING	CORRECT SPELLING	DEFINITION
____	1. i kon′ ə mē	_____	a. to abstain from buying or using
____	2. reg yə lā′ shən	_____	b. the hearing and determination of a dispute
____	3. kôr pə rā′ shən	_____	c. the management of the resources of a community or country
____	4. boi′ kot	_____	d. failure to exercise reasonable care
____	5. prə sē′ jər	_____	e. security pledged for the payment of a loan
____	6. är bi trā′ shən	_____	f. something done or performed
____	7. neg′ li jens	_____	g. law, rule, or order proscribed by authority
____	8. kə lat′ ər əl	_____	h. moneys owed; debt
____	9. ak′ shən	_____	i. a particular course of action
____	10. lī ə bil′ i tē	_____	j. an incorporated business; a company

Try to pronounce the words as they are spelled phonetically. Spell them as best you can and write them in the middle column. Then match each word to its definition.

MATCH	PHONETIC SPELLING	CORRECT SPELLING	DEFINITION
_____	1. man′ ij ment	_____	a. to ship to other countries
_____	2. ben ə fish′ ə rē	_____	b. one who keeps detailed records of a company's transactions
_____	3. ik sport′	_____	c. something given or received for services, debt, loss, or injury
_____	4. ə koun′ tnt	_____	d. the owner of a business
_____	5. kom pən sā′ shən	_____	e. practice of controlling or directing an enterprise
_____	6. boŏk′ kē pər	_____	f. an agreement between two parties to do something specific
_____	7. fran′ chīz	_____	g. steady rise in level of prices and decrease in value of currency
_____	8. kon′ trakt	_____	h. right granted by a company to an individual to sell its products
_____	9. prə prī′ i tər	_____	i. person skilled in handling financial accounts
_____	10. in flā′ shən	_____	j. person who receives benefits or profits

The following page is a reprint of a dictionary page. You will need to refer to it to answer these questions. For pronunciation questions, you may need to refer to the dictionary page used in exercise 3, since it includes a key.

1. Explain the difference between the two pronunciations of the word *aluminate*. _____

   _____

2. Which of the following words would be found on this page: *arthritis, amanuensis, alum root, association*? Explain why. _____

   _____

3. What is the plural of the word *alveolus*? What does it mean? _____

   _____

4. After whom is Alzheimer's disease named? What did you learn about him? _____

   _____

5. Which definition of *amalgamate* applies to business? _____

   _____

6. How many different entries are listed for the abbreviation *am* or *AM*? _____

7. Which entry is accompanied by an illustration? _____

8. Which Brazilian novelist is identified? (*Hint:* You can cut down on your searching time if you look only for names.) _____

9. Where would a nursemaid be called an *amah*? _____

10. What did you learn about the usage of *alumna*? _____

aluminate to **amaryllis family** 42

a•lu•mi•nate (ə lo͞o′mə nit′, -nāt′), *n.* a salt of the acid form of aluminum hydroxide, containing the group AlO_2^- or AlO_3^{-3}. [1725–35]
al•u•min•i•um (al′yə min′ē əm), *n., adj. Chiefly Brit.* ALUMINUM.
a•lu•mi•nize (ə lo͞o′mə nīz′), *v.t.,* **-nized, -niz•ing.** to treat with aluminum. [1855–60] **—a•lu′mi•ni•za′tion,** *n.*
a•lu•mi•no•sil•i•cate (ə lo͞o′mə nō sil′ə kit, -kāt′), *n.* any aluminum silicate containing alkali-metal or alkaline-earth-metal ions, as a feldspar, zeolite, or beryl. [1905–10]
a•lu•mi•nous (ə lo͞o′mə nəs), *adj.* of the nature of or containing alum or alumina. [1535–45; < F or L] **—a•lu′mi•nos′i•ty** (-nos′i tē), *n.*
a•lu•mi•num (ə lo͞o′mə nəm), *n.* **1.** a silver-white metallic element, light in weight, ductile, malleable, and not readily corroded or tarnished: used in alloys and for lightweight products. *Abbr.:* alum.; *Symbol:* Al; *at. wt.:* 26.98; *at. no.:* 13; *sp. gr.:* 2.70 at 20°C. **—*adj.*** **2.** of, pertaining to, or containing aluminum. Also, *esp. Brit.,* **aluminium.** [1812; alter. of earlier *alumium.* See ALUMINA, -IUM²] **—al•u•min•ic** (al′yə min′ik), *adj.*
alu′minum hydrox′ide, *n.* a crystalline, water-insoluble powder, $Al(OH)_3$ or $Al_2O_3{\cdot}3H_2O$, obtained chiefly from bauxite: used in the manufacture of glass, ceramics, and printing inks, in dyeing, and as an antacid. [1870–75]
alu′minum ox′ide, *n.* ALUMINA.
alu′minum potas′sium sul′fate, *n.* ALUM¹ (def. 1).
alu′minum sil′icate, *n.* any crystalline combination of silicate and aluminate.
a•lum•na (ə lum′nə), *n., pl.* **-nae** (-nē, -nī). a woman who is a graduate or former student of a specific school, college, or university. [1880–85, *Amer.;* < L: foster daughter, pupil; fem. of ALUMNUS] **—Usage.** See ALUMNUS.
a•lum•nus (ə lum′nəs), *n., pl.* **-ni** (-nī, -nē). **1.** a graduate or former student of a specific school, college, or university. **2.** a former associate, employee, member, or the like. [1635–45; < L: foster son, pupil = *al(ere)* to feed, support + **-o-m(i)nos* orig. passive participle suffix, akin to Gk *-menos*] **—Usage.** ALUMNUS (in Latin a masculine noun) refers to a male graduate or former student; the plural is ALUMNI. An ALUMNA (in Latin a feminine noun) refers to a female graduate or former student; the plural is ALUMNAE. Traditionally, the masculine plural ALUMNI has been used for groups composed of both sexes and is still widely so used. Sometimes, to avoid any suggestion of sexism, both terms are used for mixed groups: the *alumni/alumnae* (or *the alumni and alumnae*) *of Indiana University.* While not quite equivalent in meaning, the terms *graduate* and *graduates* avoid both the complexities of the Latin forms and the use of a masculine plural form to refer to both sexes.
al•um•root (al′əm ro͞ot′, -ro͝ot′), *n.* any of several North American plants belonging to the genus *Heuchera,* of the saxifrage family, esp. *H. americana,* having mottled foliage, greenish-white flowers, and an astringent root. [1805–15, *Amer.*]
al•u•nite (al′yə nīt′), *n.* a mineral, a hydrous sulfate of potassium and aluminum, $KAl_3(SO_4)_2(OH)_6$, commonly occurring in fine-grained masses. Also called **al•um•stone** (al′əm stōn′). [1865–70; < F *alun* (< L *alūmen* ALUM¹) + -ITE¹]
Al•va (äl′vä) also **Alba,** *n.* **Fernando Alvarez de Toledo, Duke of,** 1508–82, Spanish general who suppressed a Protestant rebellion in the Netherlands in 1567.
Al•va•ra•do (äl′vä rä′dō), *n.* **1. Alonso de,** c1490–1554, Spanish soldier in the conquests of Mexico and Peru. **2. Pedro de,** 1495–1541, Spanish soldier: chief aide of Cortés in the conquest of Mexico.
Al•va•rez (al′və rez′), *n.* **Luis Walter,** 1911–88, U.S. physicist.
Ál•va•rez Quin•te•ro (äl′vä reth′ kēn te′rô), *n.* **Joa•quín** (hwä kēn′), 1873–1944, and his brother **Se•ra•fín** (se′rä fēn′), 1871–1938, Spanish dramatists and coauthors.
al•ve•o•la (al vē′ə lə), *n., pl.* **-lae** (-lē′). ALVEOLUS. [< NL; L *alveolus*]
al•ve•o•lar (al vē′ə lər), *adj.* **1.** of or pertaining to an alveolus or to alveoli. **2.** (of a consonant sound) articulated with the tongue touching or close to the alveolar ridge behind the upper front teeth, as English (t), (d), or (n). **—*n.*** **3.** an alveolar sound. [1790–1800] **—al•ve′o•lar•ly,** *adv.*
alve′olar ridge′, *n.* the ridgelike border of the upper and lower jaws containing the sockets of the teeth. Also called **alve′olar proc′ess.** See diag. at MOUTH.
al•ve•o•late (al vē′ə lit, -lāt′) also **al•ve′o•lat′ed,** *adj.* having alveoli; deeply pitted, as a honeycomb. [1830–40; < L] **—al•ve′o•la′tion,** *n.*
al•ve•o•lus (al vē′ə ləs), *n., pl.* **-li** (-lī′). **1.** a little cavity, pit, or cell, as a cell of a honeycomb. **2.** any of the tiny bunched air sacs at the ends of the bronchioles of the lungs. **3.** the socket within the jawbone in which the root or roots of a tooth are set. [1700–10; < L, = *alve(us)* concave vessel + *-olus* -OLE¹]
al•way (ôl′wā), *adv. Archaic.* always. [bef. 900; ME *alle wei;* OE *ealneweg* = *ealne,* acc. sing. masc. of *eal* ALL + *weg* WAY¹]
al•ways (ôl′wāz, -wēz), *adv.* **1.** every time; on every occasion; without exception: *We always sleep late on Saturday.* **2.** all the time; continuously; uninterruptedly: *The light is always burning.* **3.** forever: *Will you always love me?* **4.** in any event; if necessary: *I can always decide not to go.* [1200–50; ME *alwayes, alles weis,* gen. of *alle wei* ALWAY]
al′yce clo′ver (al′is), *n.* a plant, *Alysicarpus vaginalis,* of the legume family, native to central Asia and grown in warm regions as forage. [1940–45; prob. by folk etym. from NL *Alysicarpus* the genus name = Gk *(h)alysi-,* comb. form of *hálysis* chain + Gk *-karpos* -CARPOUS]
a•lys•sum (ə lis′əm), *n.* **1.** any of various plants of the mustard family, having gray leaves and clusters of small yellow or white flowers. **2.** SWEET ALYSSUM. [1545–55; < NL; L *alysson* < Gk, neut. of *álysos* curing (canine) madness = *a-* A-⁶ + *-lyssos,* adj. der. of + *lýssa* madness]
Alz′hei•mer's disease′ (älts′hī mərz, alts′-, ôlts′-), *n.* a common form of dementia of unknown cause, usu. beginning in late middle age, characterized by progressive memory loss and mental deterioration associated with brain damage. [after Alois *Alzheimer* (1864–1915), German neurologist, who described it in 1907]
am (am; *unstressed* əm, m), *v.* 1st pers. sing. pres. indic. of BE. [before 900; ME; OE *am, eam, eom;* c. ON *em,* Go *im,* OIr *am,* Gk *eimí,* Skt *asmi*]
AM, 1. amplitude modulation: a method of impressing a signal on a radio carrier wave by varying its amplitude. **2.** a system of broadcasting using this method. Compare FM. [1935–40]
Am, *Chem. Symbol.* americium.
Am., 1. America. **2.** American.
A.M., Master of Arts. [< L *Artium Magister*]
a.m. or **A.M., 1.** before noon. **2.** the period from midnight to noon, esp. the period of daylight prior to noon. Compare P.M. [1755–65; < L *ante merīdiem*] **—Usage.** The abbreviation A.M. refers to the period from midnight until noon. One minute before noon is 11:59 a.m. One minute after noon is 12:01 p.m. Many people distinguish between noon and midnight by saying *12 noon* and *12 midnight.* Expressions such as *6 a.m. in the morning* and *9 p.m. at night* are redundant.
-ama, var. of -ORAMA: *rollerama; Futurama.*
A.M.A., American Medical Association.
Am•a•dis (am′ə dis), *n.* (in medieval romances) a knight-errant, model of the chivalric hero.
A•ma•do (ə mä′dō, -do͞o), *n.* **Jor•ge** (zhôr′zhə), born 1912, Brazilian novelist.
am•a•dou (am′ə do͞o′), *n.* a spongy substance prepared from tree fungi, esp. *Polyporus* species, used as tinder and to stanch blood in open wounds. [1805–15; < F, MF, appar. n. der. of *amadouer* to coax, influence by flattery. v. der. of Oc, OPr *amadou(r)* lover < L *amātōrem,* acc. of *amātor* (see AMATEUR); the name is usu. explained by the conventional assoc. between love and highly combustible substances]
A•ma•ga•sa•ki (ä′mə gə sä′kē, am′ə-), *n.* a city on SW Honshu, in S Japan. 523,657.
a•mah (ä′mə, am′ə), *n.* (in colonial India and the Far East) a female servant, esp. a nursemaid. [1830–40; < Pg *ama* wet nurse < ML *amma*]
a•main (ə mān′), *adv. Archaic.* **1.** with full force. **2.** at full speed. **3.** suddenly; hastily. **4.** exceedingly; greatly. [1530–40]
Am•a•lek•ite (am′ə lek′īt, ə mal′i kīt′), *n., pl.* **-ites,** (*esp. collectively*) **-ite.** a member of the tribe descended from Esau. Gen. 36:12. [< Heb *ʿămālēq* Amalek + -ITE¹]
a•mal•gam (ə mal′gəm), *n.* **1.** an alloy of mercury with another metal or metals. **2.** an alloy chiefly of silver mixed with mercury and variable amounts of other metals, used as a dental filling. **3.** a mixture or combination. [1425–75; late ME < MF < ML < Ar *al* the + dial. Ar *malgham* < Gk *málagma* softening agent = *malak-,* s. of *malássein* to soften + *-ma* n. suffix]
a•mal•ga•mate (ə mal′gə māt′), *v.,* **-mat•ed, -mat•ing.** **—*v.t.*** **1.** to mix or merge so as to make a combination; blend; unite: *to amalgamate two companies.* **2.** to mix or alloy (a metal) with mercury. **—*v.i.*** **3.** to combine, unite, merge, or coalesce: *The three schools decided to amalgamate.* [1635–45] **—a•mal′ga•ma•ble,** *adj.* **—a•mal′ga•ma′tor,** *n.*
a•mal•ga•ma•tion (ə mal′gə mā′shən), *n.* **1.** the act or process of amalgamating. **2.** the state or result of being amalgamated. **3.** the extraction of precious metals from their ores by treatment with mercury. [1605–15]
Am•al•the•a (am′əl thē′ə), *n.* (in Greek myth) a nurse of the infant Zeus, variously depicted as a nymph or a goat.
a•man•dine (ä′mən dēn′, am′ən-), *adj.* served or prepared with almonds: *trout amandine.* [1835–45; < F; see ALMOND, -INE¹]
am•a•ni•ta (am′ə nī′tə, -nē′-), *n., pl.* **-tas.** any of various gill fungi of the genus *Amanita,* having a cup at the base of the stalk: many species are poisonous. [1821; < NL < Gk *amānîtai* (pl.) kind of fungi]
a•man•ta•dine (ə man′tə dēn′), *n.* a water-soluble crystalline substance, $C_{10}H_{17}NHCl$, that inhibits penetration of viruses into cells and is used against certain types of influenza and in the treatment of parkinsonism. [1960–65; coinage appar. based on the chemical name *1-aminoadamantane*]
a•man•u•en•sis (ə man′yo͞o en′sis), *n., pl.* **-ses** (-sēz). a person employed to write what another dictates or to copy what has been written by another; secretary. [1610–20; < L *(servus) āmanuēnsis* = *ā-* A-⁴ + *manu-,* s. of *manus* hand + *-ēnsis* -ENSIS]
A•ma•pá (ä′mä pä′), *n.* a federal territory in N Brazil. 232,400; 54,160 sq. mi. (140,276 sq. km). *Cap.:* Macapá.
am•a•ranth (am′ə ranth′), *n.* **1.** any plant of the genus *Amaranthus,* some species of which are cultivated as food and some for their showy flower clusters or foliage. **2.** an imaginary flower that never dies. **3.** a purplish red, water-soluble powder, $C_{20}H_{11}N_2O_{10}Na_3$, used as a dye. [1545–55; < L *amarantus,* alter. of Gk *amáranton* unfading flower, n. use of neut. sing. of *amárantos* = *a-* A-⁶ + *-marantos,* v. adj. of *maraínein* to fade]
am′aranth fam′ily, *n.* a family, Amaranthaceae, of herbaceous, often weedy plants with alternate or opposite leaves and small, chaffy flowers in brightly colored dense clusters: includes the cockscomb and amaranth.
am•a•ran•thine (am′ə ran′thin, -thīn), *adj.* **1.** of or like the amaranth. **2.** undying; everlasting. **3.** of purplish-red color. [1660–70]
am•a•relle (am′ə rel′), *n.* any variety of the sour cherry, *Prunus cerasus,* having colorless juice. [< G < ML *amārellum* = L *amār(us)* bitter + *-ellum* dim. suffix; see -ELLE]
am•a•ret•to (am′ə ret′ō, ä′mə-), *n.* an almond-flavored liqueur. [1975–80; < It, dim. of *amaro* bitter < L *amārus*]
Am•a•ril•lo (am′ə ril′ō), *n.* a city in NW Texas. 166,010.
am•a•ryl•lis (am′ə ril′is), *n.* **1.** any of several bulbous plants of the genus *Hippeastrum,* esp. *H. puniceum,* which has large red or pink flowers: popular as a houseplant. **2.** Also called **belladonna lily.** a related plant, *Amaryllis belladonna,* having clusters of usu. rose-colored flowers. **3.** any of several other similar or related plants. [1785–95; < L: name of a shepherdess in Virgil's *Eclogues*]
amaryl′lis fam′ily, *n.* a family, Ama-

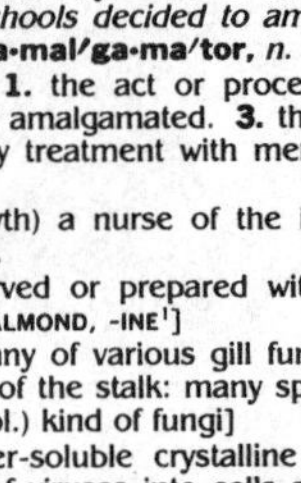

amaryllis (def. 2), *Amaryllis belladonna*

Webster's College Dictionary (New York: Random House, 1991), p. 42.

SKILL DEVELOPMENT: SKIMMING AND SCANNING

At times, it is not necessary to read an entire article or every word in a passage. For example, you may need to research a topic to write a term paper. If you are faced with a list of twenty-five journal articles on the topic, you will need a way to decide which ones to read thoroughly and take notes on, and which ones to eliminate. *Skimming* is one way to decide which articles are relevant.

When you skim, you try to get a sense or general idea about the passage. You will probably look at the title and subheadings, illustrations or pictures, words in boldface or italics. You may note how long the passage is and how many sections it has. You may select a paragraph or two (often the first and last) to read entirely to get an impression of the author's style, the difficulty of the passage, or your familiarity with the vocabulary. In this last step, you are trying to determine how this passage fits in with your reading experience. You will probably make a judgment about whether you will find the actual reading easy and interesting. This is a practical assessment since you may need to anticipate how much time and energy to allot to the reading.

There are other uses for skimming as well. Before you read a textbook chapter, for example, skimming will give you an idea what it's about. In this case, you are using the technique to *preview* the chapter. Literally, the word *preview* means "to look before."

Perhaps you have already read and studied a passage to prepare for a quiz or a test. If you underlined the important points, you may wish to skim over those points as a *review* just before your test. Another example of the usefulness of skimming relates to book selection. If you are trying to select a novel for pleasure reading from the library shelf or a bookstore rack, you may wish to skim through the book to find out about the plot and the author's style before you borrow or purchase it.

Scanning is another technique that uses selective reading. You don't read every word when you skim, and you don't read every word when you scan either. There is an important difference, though, between these two methods. As you know, when you skim, you try to get an overall impression of the reading. When you scan, on the other hand, you are looking for specific information. When you look up a friend's number in the telephone book, you don't read all the names listed on that page. You just look for your friend's name, and you may use your finger as a guide as you scan the page. If you are making up a grocery list, you may scan a recipe to see what ingredients you will have to buy. When your business professor asks you to find out information about the rules of bankruptcy, you scan the index or the library reference sources for that particular topic. If your chemistry assignment consists of a list of questions to answer based on a description of an experiment, you will probably scan for the answers rather than reread the whole account of the experiment.

Exercise 6
Previewing and Reviewing

Skimming is useful when you are about to begin reading. You should look over the material to learn as much as you can before you actually begin. Here are some questions your preview should help you answer:

- What is the selection about?

- How long is it?

- Does it seem difficult?

- Does it seem like anything I've read before?

- Are there many unfamiliar vocabulary words?

- What do I already know about this subject?

- What do I expect to learn from reading this passage?

You will practice previewing on a passage about torts. Since the passage is relatively short, your preview should only take a minute or two. If you already use a previewing strategy that works for you, stick with it. If you don't usually preview or if you want some suggestions, follow these guidelines:

1. Read the title and the subheadings.

2. Read words or phrases in italics or boldface.

3. Read any group of statements that are numbered.

4. Read the first paragraph.

5. Read the first sentence of each of the other paragraphs.

Now preview the passage that follows.

WHAT IS A TORT?

Tort is a French word that means "to twist." Torts are civil wrongs, actions that are not straight but twisted. A **tort** is an interference with someone's person or with someone's property that results in an injury to them or to their property. For example, using someone else's land is an interference with their property rights and is the tort of trespass. Damage could result if you held a concert on someone else's land and the crowd destroyed the lawn or left garbage that had to be removed. The law gives us protection

Excerpt from *Business and the Legal Environment,* 2nd ed., by Marianne Moody Jennings (Boston, PWS-Kent, 1991), pp. 203–204.

of our persons and property through the law of torts, which is a way to recover the damages done to us.

TORTS VS. CRIMES

A tort is a private wrong. When a tort is committed, the party who was injured is entitled to collect compensation for damages from the wrongdoer. A crime, on the other hand, is a public wrong and requires the wrongdoer to pay a debt to society through a fine or by going to prison.

TYPES OF TORTS

There are three types of tort liability: **intentional torts, negligence,** and **strict tort liability.** Intentional torts are harms done by people on purpose. For example, battery, or the striking of another person, is an intentional tort. A person is injured because you chose to hit him. However, suppose that you are stretching your arms in a crowd and you strike a man in the nose and hurt him. You have not committed the tort of battery, but you may have committed the tort of negligence. You did not intentionally strike the man as you would have if you were having an argument, but you were carelessly swinging your arms in a crowd of people. These careless actions, or actions done without thinking through the consequences, are torts of negligence. These accidental harms also impose liabilities on the parties. In other words, persons who cause harm may be subject to a penalty even if they did not mean to do anything wrong. The key difference between intentional torts and negligence is the state of mind, or intention. Under the intentional tort standard, the party intended to commit the act. Under negligence, the party may have been careless or may not have thought carefully through his actions. But the actions taken were not done with the intent to cause harm. (Strict tort liability is generally used in product liability and will not be discussed here.)

Torts are also classified as property torts and personal torts. The example of trespassing given earlier is an example of a property tort because the injury is done to someone's property. The tort of defamation is an example of a personal tort. It involves publishing untrue statements about a person resulting in harm to him/her. The tort of negligence can involve injury to person or property. For example, if someone runs a red light and runs into your car, he has been careless and the tort of negligence has occurred. If you are injured and your car is damaged, you have experienced both personal and property damage. Regardless of the type of tort, the remedy for the tort is recovery for the damage done to you or your property. You are entitled to compensation.

THE INTENTIONAL TORTS

Defamation and Product Disparagement. Defamation is an untrue statement about one party to another about a third party. It can consist of either **slander** or **libel.** Slander is oral or spoken defamation and libel is written (and in some cases broadcast) defamation. When an untrue statement is made about a business product or service, the defamation is referred to as **disparagement,** and is either **trade libel** or **slander of title.**

These business torts occur when representatives of one business make untrue statements about another business, its product, or its abilities. The elements for disparagement are:

1. a statement about a business' reputation, honesty, or integrity that is untrue

2. publication

3. a statement that is directed at a business and is made with malice and the intent to injure that business

4. damages

False Statements About Other Businesses. One way for a competitor to increase its business is to make statements about other businesses that would discourage customers. This type of statement is fair if it is true. But if it is false, it is disparagement. A statement that an auto parts store sells reconditioned parts when, in fact, it sells new parts, damages that store's honesty, integrity, and reputation. A statement that an accounting firm has been involved in several major securities frauds does the same. Any untrue statement that deals with the competence or quality of a business satisfies element #1 above.

Publication with Malice and Intent. For disparagement to occur, the statement must be communicated to a third party. Publication does not require a newspaper ad or radio spot. An accountant who addresses a group of lawyers at a luncheon meeting and untruthfully states that another firm has been involved in fraud has met the publication element. So has a supplier who notifies other suppliers that a certain business is bankrupt when it is not. Technically, the statement need only be made to one other person. The more persons involved, however, the easier it will be to establish damages.

Statement About a Particular Business. The general statement "All accountants are frauds" does not meet this element about disparagement. The defamatory statement must either be about a particular business, or be specific enough to include only a small group of businesses. For example, the statement "All the dress stores in Parkland Mall carry defective merchandise" is specific enough to meet this element. "All dress stores carry defective merchandise" is not.

Damages. The business that is defamed must be able to establish damages such as lost business, lost profits, lost advertising, or some economic effect resulting from the defamatory statements.

1. On the basis of your preview, without looking back at the passage, write a sentence or two telling what this passage is about. _____

    _____

    _____

2. List any words or phrases that you remember printed in italics or boldface. _____

    _____

    _____

3. Does the passage seem difficult? _____

4. Have you read anything like it? If so, what? _____

    _____

5. What do you know about torts? _____

    _____

6. List three things you expect to learn from reading this passage.

    a. _____

    b. _____

    c. _____

Now that you have finished your preview, the next step is to read carefully to try to understand and remember the information. Go back to the article, and, as you read, underline the important points.

After you have read the article carefully, you should be able to answer the following questions. Look back if you need to. Write your answer after each one.

1. What is a tort? _____

    _____

2. What are two differences between a tort and a crime?

    a. _____

    b. _____

3. List and define the three types of tort liability:

    a. _____

    b. _____

    c. _____

4. Explain the difference between property torts and personal torts. Give an example of each. _____

    _____

    _____

5. What is *defamation*? _____

6. What is the difference between *slander* and *libel*? _____

_____

7. What is *disparagement*? _____

8. List and explain the elements for disparagement:

   a. _____

   b. _____

   c. _____

   d. _____

Writing Exercise

Assume that you are a lawyer who is consulted by a hardware store owner. She believes that she has been the victim of an intentional tort as the result of a competitor's advertisement. Write a letter to her explaining the elements for disparagement. In addition, pose a series of questions you would like her to answer to decide if she has a case.

_____

_____

_____

_____

_____

_____

_____

_____

_____

_____

_____

_____

_____

_____

_____

Reviewing is the final step in a reading activity. Some people think it is the most important one. Think of it as an insurance policy. By reviewing, you can check your understanding and test your recall. Students who read an assignment, close the book, and walk away often forget half of what they have read. Some students who don't review admit they remember nothing at all about what they read. Psychologists have researched the benefit of review or recall activities. They have found significant differences in comprehension (understanding) and retention (how long the material is remembered). Students who review understand more and remember it longer than those who don't. There are many ways to review, and the technique you choose does not matter as much as the fact that you do it. Here are some ways to review (you may wish to add to the list):

- Reread your underlining and margin notes.

- Ask yourself questions about the material and answer them.

- Have someone test you by asking you for definitions or explanations.

- Take notes on the material.

- Outline the information.

- Write a summary of what you read.

- Explain what you read to someone else.

- Recite the important points aloud.

Choose one of these techniques or one of your own. Review the article on torts using the strategy you choose. Then ask a fellow student to test you on the information. Reverse roles, and test your classmate. Do the techniques seem to work? Does one seem better than the other?

Exercise 7

Scanning to Locate Information

Many authors choose to present information visually as well as verbally. Diagrams, charts, graphs, time lines, and maps are examples of graphic aids that are used to enhance text. Scanning is a strategy that is particularly appropriate for such material. In a way, scanning is a visual skill. Your eyes cruise the page, looking for specific information. Some details are easier to spot than others. For example, if you are looking for the name of a person or place, you search for words that begin with capital letters. Dates also stand out from the text of a page and can usually be located quickly because they differ visually from words. Glossaries and dictionaries list words alphabetically, so a reader can quickly scan only the appropriate section of the page.

The exercise that follows presents you with a graphic representation of the history of advertising in America. On the next page you will find information presented in a time-line fashion. In addition to the visual aspect of the presentation, the information is also arranged chronologically. Both of these features make your scanning task easier. As a thorough reader, you should preview the material to get an overall sense of the topic. As you answer the scanning questions, though, discipline yourself not to read every word and date. Rather, try to zero in on the information you are looking for.

11.2 The History of Advertising in America

1800

1837
Settlers are lured to Illinois by publications subsidized by land speculators.

1800 — Early printers like Benjamin Franklin produce promotional sheets to supplement their income.

1828 — Andrew Jackson's election to the presidency is attributed, in part, to his ability to manipulate the press.

1841 — Volney Palmer organizes the first ad agency in America.

1875 — N. W. Ayer & Son Agency begins offering ad counseling directly to advertisers.

1896 — McKinley-Bryan presidential race marks the beginning of modern political campaign methods.

1900

1929
The first Code of Ethics issued by the National Association of Broadcasters provides guidelines for the regulation of broadcast commercials.

1911 — Advertising professionals, led by industry trade paper *Printer's Ink*, begin a crusade to "clean up the industry" that spells the beginning of the end for patent-medicine vendors and other shady advertisers.

1922 — The first radio ad, for a real-estate development company, is aired in New York.

1950

1954 — For the first time, TV ad revenues top $500 million and exceed those of radio.

1957 — Vance Packard's controversial book *The Hidden Persuaders* documents excesses in the advertising industry.

1979 — Psychographics is the latest ad-industry methodology.

1980 — Ronald Reagan's election signals the deregulation of advertising thanks in part to a less aggressive Federal Trade Commission.

1973
Subliminal Seduction by Wilson Bryan Key alerts the public to the use of alleged hidden messages in advertising.

1984 — "Great Communicator" Reagan is reelected by one of the widest margins in history.

1988 — George Bush's successful presidential campaign is characterized by numerous "negative" 30-second TV spots.

1989 — Research indicates that for the first time, over half of all students enrolled in U.S. journalism and communications programs hope to find jobs in advertising and PR. Despite this, the number of news-oriented majors remains constant.

1991 — The recession is blamed for large advertising cutbacks.

1993 — With advertising revenues down, there are dire predictions of "the end of advertising." Insiders contend that reports of advertising's demise are greatly exaggerated.

From *Mediamerica, Mediaworld: Form, Content and Consequence of Mass Communications*, by Edward Jay Whetmore (Belmont, Calif.: Wadsworth, 1993), pp. 284–285.

Scan the time line for the answers to the following questions.

1. According to the time line, when did advertising in America begin? _____

2. In what year did the National Association of Broadcasters issue the first code of ethics? _____

_____

3. Who is the "Great Communicator"? _____

4. In the 1950s, how much money was spent on TV advertising? _____

5. What presidential race began modern political campaigning? _____

6. What is blamed for the cutbacks in advertising in the 1990s? _____

7. What was the name of the first ad agency? _____

8. In what year was there a campaign to "clean up the industry"? _____

9. What did the publication of *The Hidden Persuaders* do? _____

10. What characterized George Bush's presidential campaign? _____

_____

Most conscientious readers will use several strategies when dealing with a passage. For example, a reader may preview the material, underline important points, and scan to find the answers to questions as a review. In the passage that follows, you will be asked to use all of these skills. In addition to applying the strategies, you will also be applying the information presented to a particular case. Authors who provide examples of concepts and defined terms help their readers further their understanding and use the information. Readers who come up with their own examples take comprehension one step further and demonstrate that they have truly mastered the material.

The passage that follows explains the concept of *false imprisonment,* another type of *intentional tort.* Then the reader is presented with a case in which a customer charged a store with false imprisonment. Preview the material first. Then read it carefully and underline or highlight the important points. The judicial opinion is written in language that is more formal than what you usually read. There is also quite a bit of repetition as the judge explains his decision. When you underline or highlight, look for the important points and mark them only once. Scan to find the answers to the case questions, and complete the writing exercise.

Exercise 8

Applications

THE INTENTIONAL TORTS: FALSE IMPRISONMENT

This tort is often referred to as "the shopkeeper's tort" since it generally occurs because of a shoplifting accusation in a store. **False imprisonment**

Excerpt from *Business and the Legal Environment,* 2nd ed., by Marianne Moody Jennings (Boston: PWS-Kent, 1991), pp. 209–211.

is the detention of a person for any period of time (even a few minutes) against his or her will. No physical harm need result; the imprisoned party can collect minimal damages simply for being imprisoned without consent. Because shopkeepers need the opportunity to investigate matters when someone is suspected of shoplifting, the tort of false imprisonment does carry the defense of the **shopkeeper's privilege.** This privilege allows a shopkeeper to detain a suspected shoplifter for a reasonable period of time while the matter or incident is investigated. In most states, the shopkeeper must have a reasonable basis for keeping the person, that is, the shopkeeper must have reason to suspect the individual even if it turns out later that the individual has an explanation or did not do what the shopkeeper suspected. The following case deals with the issue of a shopkeeper's detention of a shopper for suspicion of shoplifting.

JOHNSON V. K-MART ENTERPRISES, INC.
297 N.W.2D 74 (WIS. 1980)

Facts. Deborah Johnson (plaintiff) went to a K-Mart (defendant) store in Madison, Wisconsin. She took her baby into the store with her; the baby was in a car seat she had purchased at K-Mart several weeks earlier. She bought some diapers and baby clothes. As she was leaving, she was stopped and confronted by the store's security guard, who asked her to come back into the store. A K-Mart employee had reported that Ms. Johnson had taken the infant seat. Ms. Johnson was kept for twenty minutes. After establishing her previous ownership by showing the K-Mart people the cat hair, stains, and food crumbs in the seat, the guard apologized and she was permitted to leave. Johnson filed suit for false imprisonment and her action was dismissed. Johnson appealed.

Judicial Opinion. (Dykman, Judge) "The essence of false imprisonment is the intentional, unlawful, and unconsented restraint by one person of the physical liberty of another." Whether plaintiff may recover depends in this case upon the unlawfulness of defendant's conduct. Section 943.50(3), Stats., makes defendant's action in restraining plaintiff lawful, if the elements of that statute are present.

The trial court identified 8 elements of sec. 943.50(3), Stats.:

1. A merchant or merchant's adult employee (who has)

2. Probable cause (for believing that a person has violated sec. 943.50, Stats.) may

3. Detain suspect in a reasonable manner,

4. For a reasonable length of time (to)

5. Deliver suspect to a peace officer

6. Detained persons must be promptly informed of the purpose for detention (and given permission)

7. To make telephone calls.

8. No interrogation or search of suspect against his will may be made before arrival of peace officer.

Plaintiff argues that her deposition shows that a factual issue exists because a reasonable jury could find that defendant had no probable cause to believe plaintiff shoplifted the infant seat.

Whether probable cause exists is a mixed question of law and fact. If material facts are in dispute, the facts are to be determined by a jury. The court will decide the question of probable cause from those facts. Where the facts are undisputed, the existence of probable cause is a question of law which is decided solely by the court.

Because defendant is a corporation, it must transact business through its officers and employees. Section 943.50(3), Stats., permits a merchant (here K-Mart) to detain a shopper if certain conditions are met, one of which is that the merchant have probable cause for believing that the shopper stole the merchant's goods. Plaintiff's deposition shows that defendant's security officer believed that plaintiff stole the infant seat because another K-Mart employee told him that she saw plaintiff steal it. There is no conflicting evidence on this point. The question is whether the employee who said she saw plaintiff steal the infant seat was fabricating her story. Our inquiry is whether there is an issue of material fact in dispute as to whether the K-Mart employee who detained the plaintiff had probable cause for believing that plaintiff stole the infant seat.

We find no material facts in dispute, nor reasonable alternative inferences to be drawn from the facts. The merchant received word, through one of its employees, that plaintiff removed an infant seat from the shelf, put her child in it, and left the store without paying for the seat. We hold as a matter of law that the merchant, through its security guard, had probable cause to believe that plaintiff had shoplifted.

Plaintiff argues that her deposition shows that the place of detention made the detention unreasonable, or at least would present an inference from which a jury could find that the manner of detention was unreasonable.

Few innocent people who are detained because they are suspected of shoplifting will feel that their detention was accomplished in a reasonable manner. Plaintiff's complaint is that the place she was detained was public. Yet, plaintiff's deposition shows that defendant's only actions were to stop plaintiff, ask her to return to the store, inform her that she was suspected of shoplifting, produce the witness who allegedly saw plaintiff steal the infant seat, apologize to plaintiff for the detention and release her. There is no suggestion in plaintiff's complaint or deposition that she asked to go to a more private place. Defendant's actions do not permit an inference that the detention was accomplished in an unreasonable manner.

In plaintiff's deposition, she testified that she was detained for 20 minutes. An inference could be drawn from the entire deposition that most of this time was spent in obtaining the presence of the K-Mart employee who said she saw plaintiff steal the infant seat. Plaintiff suggests that the employee was not produced more quickly because she was afraid of confronting the person she had falsely accused.

. . . In determining whether a 20-minute detention is reasonable as a matter of law, we must weigh the customer's important liberty interests against a merchant's need for protection against shoplifters. Such a balancing is evident in the language of the statute which gives merchants the power to detain suspected shoplifters while at the same time safeguarding the customer's rights. We hold that a merchant's interest in detaining suspected shoplifters is such that a 20-minute detention is reasonable.

Judgment affirmed.

1. What was Johnson accused of shoplifting? _____

2. Did K-Mart have probable cause to stop her? _____

3. Was the twenty-minute detention reasonable? Why? _____

_____

4. Does Johnson recover anything; that is, is she awarded any damages? Do you think she should? _____

_____

5. Think back to the unit on civil rights. Could Johnson argue that any of her civil rights had been violated? Would she be correct? _____

_____

Writing Exercise

Explain the tort of false imprisonment and give your own example of a situation where damages should be awarded.

_____

_____

_____

_____

_____

_____

_____

_____

_____

_____

_____

_____

_____

_____

_____

SKILL DEVELOPMENT: NOTE TAKING AND SUMMARIZING

To survive in college, students need to know how to take notes and how to summarize. The following sections will help you develop these skills.

NOTE TAKING

So much information is presented in each course that the student who does not know how to organize the information is overwhelmed. Students usually take notes during their professors' lectures; that is, they write down information they hear. Without their notes, the students would have no other record of the information. Students who try to write down everything the professor says usually become lost. It is impossible to listen, comprehend, and write as quickly as someone speaks. Some students bring tape recorders to class, so they can concentrate on listening to the lecture in class and then take notes from the tape. This method also allows the student to replay certain portions of the tape. Not all students have access to tape recorders or feel comfortable using them. Some professors don't allow them. Therefore, all college students need to master the art of taking notes.

Consider the similarity between underlining or highlighting text and taking notes from a lecture. In both cases, the reader or listener is trying to understand the material and select the most important points. Just like an author, a lecturer gives clues as to what is important. As a reader, you look for headings and words emphasized by bold or italicized type. As a note taker, you listen for the introduction of new topics and points that are emphasized by the speaker's tone of voice or gestures. Authors list points by numbers or key phrases such as *first of all, in addition, finally;* speakers do the same. The lecturer may also highlight important points by writing them on the board, projecting them on a screen, or providing them in a handout. In any case, you use the same thinking skills in deciding what lecture notes to write as you do in deciding what to underline.

After the lecture, though, your work is not done. If you were smart, you left plenty of space on your page of notes to fill in additional explanations or examples. Review your notes *before* you leave your classroom. With the lecture fresh in your mind, and perhaps the notes still on the board, this is the perfect time to clarify any words or phrases that are unclear. If you wait a day or so, you may be asking yourself, "I wonder what I meant by that." It is also a good idea to review your notes immediately before the next class meeting. If you have any questions, you can ask the professor for clarification at the beginning of class. It prepares you, too, for the professor's continuing discussion of the subject or shift to a new one.

You will also be taking notes on assigned readings in professional journals or in reserved library books. Many students make copies of assigned articles so they can take the information with them. One advantage of this method is that they can underline and make notes on the copy. In some cases, however, copying the article is not practical. Students must learn to identify the important information and write it in a meaningful way. In the exercises that follow, you will see some samples of students' notes and have the opportunity to practice taking your own notes.

Exercise 9

Margin Notes

Margin notes are particularly helpful when you are reviewing information you have already read and studied. They are not substitutes for underlining, but they are additional aids. It is helpful to know from your margin notes where you will find definitions and examples. You can also indicate important points by writing checkmarks, asterisks, or stars in the margin. In this exercise, you will read an article about a controversial television program's depiction of a truck crash. The article is printed with room for margin notes on the left or right. At the beginning, the notes are provided. For the remainder of the article, however, you will write your own margin notes, following the guidelines at the end of the article.

Scan the article first, paying attention to the vocabulary words printed in boldface. If you are not familiar with them, you may want to complete the vocabulary exercise that follows the article. Next, read the article, concentrating on the margin notes and how they are used. Finally, return to the article to write your own margin notes. Important points in the article are underlined to help you decide what to write your notes about.

WHERE NBC WENT WRONG

The network suffers a humiliating bout of confessions and soul-searching after admitting it rigged the crash-and-burn of a GM truck.

(1)

But for a puff of smoke, it all might have turned out differently. Last week General Motors Corp. might still have been **reeling** from a $102.2 million jury verdict, awarded to an Atlanta couple whose son died when his GM truck exploded in a collision. NBC News might have been **touting** itself for having exposed the danger of GM's controversial "sidesaddle" gas tanks in a **riveting** *Dateline NBC* segment. Instead the network **singed** its reputation, and the car company won in the court of public opinion the safety battle it had lost in the courthouse.

GM was sued because of sidesaddle gas tanks

By William A. Henry III, *Time*, February 22, 1993, p. 59.

(2)

Dateline's report on Nov. 17 featured 14 minutes of balanced debate, capped by 57 seconds of crash footage that explosively showed how the gas tanks of certain old GM trucks could catch fire in a sideways collision. Following a tip, GM hired detectives, searched 22 junkyards for 18 hours, and found evidence to **debunk** almost every aspect of the crash sequence. Last week, in a devastating press conference, GM showed that the **conflagration** was rigged, its causes **misattributed**, its severity overstated and other facts distorted. Two crucial errors: NBC said the truck's gas tank had **ruptured**, yet an X-ray showed it hadn't; NBC consultants set off explosive miniature rockets beneath the truck split seconds before the crash—yet no one told the viewers.

NBC rigged crash & fire

(3)

There was plenty of sarcastic **speculation** about what happened between Monday afternoon, when NBC was defiantly dismissing GM's charges, and Tuesday morning, when it drafted an **abject** apology largely on GM's terms. NBC News president Michael Gartner says he simply realized he had goofed by speaking first and asking questions later. "The more I learned, the worse it got. Ultimately I was troubled by almost every aspect of the crash. I knew we had to apologize. We put 225,000 minutes of news on the air last year, and I didn't want to be defined by those 57 seconds." Gartner also faced nonjournalistic pressures. GM's top management had sent word it would sue via the top management of NBC's parent company, General Electric, a big GM supplier.

(4)

Dateline co-anchor Jane Pauley, who shared the awkward duty of apologizing on air, told the staff in a pep talk the next day that she took "perverse pride" in the readiness to admit failings. But most journalists and, for that matter, most news consumers seemed to agree with former NBC News president Reuven Frank, who said, "this is the worst black eye NBC News has suffered in my experience, which goes back to 1950."

(5)

How could NBC go so far wrong? One veteran correspondent was not surprised. "The whole atmosphere" has been so competitive and overeager, he said, that the network was "an accident waiting to happen." More details may emerge from NBC's investigation, but it is already clear that employees fell into some familiar traps:

(6)

1. CHOOSE A SEXY TOPIC AND SELL IT SEXILY. Video newsmagazines are **proliferating** because they are cheaper, and thus more profitable, than comedy or drama. But to beat the **tabloid** "news" and talk shows, network magazines increasingly concentrate on crime, celebrities and scandals—and on graphic visual imagery. Gartner says NBC would have had a perfectly sound, valid and sensible 14-minute story about the controversy

without the crash. But the producers felt the story would be **stronger** with one.

(7)

2. PICTURES ARE EVERYTHING. The firm that NBC hired staged just two crashes. GM trucks do not, of course, explode in half of all sideways collisions, or there wouldn't be many left on the road. So the consultants helped things along. As GM later demonstrated, the truck that did burn—apparently because it had an ill-fitting gas-tank cap, made for a different truck—ignited only for about 15 seconds. But <u>to ensure that its images were graphic,</u> NBC used tightly edited shots in which the <u>flames looked much worse.</u>

(8)

3. TRUST THE EXPERTS. NBC's testers insisted that the rockets wouldn't matter unless fuel was spilled, and that on the actual day the explosion was sparked by a broken headlamp anyway. The producers were so taken with this reason that they forgot the basic question, Is it fair? The essential contract is not with any source or expert, but with the reader or <u>viewer</u>, who is **entitled** to the facts <u>to judge for himself</u>.

(9)

4. CIRCLE THE WAGONS. <u>Journalists</u> are so often **assailed** by news subjects protesting stories that are fair and true—but inconvenient—that they <u>tend to dismiss all complaints</u>. It was ill-advised of the story's producers to answer GM without consulting GM's legal department or journalistic superiors. It was loyal but just as unwise for Gartner to reaffirm the story later without checking. Even the ablest journalist sometimes gets things wrong.

(10)

What will this episode mean for NBC News? Theories last week ranged from short-term embarrassment all the way up to demise. The most <u>probable result</u> is that all TV-news shows will look for <u>more about celebrities, crime and vastly less complex scandals</u>. The safety of GM trucks is exactly the kind of issue that popular news programs should address. But instead of making sure they do it right, **skittish** producers and executives will probably be inclined for a while not to do it at all. —**With reporting by Joseph R. Szczesny/Detroit.**

The following underlined words appeared in the article "Where NBC Went Wrong." In this exercise, they are presented in different sentences to provide additional context. After each sentence, write your own definition for the underlined word.

1. After the hurricane hit the Florida coast, residents were <u>reeling</u> from its effects for months. _____

2. Having won the division championship two years in a row, the soccer coach is <u>touting</u> her players as being the best in the state. _____

3. The <u>riveting</u> special effects of films like *Jurassic Park, Terminator,* and *Jaws* partially account for their popularity. _____

4. The camper's fingers were <u>singed</u> as he tried to remove the fork he had dropped into the campfire. _____

_____

5. The intellectual superiority of men, a popular notion in the sixteenth century, is a myth that feminists tried to <u>debunk</u> in the twentieth century. _____

6. Many of David Koresh's followers were burned to death in the <u>conflagration</u> at their compound in Waco, Texas. _____

7. During the trial, the defendant claimed that his brother's illegal behavior had been <u>misattributed</u> to him.

_____

8. Ten minutes after arriving at the hospital, the patient's appendix <u>ruptured</u> and emergency surgery began.

_____

9. <u>Speculation</u> about the identity of the instructor grew, as the students waited for the first class meeting to begin. _____

10. After living in <u>abject</u> poverty for most of her childhood, Anita, as a successful businesswoman, enjoyed providing her children with luxuries as well as necessities. _____

_____

11. Since the introduction of cable television, the number of available programs has <u>proliferated</u> each year.

_____

12. <u>Tabloid</u> newspapers tend to sensationalize their stories by featuring graphic photos and dramatic headlines. _____

13. Recipients of social security checks feel <u>entitled</u> to the money since they contributed to the system during their working years. _____

14. Furious about the change in work schedules, the employees <u>assailed</u> the boss as she tried to explain her reasons. _____

15. Charles has been <u>skittish</u> around dogs since a violent experience, but now he is trying to overcome his fear. _____

The important points in each paragraph of the article have already been underlined for you. The following instructions provide additional suggestions for writing margin notes. The first two paragraphs already have margin notes, but the guidelines for those notes are printed here as well.

1. In the margin next to the first paragraph, write specific information about what happened to GM.

2. Next to paragraph 2, write down what NBC did.

3. For paragraph 3, explain what NBC was finally forced to do.

4. Write down what producers do to attract viewers (paragraph 6).

5. Describe a technique that NBC used in its program (paragraph 7).

6. Write down what the author recommends to producers (paragraph 8).

7. Write down *either* what journalists typically do *or* what they should do (paragraph 9).

8. Write down the probable result of this incident (paragraph 10).

Writing Exercise

Tell how you would have produced the *Dateline* story about the GM truck gas tanks to inform the viewers, keep their attention, and avoid questionable or illegal journalistic tactics.

_____

_____

_____

_____

_____

_____

_____

_____

_____

_____

_____

_____

_____

SUMMARIZING

College students are frequently asked to summarize. Not all of these requests are academic. Friends may ask for an account of a movie or a television show. Classmates may ask what happened in a class they missed. These people are not asking for a complete description of the event. They don't want to hear the dialogue, word for word, or every detail of the class session. They want a summary that includes the most important points and leaves out the others. Professors will ask you to summarize a chapter assigned for homework. You may be required to write a summary of a journal article. Essay questions are actually asking for a summary of ideas, concepts, or events. A summary is a culminating or final activity. It comes after you have used your reading strategies to understand the material. Before you summarize, you should do the following:

- Preview the passage.

- Ask questions to guide your reading.

- Read carefully to understand the main points.

- Underline or highlight important details.

- Review the material by answering questions or performing other recall activities.

As you've already learned, summarizing is one of the review or recall activities that will aid your comprehension and help you remember what you have read. You may also find a discussion of the material with a fellow reader an excellent way to prepare to write a summary. When you are ready to begin your summary, follow these steps:

1. Write out the main idea.

2. Check off the underlined points you think you should include in your summary.

3. Write sentences *in your own words* that include one or two points in the order they were mentioned

4. Review your sentences to see if one logically follows another.

5. Write transition sentences to connect the thoughts if necessary.

6. Write your sentences in paragraph form.

7. Read the whole summary to make sure it flows smoothly and includes all important points.

Exercise 10

Steps in Summarizing

In the following article, the important points have already been underlined. After your reading, you will see samples of the first few steps in writing a summary, and you will be asked to finish writing the summary. You will practice writing summaries after other reading selections as well.

CONSUMERS FINALLY RESPOND TO HIGH CREDIT CARD INTEREST

After a decade of self-deception, Americans have finally begun to face the truth about how much interest they actually pay on their credit cards. And now, for the first time, many consumers are shopping for a card that

By Saul Hansell, *The New York Times*, March 29, 1993, pp. 1, D7. ©1993 by The New York Times Company. Reprinted by permission.

will charge them a lower rate. For years, many consumers were drawn to Mastercards and Visa cards issued by banks, mainly on the basis of which one offered the highest credit limit. Studies show that the vast majority of card holders simply pretend to themselves that they did not pay any interest, when two-thirds of them did. Thus they were undisturbed by interest rates that stubbornly remained around 19% even as other rates fell sharply.

"MORE HONEST WITH THEMSELVES"

"People used to say to themselves, 'I may pay interest once in a while, but that's not really me because I'm going to pay it all off next month,'" said Ruvan N. Cohen, director of card marketing at Citibank, the nation's largest bank and largest issuer of credit cards. "In the last year, people began to be more honest with themselves. They admit they pay interest and have started to read the rate disclosure boxes. We have to respond to that."

And now the slide in credit card rates shows no sign of stopping. Citibank will announce today that it is lowering rates to 15.4% from 19.8% on nine million cards—including "affinity cards" linked to merchants, like the widely held cards that offer frequent-flier miles from American Airlines.

Last year Citibank lowered the rate for another nine million regular and gold cards for customers with good credit records. After today's rate cut, 70% of Citibank's 27 million cards will have rates below 19.8 percent, the industry standard since 1981.

LOW RATES TO NEW CUSTOMERS

And for the first time, Citibank will offer the low rates to new customers. Last week, it mailed 30 million solicitations offering a 9.9% rate to customers who transfer their debts from another bank.

The Northwest Corporation noticed in the middle of last year that many customers who were heavy borrowers were transferring balances to lower rate cards. "It became clear that our customers had fundamentally changed," said Brian O'Hare, the head of credit cards for the Minneapolis based bank. Northwest dropped its rate for most customers from 19.8% to 15% last summer."

This change in psychology is largely because the economic downturn has forced many consumers to look more closely at their finances. "The recession has had a profound impact on people's idea of value," said Mr. O'Hare of Northwest. "People are choosing to spend less and save more."

Another factor was simply the publicity given to interest rates. In 1986, Congress voted to phase out the deductibility of consumer interest, and in 1991 the Senate passed a bill introduced by Senator Alphonse D'Amato, Republican of New York, to cap interest rates for credit cards.

"Here were 30-second sound bites right from the halls of Congress, and lo and behold, 80% of the people know what their A.P.R. is," said Thomas Lynch, head of credit cards at Chase Manhattan Bank, referring to annual percentage rate.

Immediately after Senator D'Amato introduced his bill, in fact, calls began to pick up at Bank Card Holders of America, a group that sells lists of credit cards with low rates. Last year the group sold 2500 of the lists a week for $4, double the rate of the year before. "With rates for home mortgages and car loans dropping to 20-year lows, consumers were beginning to ask why they were paying almost 20% for a credit card," Gerri E. Detweiler, the group's director said.

Just two years ago, 70% of the money owed on credit cards—nearly $200 billion—was at rates higher than 18%. Last year that portion fell to 44%, according to a new study conducted for the Congressional Budget Office by Ram Research. At the same time, the portion of credit card debt with rates of 16.5% or less increased to 38% from 7%.

VARIABLE RATES

Most banks have quietly shifted to variable rates—usually about 9 percentage points above the prime rate—so this savings may not last when the prime, now 6%, rises. Even though that rate is still far higher than the best deals available on credit cards, last year the lower variable rates saved consumers more than $2 billion on the more than $30 billion paid annually for credit card interest payments.

But while the banks are responding, they are not doing so cheerfully. When consumers did not shop for interest rates, the profit margins on credit cards were as high as 4% of the amount lent, far higher than those on other bank products. In 1990, banks earned more than $4 billion from credit card lending, one-quarter of the profits of the entire banking system. Some of the largest banks might not have survived their losses from bad real estate loans if they had not been buoyed by earnings from cards.

Now losses from bad credit card debt have risen just as annual fees and interest rates have come down. As a result, credit card earnings fell to 2.5% of assets in 1990 and to 1.5% of assets today, according to Salomon Brothers.

Banks, of course, can still demand higher rates on credit cards than on other types of consumer loans, because consumers are willing to pay for the greater convenience that cards offer. Nonetheless, with industrial companies like AT&T and General Motors sponsoring very successful new card programs—and offering discounts on everything from phone calls to new cars—many banks are finding that their best defense is to cut rates.

DISCOUNTS PRODUCE NEW GROWTH

"Consumer sensitivity to interest rates was virtually nonexistent," said Donald J. Auriemma, a credit card consultant. "They didn't know their annual percentage rate and they didn't care."

What consumers focused on was whether their cards had high credit lines, and then opted for those that had no annual fee, even when paying $20 a year up front could save hundreds of dollars a year in interest.

But it was only last year, that offers of cards with lower rates started to attract more customers than no-fee cards, Mr. Auriemma said.

Amid the increased scrutiny from consumers, banks have tried to appear as if they are offering lower rates than they really are. Some banks, including Citibank, offer the new lower rate only on purchases made after a cut is announced. Existing balances are billed at the higher rate.

Others, like Discover and American Express' Optima card, give the best rate only to customers who charge more than a certain amount in a year.

Now, let's review the steps in writing a summary that were given earlier. This time, plug in information from the article on credit cards. The first three steps have been partially completed.

1. Write out the main idea.

   As a result of lower interest rates in general and consumer demand, banks have been forced to drastically lower the interest rates on credit card balances.

2. Check off the underlined points you think should be included in a summary. (The underlined version should guide you, and you should check off most of the underlined points.)

3. Write out sentences. The first four are done for you. Write at least three more.

   • For years, Americans have pretended that they pay little or no interest on credit card purchases, when they actually pay around 19 percent interest.

   • Now credit card rates are dropping dramatically.

   • Rates have been cut to as low as 9.9 percent for new customers, while current customers and transferring customers are also being offered lower rates.

   • One reason consumers are paying attention to the rates is that the economic downturn has forced them to economize.

   • Another reason _____

   _____

   • _____

   _____

   • _____

   _____

4. Review all the sentences to see if they are clear, logical, and include the important points.

5. Write transition sentences if you need them.

6. Write your summary below. Copy your sentences in paragraph form.

   _____

   _____

   _____

   _____

   _____

7. Read the whole summary to make sure it flows smoothly and includes all important points.

SKILL DEVELOPMENT: IDENTIFYING ORGANIZATIONAL PATTERNS

In the first three sections of the book, you learned to identify four different organizational patterns authors use in their writing: definition/example, list, process description, and chronological. In this section, you will learn about the last two organizational patterns: comparison/contrast and cause/effect. After two practice exercises on each of the new patterns, you will practice identifying all of the organizational patterns you have learned throughout the text.

Textbook authors often use a *comparison/contrast writing pattern* to point out the similarities and differences between two situations, recommendations, plans, terms, or procedures. Authors who deal *only* with similarities use a comparison pattern; those who include *only* differences use a contrast pattern. If the two topics share many similarities, the author may choose to compare them in the first paragraph. In this case, he or she will probably use some of the following words: *like, similarly, also, in addition.* Sometimes the author will contrast two things within the same paragraph. Key words such as *on the other hand, however, whereas, in contrast* indicate that he or she is shifting from one thing to the other. If the author is engaging in an extensive description, he or she may deal with similarities and differences throughout the passage, using a comparison/contrast pattern. In such cases, the reader's job is to identify and group the similarities and differences. As you read the sample paragraph, consider the authors' purpose, and try to decide whether their emphasis is on the similarities or the differences between centralization and decentralization.

Exercise 11

Identifying the Comparison/Contrast Pattern

CENTRALIZATION VERSUS DECENTRALIZATION

The terms **centralization** and **decentralization** refer to *a philosophy of organization and management that focuses on either the selective concentration* (centralization) *or the dispersal* (decentralization) *of authority within an organization structure.* The question of where authority resides is resolved in an operating philosophy of management—either to concentrate authority for decision making in the hands of one or a few, or to force it down the organization structure into the hands of many.

Centralization and decentralization are relative concepts when applied to organizations. Top-level management may decide to centralize all decision making: purchasing, staffing, operations. Or it may decide to set limits on what can be purchased at each level by dollar amounts; decentralize the hiring decisions to first-level management for clerical workers

Excerpt from *Introduction to Business,* 4th ed. by Joseph T. Straub and Raymond F. Attner (Boston: PWS-Kent, 1991), p. 115.

(retaining authority for managerial decisions); and let operational decisions be made where appropriate.

More and more organizations have seen decentralization as a means to greater productivity and rebuilding the organization. Decentralization is a way for managers to be closer to the action. Major corporations such as Mattell, General Foods, and Intercraft Industries Corporation are moving to a more decentralized philosophy of management.

Notice first that the title gives you a clue that the authors plan to contrast two terms. The terms are included in the title, and they are separated by the word *versus,* an indication that differences will be emphasized. You have probably seen and heard this word in other contexts. Court cases, boxing matches, and other sporting events use *v.* or *vs.,* abbreviated forms, to indicate the opponents, competitors, or rivals. The word *versus* means "against," or "in contrast to."

You should next realize that the first paragraph follows the definition pattern that you learned about in the first section of this book. In fact, there are also examples in this passage, as you have come to expect from the definition/example pattern. The emphasis, however, is on the *differences* between the two philosophies of organization. Indeed, you will find many examples in your reading where authors choose to mix or combine organizational patterns to cover a topic or to get several points across. As a reader, it is useful to determine the author's dominant pattern; this will give a good indication of his or her main point.

In this passage, your job is to understand the contrast. That is, you need to figure out the differences between *centralization* and *decentralization.* In the definition found in the first paragraph, <u>underline</u> the words that tell what these two terms have in common. Then *circle* the words that indicate their differences. Write the words below:

SIMILARITIES	DIFFERENCES
1. _____	1. _____
2. _____	2. _____
3. _____	3. _____

Words that indicate similarities would include *philosophy, organization,* and *management.* Terms that indicate differences would include *concentration* versus *dispersal, one* or *a few* versus *many.*

To grasp the concepts of centralization and decentralization, look for the examples the authors provide and then think of some of your own. In the second paragraph, notice that the authors apply the type of management to purchasing, staffing, and operations. Think of a work situation in which you or someone you know was involved in, or affected by, a business decision. Perhaps a business purchase or a change in staff schedules occurred. Describe how the decision was made and who made it. Then decide whether this decision reflects a centralized or decentralized philosophy of management. Share your example with your classmates, and see if they agree with your interpretation.

Your Example:

_____

_____

_____

_____

In the last paragraph, the authors consider the advantages of one of the two philosophies. This is a very common approach in comparison/contrast writing. After two things are compared and contrasted, it is logical to try to decide which is better. Advantages and disadvantages may be listed or described for each approach. Sometimes it isn't possible to come to a conclusion about which way is better. It may depend on the situation. In our sample passage, however, the authors give us a clear indication of which philosophy they favor. Determine which approach the authors favor and list their reasons for preferring it.

Preferred Philosophy:

_____

_____

_____

_____

Explain the difference between centralization and decentralization as philosophies of organization and management. Tell which approach you prefer and why.

Writing Exercise

_____

_____

_____

_____

_____

Exercise 12

Identifying the Cause/Effect Writing Pattern

The *cause/effect writing pattern* is often used to explain why things happen or to anticipate results or consequences. It may be found in scientific journal articles that describe the results of an experiment. Historians may explore the causes of a war. Economic analysts may predict the consequences of inflation. Some of the key words found in cause/effect passages include *because, as a result of, consequently.* It is the reader's job to identify and to understand the relationship the author is describing. Readers should be able to see why or how events or actions produced results or consequences. For example, a professor may have an attendance policy that results in a student's withdrawal from the course after five absences. If a student misses five classes, he or she can expect to be withdrawn from the class. We can assume the cause of the action is a combination of student behavior and instructor policy. The result, of course, is withdrawal from the course. In your reading, you will find that the author may not state the cause and effect as clearly as in this simple example. In such cases, the reader must identify the cause and the effect and determine how one influences the other. As you consider the following example, try to determine the result of the marketing campaign and why it was or wasn't successful.

CONSUMER BEHAVIOR AND MARKETING ACTION

Consumer *benefits, perceptions,* and *attitudes* influence development of successful marketing strategies. Kellogg Company was successful in introducing new adult cereals because it recognized that young adults sought the *benefits* of more nutritional breakfast foods. Based on research, it determined that young adults had a *perception* of cereals as kid stuff. Kellogg recognized that if it wanted to increase sales of adult cereals, it would have to change these perceptions to develop more positive *attitudes* toward adult cereals. As a result of this knowledge of the consumer, Kellogg developed different cereals aimed at health-conscious young adults. It introduced All-Bran, a high-fiber cereal, and Common Sense, containing oat bran. It even introduced fat-free Special K waffles as an extension of its Special K cereals targeted to dieters.

But the company may have gone too far in trying to capture the adult segment. Some of its health claims have been questioned by the Food and Drug Administration. For example, the FDA forced Kellogg to withdraw its claim that Heartwise cereal helps reduce cholesterol. In 1991, the company changed the name of Heartwise to Fiberwise to avoid any connotation that the cereal fights heart disease.

The title gives you some clues as to what the passage will be about. From the phrase *consumer behavior,* you can tell it will deal with what people buy. The term *marketing action* indicates that it will also include

Excerpt from *Consumer Behavior and Marketing Action,* 4th ed., by Henry Assael (Boston: PWS-Kent, 1992), p. 2.

information about trying to sell something. The title does not clearly indicate that the passage will be organized in a cause/effect pattern. However, your experience with the relationship between buying and selling may help you predict the organization. In any case, you should plan to look for the relationship between consumer behavior and marketing action. In other words, how do sellers try to persuade consumers to buy their products?

1. On the basis of the information found in the first paragraph, tell what effect or result Kellogg hoped to achieve: _____
   _____
   _____

2. As a marketing goal, Kellogg wanted to sell cereal to adults. An increase in cereal sales was the company's desired effect. Was Kellogg successful in reaching this goal? _____
   _____
   _____

Although the passage does not include support or examples, it does say that the company was successful. As you try to figure out the cause of this success, you will notice that it includes several factors. The author tells you that Kellogg took the following actions to effect this result:

1. Recognized that young adults wanted nutritional benefits from breakfast food

2. Researched the perception of cereal as kid stuff

3. Introduced new cereals aimed at the adult market

4. Developed more positive attitudes toward adult cereals through marketing

You may wish to sum up this first paragraph with a main idea sentence that includes the cause and effect. For example:

> The Kellogg company successfully introduced adult cereals through a marketing campaign that emphasized their nutritional value.

The second paragraph begins with the word *but,* an indication that different or contrasting information may follow. In contrast to the first paragraph that describes the company's success, the second describes the difficulties resulting from the marketing campaign. In this paragraph, too, we see another example of cause/effect.

3. To determine the result or effect, tell what Kellogg did. _____
   _____

You may have included one or two actions.

1. Kellogg withdrew its claim that Heartwise cereal helps reduce cholesterol.

2. It also changed the name of the cereal from Heartwise to Fiberwise.

4. To determine the cause or reason for these actions, ask yourself why the company did these things. Write the cause here. _____

_____

From the passage, we know that the first effect or action (withdrawing the reduced cholesterol claim) was required. The reason Kellogg withdrew its claim is that the FDA forced it to do so. The reason for the second action is not quite so clear. It appears that the company changed the cereal name voluntarily. We can infer that pressure from the FDA or public perception of dishonesty persuaded the company to do so.

Writing Exercise

Describe how a marketing campaign can persuade consumers to buy a product. Use your own example to illustrate how an advertising campaign can affect consumers' attitudes and behavior.

_____

_____

_____

_____

_____

_____

_____

_____

_____

_____

_____

_____

_____

_____

Read each of the following paragraphs and identify the type of organzation the author has used. Tell why you believe you have identified them correctly. Use the following identification labels:

A. Definition/example

B. List

C. Chronological or sequential

D. Comparison/contrast

E. Cause/effect

F. Process description

1. Who Is Responsible for Business Crime?

One of the major differences between nonbusiness and business crime is that more people can be convicted for business crimes. For nonbusiness crimes, only those actually involved can be convicted. For business crimes, on the other hand, those in the management of firms in which employees commit criminal acts can be held liable if they authorized the conduct, knew about the conduct but did nothing, or failed to act reasonably in their supervisory positions. (*Business and the Legal Environment,* 2nd ed., by Marianne Moody Jennings [Boston: PWS-Kent, 1991], p. 186.)

a. Pattern: _____

b. Key words: _____

c. Explanation: _____

_____

2. Arbitration

Arbitration is the mediation of disputes, which gives the parties a faster and less expensive method for settling disputes. Many contracts have mandatory arbitration clauses in them that require the parties to a contract, in the event of a dispute, to submit to arbitration.

   Using an arbitrator to resolve a dispute has an obvious advantage over seeking judicial resolution: An arbitrator is used in a particular dispute because of his or her expertise in the subject matter of the contract. In the case of construction disputes, for example, the American Arbitration Association can provide experts in everything from acoustics to tunnels. In short, arbitrators bring expertise to a dispute. (*Business and the Legal Environment,* 2nd ed., by Marianne Moody Jennings [Boston: PWS-Kent, 1991], p. 65.)

a. Pattern: _____

b. Key words: _____

c. Explanation: _____

_____

3. Historical Antecedents of Consumerism

The consumer movement is not new. The first recorded consumer protest occurred in 1775 when a Massachusetts law sentenced people who sold tainted food to the pillory. The real consumer movement started at the turn of the century, and there have been three distinct periods since then in which consumer protection has become a national issue. Each of these periods was marked by rising consumer prices coupled with muckraking exposes resulting in consumer protection legislation. After these three periods, which lasted until the late 1970's, the 1980's saw a decline in the emphasis on consumerism as a result of deregulation of business activities in the Reagan era. The 1990's are seeing a rebirth of consumerism, particularly as it relates to environmental concerns, health and nutritional claims, and protection of children. (*Consumer Behavior and Marketing Action*, 4th ed., by Henry Assael [Boston: PWS-Kent, 1992], p. 679.)

a. Pattern: _____

b. Key words: _____

c. Explanation: _____

_____

4. Indirect Compensation: Employee Fringe Benefits

In addition to direct compensation for the job being performed, human resources managers build into the work environment **fringe benefits**—*nonfinancial rewards provided for employees.* Most of them fall into one of the following categories:

• Life, health, and dental insurance

• Paid vacations

• Sick pay

• Holidays, funeral leave, and emergency leave

• Discounts on merchandise or services

• Paid lunches and rest periods

• Tuition reimbursement

• Child care

Indirect benefits typically have averaged between 22 and 35 percent of a company's payroll. (*Introduction to Business*, 4th ed., by Joseph T. Straub and Raymond F. Attner [Boston: PWS-Kent, 1991], p. 158.)

a. Pattern: _____

b. Key words: _____

c. Explanation: _____

_____

5. Motor Vehicle Insurance

Bodily injury liability, *sometimes called PIP (personal injury protection) is motor vehicle insurance that pays court-awarded damages for bodily injury, up to the face value of the policy, if the insured person is judged liable* *for a motor vehicle accident.* If you are held responsible for an accident that permanently handicaps another, that person is sure to sue you. If you lose, and the court judgment against you exceeds the face value of your insurance policy, you may have to pay the injured person a regular sum of money for the rest of your life. Because bodily injury liability suits often result in multimillion-dollar settlements today, businesses and individuals alike should be well insured against this risk. (*Introduction to Business,* 4th ed., by Joseph T. Straub and Raymond F. Attner [Boston: PWS-Kent, 1991], p. 458.)

a. Pattern: _____

b. Key words: _____

c. Explanation: _____

_____

6. Consumer Information Processing

Consumer information processing involves a search for and organization of information from various sources. Information processing is selective; consumers choose information that is (1) most relevant to the benefits they seek and (2) likely to conform to their beliefs and attitudes. Processing of information involves a series of steps—exposure, attention, comprehension, retention in memory, and search for additional information (*Consumer Behavior and Marketing Action,* 4th ed., by Henry Assael [Boston: PWS-Kent, 1992], p. 61)

a. Pattern: _____

b. Key words: _____

c. Explanation: _____

_____

Students of economics and business need a basic understanding of the role money plays in our economic system. Although most people handle money and understand its value and function, the national and international economic picture remains confusing. The selection that follows provides some basic information about how money works in our economic system and defines terms you may have heard in business and economic reports. As with previous reading selections, guide questions are interspersed with the text to help increase your comprehension.

> **Money** is *any object that a group of people uses to pay its debts and buy the goods and services that it needs.* In addition to money, however, an advanced economic system needs financial institutions that regulate demand for that money and make it possible for organizations and individuals to save, borrow, and transfer money as they carry out daily

Selection 1

Putting Money in Perspective

Read the first section to learn what money is and what it does.

Excerpts from *Introduction to Business,* 4th ed., by Joseph T. Straub and Raymond F. Attner (Boston: PWS-Kent, 1991), pp. 361–367.

transactions. We will examine money and the various institutions, such as commercial banks, the Federal Reserve Bank, the Federal Deposit Insurance Corporation, and the major thrift institutions, that affect its flow within our economy.

WHAT MONEY DOES

A society's money functions as a medium of exchange, a measure of value, and a store of value. To do so it must be relatively scarce and widely accepted. Objects that are used as money also must be durable, portable, and divisible if they are to serve people conveniently over a long period of time. Money must not wear out, it must be easy to carry, and you must be able to divide it up to use it.

A Medium of Exchange. Money makes it easier for us to accomplish the exchange functions of marketing—buying and selling. Although we sometimes think of money only as the bills and coins we carry in our wallets and pockets, certain societies and cultures have used some of the following objects as currency:

Bison robes

Bird-of-paradise feathers

Bricks of tea

Woodpecker scalps

Manga bird feathers

Elephant-tail hair

A Measure of Value. A society's money is a universal measure of wealth. The value of everything from livestock to common stock can be expressed in a common denominator: money. This makes communication easier, because the parties to a transaction can express worth in the same units. If one U.S. resident says to another that a product or service is worth $20, both of them know what that figure represents.

A Store of Value. We can <u>convert</u> our labor and any products we own into money of a certain value and store it in that form indefinitely. People regularly store their value in such other objects as real estate, precious metals, gems, and rare coins, but these are not as *liquid* (easily disposed of) as money. If you have stored your value in nonmonetary objects and want to purchase something like a stereo, you will have to convert those valued objects into money. This process can be costly and time-consuming; you may need to have the items <u>appraised</u> to establish their value, and then find a buyer. Money is the most liquid asset of all—easily transferred from hand to hand.

It should be obvious, of course, that money must have a relatively stable value before people will be willing to store very much of their wealth in it. When the value of money declines, people rush to convert it to something whose value will hold steady or increase as time passes.

Answer the following questions based on your reading and on your experience.

1. What is money? _____

_____

2. What is the meaning of the word *convert* as it is used in the passage? _____

_____

3. What is the meaning of the word *appraised* as it is used in the passage? _____

_____

4. Give an example of a recent transaction in which you gave or received money. _____

_____

5. Give an example of a situation in which you, or someone you know, were paid with something other than

money. _____

_____

6. According to the article, money "does" three things. List them:

a. _____

b. _____

c. _____

7. Identify each of the following transactions as one of the three functions of money.

a. A bulletin-board notice says an algebra tutor is available for $15 per hour. _____

_____

b. Your cousin agrees to pay you $50 to use your car for one week. _____

_____

c. Your parents have purchased a savings bond for you as a graduation gift. _____

_____

d. Before leaving for a two-year assignment in China, the scientist bought a fifteen-unit apartment building.

_____

e. The cashier received her biggest paycheck ever due to all the overtime she had worked. _____

_____

f. Sandra checked the blue book listing for her Mustang before she decided on a sales price. _____

_____

MONEY IN THE UNITED STATES

The money supply of the United States consists of three items: coins and paper (collectively called *currency*) and checking accounts. Federal law has declared coins and paper money to be <u>legal tender</u>, which means they must be accepted as payments for debts.

Now read the next section to learn about money in our country.

Paper money takes three days to print—one day for the front, one day for the back, and one for the overprinting of such data as the serial number and the seal of the Federal Reserve Bank that will issue it. The Bureau of Engraving and Printing produces approximately 1.6 billion $1 bills each year.

The mechanics of printing and replacing paper money pose problems. Constant passing from hand to hand wears out $1 bills in eighteen months. Larger <u>denominations</u> last slightly longer. Commercial banks return worn, damaged, and dirty bills to the Federal Reserve Bank in their district, where the Treasury Department exchanges the bills for new ones and destroys them. Damaged coins are melted down and recycled by the U.S. Assay Office.

A **check** *or* **demand deposit**, the third component of the United States money supply, is *a bank depositor's written order instructing the bank to pay a certain sum to a third party.* The bank, which owes the deposited money to the customer, provides this third-party payment, usually for a fee or service charge. Although they are not legal tender, 90 percent of all money spent is in the form of checks. Three of every four persons in America have a checking account.

A **savings account** *or* **time deposit** is *a sum of money, deposited with a bank, that cannot be withdrawn by writing a check.* Because the bank may require advance notice before withdrawal, time deposits are not considered part of the money supply.

Answer the following questions on the basis of your reading.

8. What items does the U.S. money supply include? _____

_____

9. What is *legal tender*? _____

10. What does the word *denominations* mean as it is used in the passage? _____

_____

11. What did you learn about printing and replacing money? _____

_____

_____

12. Explain the differences between a checking account and a savings account. _____

_____

_____

Read the following section to find out about banks.

COMMERCIAL BANKS

What Do Banks Do? A **commercial bank** is *a profit-making corporation that accepts customers' deposits and lends them out to businesses and individual borrowers.* These banks accept both demand deposits (checking accounts) and time deposits (savings accounts), paying interest on the second type of account. Since December 31, 1980, both banks and savings and loan associations have been permitted to offer customers interest-bearing checking accounts called *NOW* accounts (for "negotiable order of withdrawal").

Commercial banks earn most of their income from interest on loans, but they also invest large amounts in interest-bearing United States government securities. The balances in depositors' accounts are actually debts that the bank must pay at some future date, and a bank could have difficulty paying depositors if many of them demanded their money at the same time.

Given their role as money lenders, commercial banks occupy an influential position in our economic system. Their widespread lending operations can act as an <u>accelerator</u> or brake on inflation and profoundly affect growth trends and public attitudes nationwide.

Commercial banks give their largest, most secure corporate borrowers a **prime rate of interest**, traditionally defined as *a lower rate of interest than that charged to most borrowers*. Although this definition has some validity, the concept of a prime rate has lost credibility within the last several years. A House Banking Committee survey of the nation's largest banks disclosed that each regularly lent money at less than its publicized prime rate. That figure was often merely a point at which potential big borrowers could begin interest-rate negotiations. A Federal Reserve Board study found that more than half the large business loans made by several New York banks in one month were at less than the prime rate—by an average of 4.26.

This <u>discrepancy</u> implies that the prime rate is a benchmark, or general guideline, and not the lowest rate available.

Certificates of Deposit. Commercial banks also issue **certificates of deposit (CD's)**, *bank obligations that pay higher interest than regular savings accounts because the depositor agrees to leave the money on deposit for a certain length of time.* Depositors who need the funds before the certificates mature may cash them in, but the bank will pay a lower rate of interest than if they had been held until maturity. Certificates of deposit are sold in denominations from $100 to $100,000 and up, generally for terms of six months to five years.

Answer the following questions
based on your reading and on your
experience.

13. Do you use a commercial bank? What for? _____
    _____

14. Why might you choose an interest-bearing checking account over a savings account? _____
    _____

15. How do commercial banks make money? _____
    _____

16. What is the meaning of the word *accelerator* as it is used in the passage? _____
    _____

17. What does the word *discrepancy* mean as it is used in the passage? _____
    _____

18. Do you think the Colgate-Palmolive Corporation would pay an interest rate higher or lower than the
    prime rate on a loan to expand their health-care product line? Explain why. _____
    _____
    _____

19. If you applied to your bank for a car loan, would you expect to pay an interest rate that was higher or
    lower than the prime rate? Explain why. _____
    _____

20. In which of the following circumstances would you consider buying a certificate of deposit? Tell why or
    why not.

    a. You are saving for the college education of a five-year-old. _____
       _____

    b. You have just received your weekly paycheck. _____
       _____

    c. You expect to pay cash for a new car this month. _____
       _____

    d. You have saved $500 in a year toward the purchase of a $5,000 car. _____
       _____

What role do commercial banks play in the U.S. economic system?

Writing Exercise

_____
_____
_____
_____
_____
_____

Selection 2

Advertising: Making a Living

Over the years, advertising has grown in popularity as a college major and as a career. It is such a varied field that it attracts people of very different temperaments and talents. Psychologists may be interested in studying what appeals to a particular group of consumers. Statisticians may plot population trends to help plan a promotional campaign. The article that follows provides information about careers in advertising and about how the advertising process works. Before you begin to read, think about what you already know about advertising. Write down your answers to the following questions.

1. How do manufacturers advertise their products? _____
_____

2. What forms of advertisement do you think are the most effective? _____
_____
_____

3. Where do you think the ideas for ads come from? _____
_____

4. Describe the best ad you have ever seen. Why is it so good? _____
_____
_____

5. If you were a clothing manufacturer, how would you try to sell your product? ___
_____
_____

Read the first section to learn about career opportunities in the field of advertising.

More than half a million people are employed in advertising in America today. Some of them are radio and television station reps and time buyers. Some deal exclusively in print: layout, design, illustrations, and graphics. Others work for newspapers, magazines, or other media outlets. Some are involved with broadcast copywriting and production.

A typical advertising agency is run by a board of directors that chooses a president, who deals with department heads, each with a specialized staff. These typically include the following:

Market Research. This is the agency's statistical arm, which informs clients of the most lucrative geographic and demographic targets for their products. Often market research involves field interviews with potential buyers. Market researchers gather numbers that indicate what groups of people might buy a product and where these potential customers might be found.

Media Selection. This is done by print-space buyers and broadcast-time buyers as well as those who handle outdoor, yellow pages, direct mail, and specialty buys. All do their best to place the client's message where it is likely to get maximum response for minimal expense.

Creative Activity. Creativity is what most of us think of when we imagine an advertising agency. It involves the people who write the words and create the visuals of the ads we see and hear each day. Photographers, graphics experts, copywriters and others are often employed by the agency on a full-time basis. Much of this work is also farmed out to production companies or freelancers.

Account Management. These are the executives who deal directly with the client and are constantly on the lookout for new clients to bring to the agency. Account executives, like radio and TV salespeople, are generally among the highest-paid staffers. Without them, there would be no need for other staff members, because there would be no clients.

Many college graduates fortunate enough to land an entry-level advertising position start as salespeople at local media outlets. If you go to an agency, you might start in the media department, planning and buying time and space. Many of these positions were traditionally filled by men. However, an increasing number of entry-level opportunities for women are found in account management.

Women will find that initiative is rewarded more rapidly in advertising than anywhere else in media—not because ad agencies are pro-feminist but because they are pro-achievement. Advertising is an upwardly mobile business. Once you get over the demeaning lower hurdles, you'll be able to rise as far as your brains and talent will take you. And even at the lowest level, advertising positions tend to pay substantially more than comparable media jobs. A beginning copywriter at an agency can expect to earn 20% more than someone doing comparable work at a radio or TV station. This holds true for employees in production, art, and other areas as well.

Excerpts from *Mediamerica, Mediaworld: Form, Content and Consequence of Mass Communication,* by Edward Jay Whetmore (Belmont, Calif.: Wadsworth, 1993), pp. 288–295.

You'll have a much better chance at success if you're competitive, aggressive, hardworking, and mix well with all kinds of people. The world of advertising is one of *compromise*. Ad people are hardheaded realists: Their business is to help clients sell. *What* they're selling makes little difference.

Advertising can be used effectively in "selling" many things that are not products in the traditional sense. It was the public-service antismoking spots on TV that helped lead to a ban on cigarette commercials in the medium. Many top advertising agencies regularly contribute their time and energies to charities (cause-related marketing) and environmental groups (green-marketing).

Answer the following questions based on your reading and knowledge.

1. There are four areas of advertising employment mentioned in the text. What are they?

   a. _____

   b. _____

   c. _____

   d. _____

2. What is the meaning of the word *statistical* as it is used in the passage? _____

   _____

3. What does the expression *farmed out* mean as it is used in the text? _____

   _____

4. Which of the advertising positions mentioned sounds interesting to you? Why? _____

   _____

5. What benefits to working in the advertising industry are mentioned? _____

   _____

6. What personal qualities seem to be valued in advertising employees? _____

   _____

FORM AND CONTENT: HOW ADVERTISING WORKS

Read the next section to learn about the advertising process.

The effectiveness of advertising is attributable to the considerable media skills of people in the industry. The most clever copywriters, best artists, and most talented graphics designers labor over the national advertising campaign that bombards us. This collaboration led Marshell McLuhan to observe: "The ad is the meeting place for all the arts, skills, and all the media of the American environment."

The television-commercial scriptwriter has only 30 seconds to tell the story. Television advertising <u>dispenses with</u> plot line and brings us action, music, and visuals. The scene may shift several dozen times in those 30 seconds. First a close-up of a hand holding a drink—suddenly a plane flies overhead—a flight attendant pours a cup of coffee—a child laughs in <u>glee</u> while being served a hot dog as the clouds roll by outside the window.

Form is the important thing; content is secondary. The ad for a shirt company shows a field of daisies—no shirt and no people. The voice-over tells us: "This shirt makes you *feel* like a daisy." It's like Picasso's painting *Man in Chair*. There's no man, no chair, only a collection of skewed lines that, according to McLuhan, represent what it *feels* like to sit in a chair.

Print media, particularly magazines, are *replete* with examples. A full-page ad for vodka pictures a lone fingerprint. In another ad, a "machine wash" tag somehow symbolizes Nike apparel. A Marlboro billboard plants a colossal cowboy in an urban landscape. In each case, visual space is given over to a scene that has a minimal "logical" connection with the product. The theory is that by surrounding the product with an unusual environment, the ad can entice the consumer to try it.

But the consumer is also busy learning other things. Ads tell us a great deal about our society, and they help influence and change that society. Although the first business of ads is to sell products, their influence doesn't stop there. In fact, that's where it begins. As McLuhan points out, "Advertising itself is an information commodity far greater than anything it advertises." In their rush to sell a product, advertisers sometimes don't even recognize the more important effects of their collective art—selling life styles and social values to generation after generation of Americans.

Advertising is the first to reflect and encourage social trends. According to McLuhan, advertising "responds instantly to any social change, making ads in themselves invaluable means of knowing where it's at." For example, America's interest in ecology during the 1970s showed up often in advertising: Ads featuring the "natural" environment sold everything from cigarettes to silverware. The women's movement had barely gotten started when television ads began picturing women as mechanics and bank presidents. Ads are first to reflect social trends because they *have* to be one step ahead. Competition in advertising is far more fierce than in programming. Thus, advertising is often more arresting than the program it interrupts.

Advertising also teaches us how to behave through little socialization lessons. They show us how and when to love one another. A wife makes her husband happy by straining his coffee through a special filter. A husband amazes his wife with the latest innovation in diapers. In many ways, advertising provides a context and a meaning for all sorts of everyday experiences. In contemporary society, virtually all our everyday experiences are somehow influenced by advertising.

Answer the following questions based on your reading and on your experience.

7. Explain what the author means when he says about advertising that "form is the important thing; content is secondary." _____

_____

8. Give an example of an ad that you have seen in which the advertiser presents the product in an unusual setting. Do you think this technique is effective? _____

_____

9. What does the phrase *dispenses with* mean as it is used in the passage? _____

_____

10. What does the word *glee* mean as it is used in the passage? _____

_____

11. What does the word *replete* mean as it is used in the passage? _____

_____

12. In addition to persuading us to buy certain products, what other influences does advertising have on our lives? _____

_____

13. Do you think the author presents a positive view of advertising? Support your answer. _____

_____

14. What do you think the author means by this sentence, "Thus, advertising is often more arresting than the programming it interrupts"? Do you agree? _____

_____

15. Give an example of how young children may be socialized by advertising. _____

_____

Describe a situation in which you, or someone you know, were persuaded to purchase something or behave in a certain way as a result of advertising. Explain how the advertising influenced the behavior.

Writing Exercise

_____

_____

_____

_____

_____

Selection 3
Consumer Rights

Read this section to learn about consumer rights.

You are now, and always will be, a consumer; and, as a consumer, you have certain legal rights that producers, manufacturers, vendors, and advertisers must respect. To be an intelligent consumer, you should be aware of your rights, so you will know if you are being treated unfairly. As a businessperson, too, it is your obligation to know and protect the rights of consumers. The reading selection that follows lists the rights of consumers. Then it explains two of those rights in detail and provides some examples.

The recent trend toward greater consumer protection reflects certain basic rights that were first formulated in 1962 in a message President John F. Kennedy sent to Congress titled *Special Message on Protecting the Consumer Interest*. This was the first message ever delivered by a president on this topic. Kennedy stated that legislative and administrative action was required for the federal government to meet its responsibilities to consumers in the exercise of their rights. He spelled out four rights that have come to serve as the basis of consumer protection:

1. **The right to safety**—to be protected against the marketing of goods that are hazardous to health or life.

2. **The right to be informed**—to be protected against fraudulent or misleading information, advertising, labeling, or other practices, and to be given the facts needed to make an informed choice.

3. **The right to choose**—to be assured access to a variety of products and services at competitive prices.

4. **The right to be heard**—to be assured that consumer interests will receive full and sympathetic consideration in the formulation of government policy.

Another right that should be added to this list is:

5. **The right to be a minority consumer without disadvantage**—to ensure that minority groups or low-income consumers will not be at a disadvantage in relation to any of the above rights compared to other groups.

Excerpts from *Consumer Behavior and Marketing Action*, by Henry Assael, pp. 692–695.

Answer the following questions based on your reading and on your experience.

1. How do you think these five rights will protect consumers? _____
   _____
   _____

2. From your own experience, or from what you have read or heard, can you think of a situation in which a consumer was denied one of those rights? Tell about your example. _____
   _____
   _____

THE RIGHT TO SAFETY

Read the next section to learn more about the consumer's right to safety.

There is general agreement among government agencies, business people, and consumerists that abuses related to product safety must be eliminated. Most companies try to <u>ensure</u> product safety and reliability, but abuses occasionally exist.

The primary government agency responsible for eliminating these abuses is the Consumer Product Safety Commission (CPSC), established in 1972. The commission can ban the sale of products, require manufacturers to perform safety tests, and require repair or recall of unsafe products. It operates a hotline to report hazardous products and also runs the National Electronic Injury Surveillance System, a computer-based system that monitors 119 hospital emergency rooms across the country. On the basis of this system, the commission computes a product Hazard Index. Among products with the highest hazard index are cleaning agents, swings and slides, liquid fuels, snowmobiles, and all-terrain vehicles (ATVs).

The CPSC's action against manufacturers of ATVs demonstrates how the commission tries to <u>ensure</u> product safety. All-terrain vehicles had been linked to over 900 deaths since 1982. In 1987, the commission filed suit against ATV manufacturers. In April, 1988, all ATV manufacturers signed a consent decree agreeing not to sell any three-wheeled ATVs and to restrict the sale of four-wheeled models to certain age groups.

One of the positive outcomes of the commission's work is its influence on firms such as Westinghouse and Philco to formalize their product safety procedures. Philco has established a National Safety Alert program to speed up detection of potentially unsafe products.

The CPSC has also been active in recalling products. It recalls an average of 200 products per year. Another agency with recall powers is the National Highway Traffic Safety Administration, which sued General Motors to force a recall of 1.1 million X-body cars because of faulty brakes.

Some companies have recognized their responsibility for product safety and have attempted to regulate their product development to ensure safety. For example, Gillette has a twenty-nine member quality inspection group whose head is empowered to stop the development of a new product or to recommend a change in its ingredients if there is a potential danger. On the team's recommendation, Gillette pulled a product off the market just when it was introduced. The product was an aerosol antiperspirant containing zirconium salt, an ingredient later found to inflame lungs.

Answer the following questions based on your reading and your thinking.

3. What can the CPSC do? _____

_____

4. What is the meaning of the word *ensure* as it is used in the passage? _____

_____

5. Why do you think cleaning agents are among the most hazardous products? _____

_____

6. On what basis are products judged hazardous? _____

_____

7. Do you think the CPSC should ban all hazardous products such as swings and slides? Explain your answer.

_____

8. Explain the difference between the recall of X-body cars and the recall of Gillette's antiperspirant. _____

_____

Read the next section to learn how deceptive advertising violates the consumer's right to be informed.

THE RIGHT TO BE INFORMED

President Kennedy's statement regarding the right to be informed covers two components, the right to be protected against misleading and deceptive information and the right to be given sufficient information to make an informed choice.

DECEPTIVE ADVERTISING

Over the years, the Federal Trade Commission has established a set of clearly defined guidelines for determining what is deceptive advertising under the Wheeler-Lea Amendment of the Federal Trade Commission Act. Advertising need only have the capacity to deceive in order to be considered deceptive; there is no need for the FTC to prove that deception has actually occurred. Furthermore, the advertiser can be ignorant of any false claim and still be liable. Consumer researchers have tried to grapple with the question, Where does puffery end and deception begin?

Gardner identified three types of deceptive advertising. The first is *fraudulent advertising*, that is, a straightforward lie. The second is *false advertising*, which involves a claim-fact <u>discrepancy</u>. That is, the benefits claimed by the product are fulfilled only under certain conditions that may not be clear in the advertising, or the product must be used in a certain manner or with certain precautions. For example, Superior Rent A Car advertised a $69-a-week rate in Miami's Yellow Pages, but it never disclosed that the rate applied only to cars with manual transmissions. A third type of deception is *misleading advertising*. It involves a claim-belief interaction. In this case, an advertisement interacts with certain consumer beliefs and results in a misleading claim. For example, manufacturers of cold medicines have advertised the exact same drug under different brand names for different ailments. Johnson & Johnson sells Tylenol cold formula and an identical cold and flu formula, and American Home Products markets Dristan Sinus and an identical CoAdvil. In these cases, advertising promoting the belief that products are different interacts with the logical belief on the part of consumers that products with different names in different packages are in fact different. The result is misleading advertising.

The 1970s saw heightened activity by the FTC in prosecuting deceptive advertising. The commission has asked some companies to desist from making deceptive claims. For example, it asked several major firms to stop claiming that enzymes in detergents eliminate stains. In some cases, the FTC asked certain companies not only to stop making deceptive claims but to publicly correct these claims. The rationale for requiring corrective advertising was that deceptive claims have a residual effect and, if uncorrected, could remain in consumer memory for a period of time. Without corrective advertising, companies continue to benefit from such past claims. The FTC required corrective advertising in the following cases:

- ITT-Continental had to correct past advertising that its Profile Bread was effective in weight reduction.

- Warner-Lambert had to correct the claim that Listerine helps prevent colds.

- Hawaiian Punch had to correct its claim that its drink was composed of natural fruit juices, when actually it contained only 11–15 percent fruit juice.

Do corrected claims have an impact on consumer beliefs? One study found that the proportion of consumers who believed that Hawaiian Punch contained little fruit juice went from 20 percent to 70 percent during the period of corrective advertising.

In the 1980s, the FTC was less rigorous in restricting deceptive advertising. In the 1970s it acted if advertising had even the capacity to deceive, but under the Reagan administration advertising had to be clearly deceptive to warrant FTC concern. The commission said that it would no longer take action against advertisements that only seemed deceptive. Rather, it would have to prove that consumers suffered actual injury before filing a complaint. In other words, the burden of proof shifted from the advertiser to the consumer.

As we saw, the FTC seemed to be taking a more activist role under the Bush administration in controlling advertising. The criterion for taking action seemed to have reverted to that used in the 1970s, namely, the capacity to deceive rather than actual deception.

The role of the FTC in the Clinton and future administrations remains to be seen.

**Answer the following questions
based on your reading.**

9. What is the meaning of the word *discrepancy* as it is used in the passage? _____

_____

10. What are the three types of deceptive advertising?

    a. _____

    b. _____

    c. _____

11. Identify the type of deceptive advertising illustrated by each of the following examples:

    a. A breakfast cereal company claims its product provides all the daily nutritional needs of a ten-year-old.
       The ad neglects to say the cereal must be eaten with milk and fruit to satisfy those needs. _____

       _____

    b. Dr. Brown's vitamins claim to add five years to the lives of those who take them daily. _____

       _____

    c. A frozen-yogurt manufacturer advertises the product as fat-free and sugar-free although certain flavors
       contain fudge, nuts, and pieces of brownies. _____

       _____

    d. A frozen food manufacturer claims that its vegetable-medley product reduces the risk of cancer.

       _____

    e. A drug company's product advertised to ease arthritic pain contains only aspirin. _____

       _____

12. What is the role of the FTC? _____

    _____

13. What is corrective advertising? _____

    _____

14. Do you think the FTC should play an activist role? Explain why you feel the way you do. _____

    _____

15. Give an example of an advertisement you believe is deceptive. Tell what the product is and describe the
    claim you find to be deceptive. _____

    _____

    _____

Review the article making margin notes and underlining important points. Use your notes and underlined material as the basis of a summary describing the FTC's role in assuring truth in advertising.

Writing Exercise

_____

_____

_____

_____

_____

_____

_____

_____

_____

_____

_____

_____

_____

_____

_____

The last reading selection deals with business ethics. What responsibilities do companies and their decision makers have to the public and to their employees? What standards of honesty and fairness can we apply to businesses whose stated purpose is to make money?

Selection 4

Business Ethics

Before you begin to read, explore your own feelings about business ethics in industry and the workplace. Write your responses to the following statements and questions.

1. Try to recall a situation in which an individual or company behaved ethically or unethically. Describe it. ___

   _____

2. What kind of regulations do you think the government should impose on businesses? _____

   _____

3. Who should decide if business people have behaved unethically? _____

   _____

4. What kind of penalties should be imposed for unethical actions? _____

   _____

Read the selection to learn more about business ethics. Answer the guide questions as you go along.

Read the first section to learn about some ethical dilemmas.

Every business and every businessperson will at some time face an ethical <u>dilemma</u>. That dilemma may be deciding whether to hire a top salesperson who has come to the job interview with sensitive data from a competitor and former employer. The dilemma may be deciding whether to market in Third World countries a toy that has been <u>banned</u> in the United States by the Consumer Product Safety Division. An ethical dilemma could be as simple as determining your company's level of quality or disclosing long-term exposure hazards to employees. The old philosophy of "what's good for business is good for the country" is no longer adequate to ensure a business's long-term survival and earnings.

Businesses today must answer not only to their shareholders but also to others. For example, one consumer was outraged about a company's sponsorship of a television program not suitable for family-hour viewing. She succeeded in persuading the company to withdraw from the show. Both ethical and socially responsible behavior are demanded by shareholders to ensure long-term earnings growth, by customers in return for their loyalty, and by communities as a condition for locating in their areas.

Answer the following questions based on your reading, experience, and beliefs.

1. What is the meaning of the word *dilemma* as it is used in the passage? _____

_____

2. What is the meaning of the word *banned* as it is used in the passage? _____

_____

3. What would you do in the following situations?

   a. Would you hire a salesperson with insider information? _____

   _____

   b. Would you market a toy banned in the United States in other countries? _____

   _____

   c. Would you tell employees about the health risks from their jobs? _____

   _____

4. Do you think consumer pressure on advertisers (and indirectly on network programmers) is appropriate? Explain. _____

_____

_____

Excerpts from *Business and the Legal Environment,* 2nd ed., by Marianne Moody Jennings (Boston: PWS-Kent, 1991), pp. 74–79.

WHY BUSINESS ETHICS?

Profitability as a Return on Ethical Behavior. Business is driven by the bottom line. Profits control whether the firm can get loans or attract investors. They indicate the firm's and, in most cases, its employees' success. Indeed, business firms can be defined as groups of people working together to obtain maximum profit. At times, the pursuit of profit can cause people to do things that, while not illegal, are unethical. Successful business, however, is a long-term project, and those firms that stick to ethical standards perform better financially in the long run. For example, the Ethics Resource Center compared the performance of companies that have codes of ethics to others. Over a 30-year period, a $30,000 investment in the companies with ethics codes would have earned more than $800,000 more than a similar investment in those without the codes. U.S. corporations that have paid <u>dividends</u> for 100 years or more are known for their emphasis on ethical behavior. In a 1988 survey of American companies with annual sales of $500 million or more, 63% considered ethical standards a competitive business strength. However, 94% of the respondents felt that businesses were troubled by ethical issues today.

Read the following section to learn about an incentive for businesses to behave ethically.

Answer the following questions based on your reading.

5. According to the author, what is the relationship between ethical conduct and business success? _____

_____

6. How does the author support her argument for this relationship? _____

_____

7. What is the meaning of the word *dividends* as it is used in the passage? _____

_____

The Tylenol tampering incident of 1982 offers an example of the rewards of being ethical. When some Tylenol capsules were discovered to have been <u>tainted</u> with deadly poison, McNeil Consumer Products Company, a subsidiary of Johnson & Johnson, followed its code of ethics and put the consumers' interest first. McNeil recalled all Tylenol capsules from the market—thirty-one million bottles with a retail value of $100 million. A new and safer form of non-capsule Tylenol caplet was developed. Within a few months, Tylenol regained its majority share of the market. Contrary to financial analysts' predictions, the recall turned out to be neither a poor decision nor a financial disaster. Rather, the company's decision enhanced its reputation. It also made Tylenol customers trust and respect the <u>integrity</u> of the company and the product.

In contrast to the positive side of ethical behavior is the negative side of unethical behavior. For example, defense contractors who were part of the spending and overcharging scandal several years ago have not regained their credibility. Beech-Nut suffered tremendous earnings losses as a result of the discovery that their baby "apple juice" did not in fact

Read the next section to find out about ethical and unethical business decisions.

contain any real apple juice. Many boycotts have targeted Nestle for its marketing of infant formula in Third World nations. In countries that lack sanitation, refrigeration, and education, infants can suffer serious health problems as a result of misuse of baby formula. The public saw Nestle's intense marketing efforts in these countries as unethical and exploitative. In 1989, nearly 20 years after the infant formula crisis, Nestle was still feeling its effects. The company withdrew its new "Good Start" formula because of continuing consumer resistance. As the Nestle case shows, a firm's reputation for ethical behavior is the same as an individual's reputation. It takes a long time to gain but it can be lost instantly as the result of one bad choice.

Answer the following questions based on your reading, experience, and beliefs.

8. What is the meaning of the word *tainted* as it is used in the passage? _____

_____

9. How would you feel about buying Johnson & Johnson products? _____

_____

10. What is your opinion of the Nestle company? _____

_____

11. What is the meaning of the word *integrity* as it is used in the passage? _____

_____

12. Can you think of an example of how a reputation for ethical (or unethical) behavior affected the success of a local merchant, store, or restaurant? Tell about it. _____

_____

_____

Read the next section to learn about other reasons to be an ethical businessperson.

Business Ethics for Personal Reasons. It would be misleading to say that every ethical business is a profitable business. First, not all ethical people are good and successful managers. But there are many competent business people who have suffered for being ethical and many others who seem to survive despite their lack of ethics. Columnist Dave Barry has said that every time there is an oil spill, the oil companies ready themselves for the higher prices and profits that come from all that oil lost at sea. Despite many lawsuits related to employees' lung diseases resulting from exposure to asbestos, Johns-Manville has emerged from a Chapter 11 bankruptcy as a profitable business selling non-asbestos insulation. There are many whistle-blowers who, while respected by many, have been unable to find jobs in their industry. If ethical behavior does not guarantee success, then why have ethics? The answer has to do with personal ethics applied to business. Ivan Boesky, an infamous stock broker, was convicted of insider trading. He was once described as follows: "He tricked everybody with his research and stock analysis when he really made money the old-fashioned way. He stole it." Business ethics is really nothing more than a standard of personal behavior applied to a group of people working together to make a profit. Some people are ethical because they can sleep better at night. Some people are ethical because they are afraid of getting caught. But being personally ethical is the justification for business ethics—it is simply the correct thing to do.

Answer the following questions based on your reading, experience, and beliefs.

13. Do ethical behavior and business success always go together? Give an example to support your answer.

   _____

14. Why is business ethics necessary? _____

   _____

15. Do you think there is a relationship between personal ethics and business ethics? Explain. _____

   _____

Assume you are about to open your own clothing store. As the owner of the business, you have decided to draw up a code of ethics. Write at least five sentences describing your commitment to ethical behavior toward your customers and employees.

Writing Exercise

_____

_____

_____

_____

_____

_____

_____

_____

_____

_____

_____

References

Assael, Henry. *Consumer Behavior and Marketing Action.* 4th ed. Boston: PWS-Kent, 1992.

Bly, Robert. *Iron John: A Book About Men.* Reading, Mass.: Addison Wesley, 1990.

Frazier, Thomas R. *Afro-American History, Primary Sources.* 2nd ed. Belmont, Calif: Wadsworth, The Dorsey Press, 1988.

Goldberg, Robert A. *Grassroots Resistance: Social Movements in Twentieth Century America.* Belmont, Calif.: Wadsworth, 1991.

Hansell, Saul. "Consumers Finally Respond to High Credit Card Interest." *New York Times,* March 26, 1993, pp. 1, D7.

Henry, William A. III. "Where NBC Went Wrong." *Time,* February 22, 1993, pp. 59.

Hughes, Langston. *Selected Poems.* New York: Knopf, 1926, 1954. In *Afro-American History, Primary Sources,* 2nd ed., Thomas R. Frazier (Chicago: The Dorsey Press).

Jennings, Marianne Moody. *Business and the Legal Environment.* 2nd ed. Boston: PWS-Kent, 1991.

Kalat, James W. *Introduction to Psychology.* 3rd ed. Belmont, Calif.: Wadsworth, 1993.

Melosi, Martin V. *Garbage in the Cities: Refuse, Reform, and the Environment.* Chicago: The Dorsey Press, 1981.

Miller, G. Tyler, Jr. *Living in the Environment.* 7th ed. Belmont, Calif.: Wadsworth, 1992.

Nanda, Serena. *Cultural Anthropology.* 4th ed. Belmont, Calif.: Wadsworth, 1991.

O'Donnell, Frank. *Annual Report of the Nature Conservancy.* Washington, D.C., 1993.

Roberts, Sam. "The Unfulfilled Legacy of a Daring Experiment." *The New York Times.* April 5, 1993, p. B3.

Robertson, Nan. *The Girls in the Balcony: Women, Men, and* The New York Times. New York: Random House, 1992.

Specter, Michael. "Sea-Dumping Ban: Good Politics but Not Necessarily Good Policy." *The New York Times.* March 23, 1993, p. 1.

Straub, Joseph T., & Raymond F. Attner. *Introduction to Business.* 4th ed. Boston: PWS-Kent, 1991.

Verderber, Rudolph F. *Communicate*. 7th ed. Belmont, Calif.: Wadsworth, 1993.

Whetmore, Edward Jay. *Mediamerica, Mediaworld: Form, Content, and Consequences of Mass Communication*. Belmont, Calif.: Wadsworth, 1993.

Wilson, R. Jackson, James Gilbert, Stephen Nissenbaum, Karen Ordahl Kupperman, & Donald Scott. *The Pursuit of Liberty: A History of the American People*. Vols. 1 and 2, 2nd ed. Belmont, Calif.: Wadsworth, 1990.